Intrusion Detection Systems
with Snort

Advanced IDS Techniques Using
Snort, Apache, MySQL, PHP, and ACID

BRUCE PERENS' OPEN SOURCE SERIES

Intrusion Detection Systems with Snort

Advanced IDS Techniques Using Snort, Apache, MySQL, PHP, and ACID

Rafeeq Ur Rehman

PRENTICE
HALL
PTR
Prentice Hall PTR
Upper Saddle River, New Jersey 07458
www.phptr.com

Library of Congress Cataloging-in-Publication Data

A CIP catalog record for this book can be obtained from the Library of Congress.

Editorial/production supervision: *Mary Sudul*
Cover design director: *Jerry Votta*
Cover design: *DesignSource*
Manufacturing manager: *Maura Zaldivar*
Acquisitions editor: *Jill Harry*
Editorial assistant: *Noreen Regina*
Marketing manager: *Dan DePasquale*

© 2003 Pearson Education, Inc.
Publishing as Prentice Hall PTR
Upper Saddle River, New Jersey 07458

This material may be distributed only subject to the terms and conditions set forth in the Open
Publication License, v1.0 or later (the latest version is presently available at
<http://www.opencontent.org/openpub/>).

Prentice Hall books are widely used by corporations and government agencies for training, marketing,
and resale.
The publisher offers discounts on this book when ordered in bulk quantities. For more information,
contact Corporate Sales Department, Phone: 800-382-3419; FAX: 201-236-7141;
E-mail: corpsales@prenhall.com
Or write: Prentice Hall PTR, Corporate Sales Dept., One Lake Street, Upper Saddle River, NJ 07458.

Other product or company names mentioned herein are the trademarks or registered trademarks of their
respective owners.

Printed in the United States of America

Fourth Printing

ISBN 0-13-140733-3

Pearson Education LTD.
Pearson Education Australia PTY, Limited
Pearson Education Singapore, Pte. Ltd.
Pearson Education North Asia Ltd.
Pearson Education Canada, Ltd.
Pearson Educación de Mexico, S.A. de C.V.
Pearson Education — Japan
Pearson Education Malaysia, Pte. Ltd.

To open source and free software developers

CONTENTS

## CHAPTER 1

Introduction to Intrusion Detection and Snort

Security is a big issue for all networks in today's enterprise environment. Hackers and intruders have made many successful attempts to bring down high-profile company networks and web services. Many methods have been developed to secure the network infrastructure and communication over the Internet, among them the use of firewalls, encryption, and virtual private networks. Intrusion detection is a relatively new addition to such techniques. Intrusion detection methods started appearing in the last few years. Using intrusion detection methods, you can collect and use information from known types of attacks and find out if someone is trying to attack your network or particular hosts. The information collected this way can be used to harden your network security, as well as for legal purposes. Both commercial and open source products are now available for this purpose. Many vulnerability assessment tools are also available in the market that can be used to assess different types of security holes present in your network. A comprehensive security system consists of multiple tools, including:

- Firewalls that are used to block unwanted incoming as well as outgoing traffic of data. There is a range of firewall products available in the market both in Open Source and commercial products. Most popular commercial firewall products are from Checkpoint (http://www.checkpoint.com), Cisco (http://www.cisco.com) and Netscreen (http://www.netscreen.com). The most popular Open Source firewall is the Netfilter/Iptables (http://www.netfilter.org)-based firewall.

- Intrusion detection systems (IDS) that are used to find out if someone has gotten into or is trying to get into your network. The most popular IDS is Snort, which is available at http://www.snort.org.

- Vulnerability assessment tools that are used to find and plug security holes present in your network. Information collected from vulnerability assessment tools is used to set rules on firewalls so that these security holes are safeguarded from malicious Internet users. There are many vulnerability assessment tools including Nmap (http://www.nmap.org) and Nessus (http://www.nessus.org).

These tools can work together and exchange information with each other. Some products provide complete systems consisting of all of these products bundled together.

Snort is an open source *Network Intrusion Detection System* (NIDS) which is available free of cost. NIDS is the type of Intrusion Detection System (IDS) that is used for scanning data flowing on the network. There are also host-based intrusion detection systems, which are installed on a particular host and detect attacks targeted to that host only. Although all intrusion detection methods are still new, Snort is ranked among the top quality systems available today.

The book starts with an introduction to intrusion detection and related terminology. You will learn installation and management of Snort as well as other products that work with Snort. These products include MySQL database (http://www.mysql.org) and Analysis Control for Intrusion Database (ACID) (http://www.cert.org/kb/acid). Snort has the capability to log data collected (such as alerts and other log messages) to a database. MySQL is used as the database engine where all of this data is stored. Using Apache web server (http://www.apache.org) and ACID, you can analyze this data. A combination of Snort, Apache, MySQL, and ACID makes it possible to log the intrusion detection data into a database and then view and analyze it later, using a web interface.

This book is organized in such a way that the reader will be able to build a complete intrusion detection system by going through the following chapters in a step-by-step manner. All steps of installing and integrating different tools are explained in the book as outlined below.

Chapter 2 provides basic information about how to build and install Snort itself. Using the basic installation and default rules, you will be able to get a working IDS. You will be able to create log files that show intrusion activity.

Chapter 3 provides information about Snort rules, different parts of Snort rules and how to write your own rules according to your environment and needs. This chapter is very important, as writing good rules is the key to building a detection system. The chapter also explains different rules that are part of Snort distribution.

Chapter 4 is about input and output plug-ins. Plug-ins are parts of the software that are compiled with Snort and are used to modify input or output of the Snort detection engine. Input plug-ins prepare captured data packets before the actual detection process is applied on these packets. Output plug-ins format output to be used for a particular purpose. For example, an output plug-in can convert the detection data to a Simple Network Management Protocol (SNMP) trap. Another output plug-in is used to log Snort output data into databases. This chapter provides a comprehensive overview of how these plug-ins are configured and used.

Chapter 5 provides information about using MySQL database with Snort. MySQL plug-in enables Snort to log data into the database to be used in the analysis later on. In this chapter you will find information about how to create a database in MySQL, configure a database plug-in, and log data to the database.

Chapter 6 describes ACID, how to use it to get data from the database you configured in Chapter 5, and how to display it using Apache web server. ACID is a very important tool that provides rich data analysis capabilities. You can find frequency of attacks, classify different attacks, view the source of these attacks and so on. ACID uses PHP (Pretty Home Page) scripting language, graphic display library (GD library) and PHPLOT, which is a tool to draw graphs. A combination of all of these results in web pages that display, analyze and graph data stored in the MySQL database.

Chapter 7 is devoted to information about some other useful tools that can be used with Snort.

The system that you will build after going through this book is displayed in Figure 1-1 with different components.

As you can see, data is captured and analyzed by Snort. Snort then stores this data in the MySQL database using the database output plug-in. Apache web server takes help from ACID, PHP, GD library and PHPLOT package to display this data in a browser window when a user connects to Apache. A user can then make different types of queries on the forms displayed in the web pages to analyze, archive, graph and delete data.

In essence, you can build a single computer with Snort, MySQL database, Apache, PHP, ACID, GD library and PHPLOT. A more realistic picture of the system that you will be able to build after reading this book is shown in Figure 1-2.

In the enterprise, usually people have multiple Snort sensors behind every router or firewall. In that case you can use a single centralized database to collect data from all of the sensors. You can run Apache web server on this centralized database server as shown in Figure 1-3.

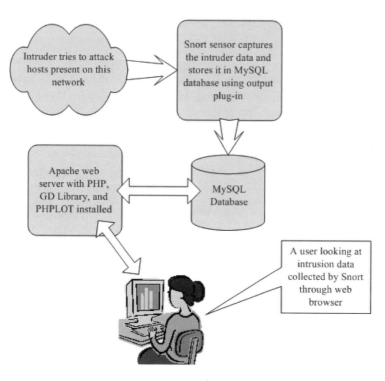

Figure 1-1 Block diagram of a complete network intrusion detection system consisting of Snort, MySQL, Apache, ACID, PHP, GD Library and PHPLOT.

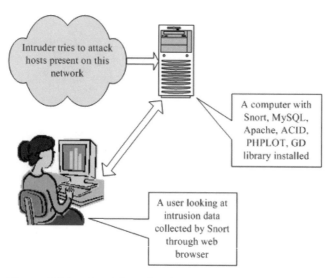

Figure 1-2 A network intrusion detection system with web interface.

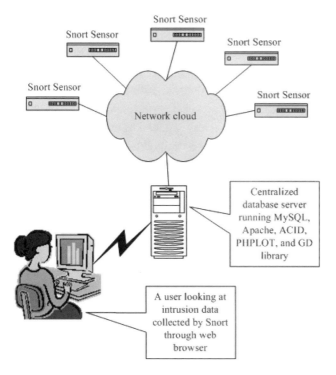

Figure 1-3 Multiple Snort sensors in the enterprise logging to a centralized database server.

1.1 What is Intrusion Detection?

Intrusion detection is a set of techniques and methods that are used to detect suspicious activity both at the network and host level. Intrusion detection systems fall into two basic categories: signature-based intrusion detection systems and anomaly detection systems. Intruders have signatures, like computer viruses, that can be detected using software. You try to find data packets that contain any known intrusion-related signatures or anomalies related to Internet protocols. Based upon a set of signatures and rules, the detection system is able to find and log suspicious activity and generate alerts. Anomaly-based intrusion detection usually depends on packet anomalies present in protocol header parts. In some cases these methods produce better results compared to signature-based IDS. Usually an intrusion detection system captures data from the network and applies its rules to that data or detects anomalies in it. Snort is primarily a rule-based IDS, however input plug-ins are present to detect anomalies in protocol headers.

Snort uses rules stored in text files that can be modified by a text editor. Rules are grouped in categories. Rules belonging to each category are stored in separate files. These files are then included in a main configuration file called snort.conf. Snort reads these rules at the start-up time and builds internal data structures or chains to apply these rules to captured data. Finding signatures and using them in rules is a tricky job, since the more rules you use, the more processing power is required to process captured data in real time. It is important to implement as many signatures as you can using as few rules as possible. Snort comes with a rich set of pre-defined rules to detect intrusion activity and you are free to add your own rules at will. You can also remove some of the built-in rules to avoid false alarms.

1.1.1   Some Definitions

Before we go into details of intrusion detection and Snort, you need to learn some definitions related to security. These definitions will be used in this book repeatedly in the coming chapters. A basic understanding of these terms is necessary to digest other complicated security concepts.

1.1.1.1   IDS

Intrusion Detection System or IDS is software, hardware or combination of both used to detect intruder activity. Snort is an open source IDS available to the general public. An IDS may have different capabilities depending upon how complex and sophisticated the components are. IDS appliances that are a combination of hardware and software are available from many companies. As mentioned earlier, an IDS may use signatures, anomaly-based techniques or both.

1.1.1.2   Network IDS or NIDS

NIDS are intrusion detection systems that capture data packets traveling on the network media (cables, wireless) and match them to a database of signatures. Depending upon whether a packet is matched with an intruder signature, an alert is generated or the packet is logged to a file or database. One major use of Snort is as a NIDS.

1.1.1.3   Host IDS or HIDS

Host-based intrusion detection systems or HIDS are installed as agents on a host. These intrusion detection systems can look into system and application log files to detect any intruder activity. Some of these systems are reactive, meaning that they inform you only when something has happened. Some HIDS are proactive; they can sniff the network traffic coming to a particular host on which the HIDS is installed and alert you in real time.

1.1.1.4   Signatures

Signature is the pattern that you look for inside a data packet. A signature is used to detect one or multiple types of attacks. For example, the presence of "scripts/iisadmin" in a packet going to your web server may indicate an intruder activity.

Signatures may be present in different parts of a data packet depending upon the nature of the attack. For example, you can find signatures in the IP header, transport layer header (TCP or UDP header) and/or application layer header or payload. You will learn more about signatures later in this book.

Usually IDS depends upon signatures to find out about intruder activity. Some vendor-specific IDS need updates from the vendor to add new signatures when a new type of attack is discovered. In other IDS, like Snort, you can update signatures yourself.

1.1.1.5   Alerts

Alerts are any sort of user notification of an intruder activity. When an IDS detects an intruder, it has to inform security administrator about this using alerts. Alerts may be in the form of pop-up windows, logging to a console, sending e-mail and so on. Alerts are also stored in log files or databases where they can be viewed later on by security experts. You will find detailed information about alerts later in this book.

Snort can generate alerts in many forms and are controlled by output plug-ins. Snort can also send the same alert to multiple destinations. For example, it is possible to log alerts into a database and generate SNMP traps simultaneously. Some plug-ins can also modify firewall configuration so that offending hosts are blocked at the firewall or router level.

1.1.1.6   Logs

The log messages are usually saved in file. By default Snort saves these messages under /var/log/snort directory. However, the location of log messages can be changed using the command line switch when starting Snort. Log messages can be saved either in text or binary format. The binary files can be viewed later on using Snort or tcpdump program. A new tool called Barnyard is also available now to analyze binary log files generated by Snort. Logging in binary format is faster because it saves some formatting overhead. In high-speed Snort implementations, logging in binary mode is necessary.

1.1.1.7   False Alarms

False alarms are alerts generated due to an indication that is not an intruder activity. For example, misconfigured internal hosts may sometimes broadcast messages that trigger a rule resulting in generation of a false alert. Some routers, like Linksys home routers, generate lots of UPnP related alerts. To avoid false alarms, you have to modify and tune different default rules. In some cases you may need to disable some of the rules to avoid false alarms.

1.1.1.8   Sensor

The machine on which an intrusion detection system is running is also called the sensor in the literature because it is used to "sense" the network. Later in this book if the word sensor is used, it refers to a computer or other device where Snort is running.

1.1.2   Where IDS Should be Placed in Network Topology

Depending upon your network topology, you may want to position intrusion detection systems at one or more places. It also depends upon what type of intrusion activities you want to detect: internal, external or both. For example, if you want to detect only external intrusion activities, and you have only one router connecting to the Internet, the best place for an intrusion detection system may be just inside the router or a firewall. If you have multiple paths to the Internet, you may want to place one IDS box at every entry point. However if you want to detect internal threats as well, you may want to place a box in every network segment.

In many cases you don't need to have intrusion detection activity in all network segments and you may want to limit it only to sensitive network areas. Note that more intrusion detection systems mean more work and more maintenance costs. Your decision really depends upon your security policy, which defines what you really want to protect from hackers. Figure 1-4 shows typical locations where you can place an intrusion detection system.

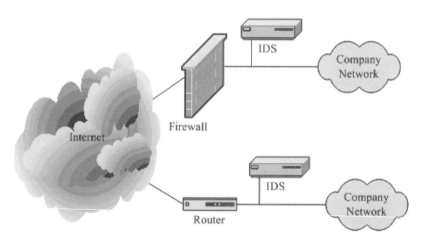

Figure 1-4 Typical locations for an intrusion detection system.

As you can see from Figure 1-4, typically you should place an IDS behind each of your firewalls and routers. In case your network contains a demilitarized zone (DMZ), an IDS may be placed in that zone as well. However alert generation policy should not be as strict in a DMZ compared to private parts of the network.

1.1.3 Honey Pots

Honey pots are systems used to lure hackers by exposing known vulnerabilities deliberately. Once a hacker finds a honey pot, it is more likely that the hacker will stick around for some time. During this time you can log hacker activities to find out his/her actions and techniques. Once you know these techniques, you can use this information later on to harden security on your actual servers.

There are different ways to build and place honey pots. The honey pot should have common services running on it. These common services include Telnet server (port 23), Hyper Text Transfer Protocol (HTTP) server (port 80), File Transfer Protocol (FTP) server (port 21) and so on. You should place the honey pot somewhere close to your production server so that the hackers can easily take it for a real server. For example, if your production servers have Internet Protocol (IP) addresses 192.168.10.21 and 192.168.10.23, you can assign an IP address of 192.168.10.22 to the honey pot. You can also configure your firewall and/or router to redirect traffic on some ports to a honey pot where the intruder thinks that he/she is connecting to a real server. You should be careful in creating an alert mechanism so that when your honey pot is compromised, you are notified immediately. It is a good idea to keep log files on some other machine so that when the honey pot is compromised, the hacker does not have the ability to delete these files.

So when should you install a honey pot? The answer depends on different criteria, including the following:

- You should create a honey pot if your organization has enough resources to track down hackers. These resources include both hardware and personnel. If you don't have these resources, there is no need to install a honey pot. After all, there is no need to have data if you can't use it.
- A honey pot is useful only if you want to use the information gathered in some way.
- You may also use a honey pot if you want to prosecute hackers by gathering evidence of their activities.

Ideally a honey pot should look like a real system. You should create some fake data files, user accounts and so on to ensure a hacker that this is a real system. This will tempt the hacker to remain on the honey pot for a longer time and you will be able to record more activity.

To have more information and get a closer look at honey pots, go to the Honey Pot Project web site http://project.honeynet.org/ where you will find interesting material. Also go to the Honeyd web site at http://www.citi.umich.edu/u/provos/honeyd/ to find out information about this open source honey pot. Some other places where you can find more information are:

- South Florida Honeynet Project at http://www.sfhn.net
- Different HOWTOs at http://www.sfhn.net/whites/howtos.html

1.1.4 Security Zones and Levels of Trust

Some time ago people divided networks into two broad areas, secure area and unsecure area. Sometimes this division also meant a network is inside a firewall or a router and outside your router. Now typical networks are divided into many different areas and each area may have a different level of security policy and level of trust. For example, a company's finance department may have a very high security level and may allow only a few services to operate in that area. No Internet service may be available from the finance department. However a DMZ or de-militarized zone part of your network may be open to the Internet world and may have a very different level of trust.

Depending upon the level of trust and your security policy, you should also have different policies and rules for intruder detection in different areas of your network. Network segments with different security requirements and trust levels are kept physically separate from each other. You can install one intrusion detection system in each zone with different types of rules to detect suspicious network activity. As an example, if your finance department has no web server, any traffic going to port 80 in the finance department segment may come under scrutiny for intruder activity. The same is not true in the DMZ zone where you are running a company web server accessible to everyone.

1.2 IDS Policy

Before you install the intrusion detection system on your network, you must have a policy to detect intruders and take action when you find such activity. A policy must dictate IDS rules and how they will be applied. The IDS policy should contain the following components; you can add more depending upon your requirements.

- Who will monitor the IDS? Depending on the IDS, you may have alerting mechanisms that provide information about intruder activity. These alerting systems may be in the form of simple text files, or they may be more complicated, perhaps integrated to centralized network management systems like HP OpenView or MySQL database. Someone is needed to monitor the intruder activity and the policy must define the responsible person(s). The intruder activity may also be monitored in real time using pop-up windows or web interfaces. In this case operators must have knowledge of alerts and their meaning in terms of severity levels.
- Who will administer the IDS, rotate logs and so on? As with all systems, you need to establish routine maintenance of the IDS.
- Who will handle incidents and how? If there is no incident handling, there is no point in installing an IDS. Depending upon the severity of the incident, you may need to get some government agencies involved.
- What will be the escalation process (level 1, level 2 and so on)? The escalation process is basically an incident response strategy. The policy should clearly describe which incidents should be escalated to higher management.
- Reporting. Reports may be generated showing what happened during the last day, week or month.
- Signature updates. Hackers are continuously creating new types of attacks. These attacks are detected by the IDS if it knows about the attack in the form of signatures. Attack signatures are used in Snort rules to detect attacks. Because of the continuously changing nature of attacks, you must update signatures and rules on your IDS. You can update signatures directly from the Snort web site on a periodic basis or on your own when a new threat is discovered.
- Documentation is required for every project. The IDS policy should describe what type of documentation will be done when attacks are detected. The documentation may include a simple log or record of complete intruder activity. You may also need to build some forms to record data. Reports are also part of regular documentation.

Based on the IDS policy you will get a clear idea of how many IDS sensors and other resources are required for your network. With this information, you will be able to calculate the cost of ownership of IDS more precisely.

1.3 Components of Snort

Snort is logically divided into multiple components. These components work together to detect particular attacks and to generate output in a required format from the detection system. A Snort-based IDS consists of the following major components:

- Packet Decoder
- Preprocessors
- Detection Engine
- Logging and Alerting System
- Output Modules

Figure 1-5 shows how these components are arranged. Any data packet coming from the Internet enters the packet decoder. On its way towards the output modules, it is either dropped, logged or an alert is generated.

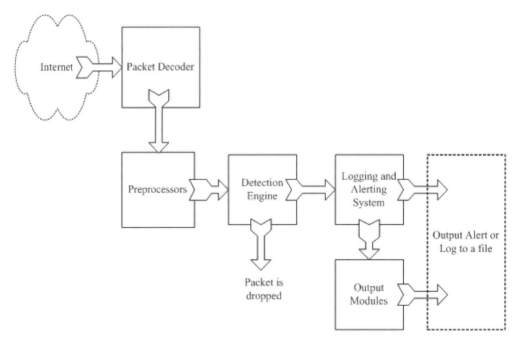

Figure 1-5 Components of Snort.

A brief introduction to these components is presented in this section. As you go through the book and create some rules, you will become more familiar with these components and how they interact with each other.

1.3.1 Packet Decoder

The packet decoder takes packets from different types of network interfaces and prepares the packets to be preprocessed or to be sent to the detection engine. The interfaces may be Ethernet, SLIP, PPP and so on.

1.3.2 Preprocessors

Preprocessors are components or plug-ins that can be used with Snort to arrange or modify data packets before the detection engine does some operation to find out if the packet is being used by an intruder. Some preprocessors also perform detection by finding anomalies in packet headers and generating alerts. Preprocessors are very important for any IDS to prepare data packets to be analyzed against rules in the detection engine. Hackers use different techniques to fool an IDS in different ways. For example, you may have created a rule to find a signature "scripts/iisadmin" in HTTP packets. If you are matching this string exactly, you can easily be fooled by a hacker who makes slight modifications to this string. For example:

- "scripts/./iisadmin"
- "scripts/examples/../iisadmin"
- "scripts\iisadmin"
- "scripts/.\iisadmin"

To complicate the situation, hackers can also insert in the web Uniform Resource Identifier (URI) hexadecimal characters or Unicode characters which are perfectly legal as far as the web server is concerned. Note that the web servers usually understand all of these strings and are able to preprocess them to extract the intended string "scripts/iisadmin". However if the IDS is looking for an exact match, it is not able to detect this attack. A preprocessor can rearrange the string so that it is detectable by the IDS.

Preprocessors are also used for packet defragmentation. When a large data chunk is transferred to a host, the packet is usually fragmented. For example, default maximum length of any data packet on an Ethernet network is usually 1500 bytes. This value is controlled by the Maximum Transfer Unit (MTU) value for the network interface. This means that if you send data which is more than 1500 bytes, it will be split into multiple data packets so that each packet fragment is less than or equal to 1500 bytes. The receiving systems are capable of reassembling these smaller units again to form the original data packet. On IDS, before you can apply any rules or try to find a signature, you have to reassemble the packet. For example, half of the signature may be present in one segment and the other half in another segment. To detect the signature correctly you have to combine all packet segments. Hackers use fragmentation to defeat intrusion detection systems.

The preprocessors are used to safeguard against these attacks. Preprocessors in Snort can defragment packets, decode HTTP URI, re-assemble TCP streams and so on. These functions are a very important part of the intrusion detection system.

1.3.3   The Detection Engine

The detection engine is the most important part of Snort. Its responsibility is to detect if any intrusion activity exists in a packet. The detection engine employs Snort rules for this purpose. The rules are read into internal data structures or chains where they are matched against all packets. If a packet matches any rule, appropriate action is taken; otherwise the packet is dropped. Appropriate actions may be logging the packet or generating alerts.

The detection engine is the time-critical part of Snort. Depending upon how powerful your machine is and how many rules you have defined, it may take different amounts of time to respond to different packets. If traffic on your network is too high when Snort is working in NIDS mode, you may drop some packets and may not get a true real-time response. The load on the detection engine depends upon the following factors:

- Number of rules
- Power of the machine on which Snort is running
- Speed of internal bus used in the Snort machine
- Load on the network

When designing a Network Intrusion Detection System, you should keep all of these factors in mind.

Note that the detection system can dissect a packet and apply rules on different parts of the packet. These parts may be:

- The IP header of the packet.
- The Transport layer header. This header includes TCP, UDP or other transport layer headers. It may also work on the ICMP header.

- The application layer level header. Application layer headers include, but are not limited to, DNS header, FTP header, SNMP header, and SMTP header. You may have to use some indirect methods for application layer headers, like offset of data to be looked for.
- Packet payload. This means that you can create a rule that is used by the detection engine to find a string inside the data that is present inside the packet.

The detection engine works in different ways for different versions of Snort. In all 1.x versions of Snort, the detection engine stops further processing of a packet when a rule is matched. Depending upon the rule, the detection engine takes appropriate action by logging the packet or generating an alert. This means that if a packet matches criteria defined in multiple rules, only the first rule is applied to the packet without looking for other matches. This is fine except for one problem. A low priority rule generates a low priority alert, even if a high priority rule meriting a high priority alert is located later in the rule chain. This problem is rectified in Snort version 2 where all rules are matched against a packet before generating an alert. After matching all rules, the highest priority rule is selected to generate the alert.

The detection engine in Snort version 2.0 is completely rewritten so that it is a lot faster compared to detection in earlier versions of Snort. While Snort 2.0 is still not in release at the time of writing this book, earlier analysis shows that the new detection engine may be up to eighteen times faster.

1.3.4   Logging and Alerting System

Depending upon what the detection engine finds inside a packet, the packet may be used to log the activity or generate an alert. Logs are kept in simple text files, tcp-dump-style files or some other form. All of the log files are stored under /var/log/snort folder by default. You can use -l command line options to modify the location of generating logs and alerts. Many command line options discussed in the next chapter can modify the type and detail of information that is logged by the logging and alerting system.

1.3.5   Output Modules

Output modules or plug-ins can do different operations depending on how you want to save output generated by the logging and alerting system of Snort. Basically these modules control the type of output generated by the logging and alerting system. Depending on the configuration, output modules can do things like the following:

- Simply logging to `/var/log/snort/alerts` file or some other file
- Sending SNMP traps
- Sending messages to syslog facility
- Logging to a database like MySQL or Oracle. You will learn more about using MySQL later in this book
- Generating eXtensible Markup Language (XML) output
- Modifying configuration on routers and firewalls.
- Sending Server Message Block (SMB) messages to Microsoft Windows-based machines

Other tools can also be used to send alerts in other formats such as e-mail messages or viewing alerts using a web interface. You will learn more about these in later chapters. Table 1-1 summarizes different components of an IDS.

Table 1-1 Components of an IDS

Name	Description
Packet Decoder	Prepares packets for processing.
Preprocessors or Input Plugins	Used to normalize protocol headers, detect anomalies, packet re-assembly and TCP stream re-assembly.
Detection Engine	Applies rules to packets.
Logging and Alerting System	Generates alert and log messages.
Output Modules	Process alerts and logs and generate final output.

1.4 Dealing with Switches

Depending upon the type of switches used, you can use Snort on a switch port. Some switches, like Cisco, allow you to replicate all ports traffic on one port where you can attach the Snort machine. These ports are usually referred to as spanning ports. The best place to install Snort is right behind the firewall or router so that all of the Internet traffic is visible to Snort before it enters any switch or hub. As an example, if you have a firewall with a T1 connection to the Internet and a switch is used on the inside, the typical connection scheme will be as shown in Figure 1-6.

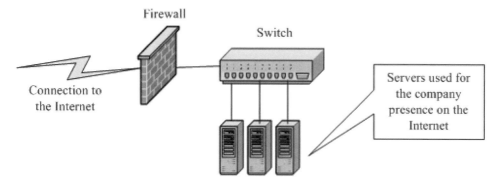

Figure 1-6 A typical connection scheme with one firewall and switched network.

If the switch you are using has a spanning port, you can connect the IDS machine to the spanning port as shown in Figure 1-7. All network traffic, including internal data flowing among company servers and the Internet data, will be visible to the IDS.

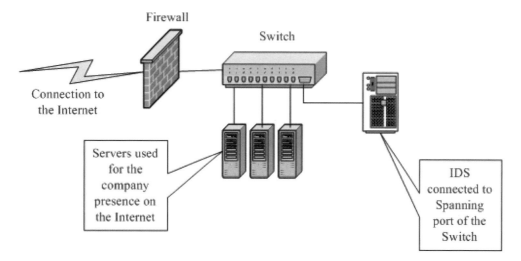

Figure 1-7 IDS connected a spanning port.

You can also connect the IDS to a small HUB or a Network TAP right behind the firewall, i.e., between firewall and the switch. In this case all incoming and outgoing traffic is visible to the IDS. The scheme is shown in Figure 1-8.

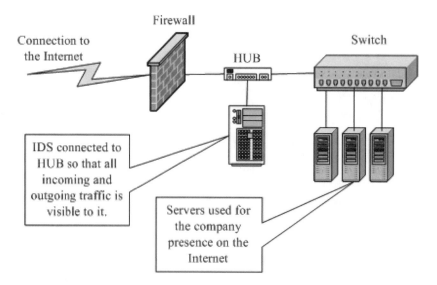

Figure 1-8 Connecting an IDS in a switched environment.

Note that when the IDS is connected as shown in Figure 1-8, data flowing among the company servers is not visible to the IDS. The IDS can see only that data which is coming from or going to the Internet. This is useful if you expect attacks from outside and the internal network is a trusted one.

1.5 TCP Stream Follow Up

A new preprocessor named Stream4 has been added to Snort. This preprocessor is capable of dealing with thousands of simultaneous streams and its configuration will be discussed in Chapter 4. It allows TCP stream reassembly and stateful inspection of TCP packets. This means that you can assemble packets in a particular TCP session to find anomalies and attacks that use multiple TCP packets. You can also look for packets coming to and/or originating from a particular server port.

1.6 Supported Platforms

Snort is supported on a number of hardware platforms and operating systems. Currently Snort is available for the following operating systems:

- Linux
- OpenBSD

- FreeBSD
- NetBSD
- Solaris (both Sparc and i386)
- HP-UX
- AIX
- IRIX
- MacOS
- Windows

For a current list of supported platforms, refer to the Snort home page at http://www.snort.org.

1.7 How to Protect IDS Itself

One major issue is how to protect the system on which your intrusion detection software is running. If security of the IDS is compromised, you may start getting false alarms or no alarms at all. The intruder may disable IDS before actually performing any attack. There are different ways to protect your system, starting from very general recommendations to some sophisticated methods. Some of these are mentioned below.

- The first thing that you can do is not to run any service on your IDS sensor itself. Network servers are the most common method of exploiting a system.
- New threats are discovered and patches are released by vendors. This is almost a continuous and non-stop process. The platform on which you are running IDS should be patched with the latest releases from your vendor. For example, if Snort is running on a Microsoft Windows machine, you should have all the latest security patches from Microsoft installed.
- Configure the IDS machine so that it does not respond to ping (ICMP Echo-type) packets.
- If you are running Snort on a Linux machine, use netfilter/iptable to block any unwanted data. Snort will still be able to see all of the data.
- You should use IDS only for the purpose of intrusion detection. It should not be used for other activities and user accounts should not be created except those that are absolutely necessary.

In addition to these common measures, Snort can be used in special cases as well. Following are two special techniques that can be used with Snort to protect it from being attacked.

1.7.1 Snort on Stealth Interface

You can run Snort on a stealth interface which only listens to the incoming traffic but does not send any data packets out. A special cable is used on the stealth interface. On the host where Snort is running, you have to short pins 1 and 2. Pins 3 and 6 are connected to same pins on the other side. Please see Snort FAQ at http://www.snort.org/docs/faq.html for more information on this arrangement.

1.7.2 Snort with no IP Address Interface

You can also use Snort on an interface where no IP address is assigned. For example, on a Linux machine, you can bring up interface eth0 using command "ifconfig eth0 up" without assigning an actual IP address. The advantage is that when the Snort host doesn't have an IP address itself, nobody can access it. You can configure an IP address on eth1 that can be used to access the sensor itself. This is shown in Figure 1-9.

On Microsoft Windows systems, you can use an interface without binding TCP/IP to the interface, in which case no IP address will be assigned to the interface. Don't forget to disable other protocols and services on the interface as well. In some cases it has been noted that winpcap (library used on Microsoft Windows machines to capture packets) does not work well when no IP address is assigned on the interface. In such a case, you can use the following method.

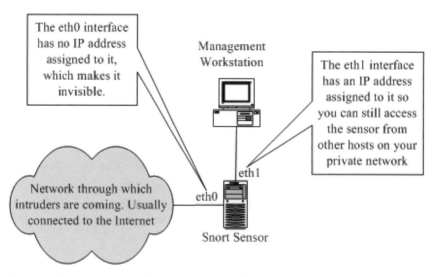

Figure 1-9 Snort sensor with two interfaces. One of these has no IP address assigned.

• Enable TCP/IP on the network interface that you want to use in the stealth mode. Disable everything other than TCP/IP.
• Enable DHCP client.
• Disable DHCP service.

This will cause no address to be assigned to the interface while the interface is still bound to TCP/IP networking.

1.8 References

1. Intrusion detection FAQ at http://www.sans.org/newlook/resources/IDFAQ/ID_FAQ.htm
2. Honey Pot Project at http://project.honeynet.org/
3. Snort FAQ at http://www.snort.org/docs/faq.html
4. Honeyd Honey Pot at http://www.citi.umich.edu/u/provos/honeyd/
5. Winpcap at http://winpcap.polito.it/
6. Cisco systems at http://www.cisco.com
7. Checkpoint web site at http://www.checkpoint.com
8. Netscreen at http://www.netscreen.com
9. Netfilter at http://www.netfilter.org
10. Snort at http://www.snort.org
11. The Nmap tool at http://www.nmap.org
12. Nessus at http://www.nessus.org
13. MySQL database at http://www.mysql.org
14. ACID at http://www.cert.org/kb/acid
15. Apache web server at http://www.apache.org

## CHAPTER 2

Installing Snort and Getting Started

A Snort installation may consist of only a working Snort daemon or of a complete Snort system with many other tools. If you install only Snort, you can capture intrusion data in text or binary files and then view these files later on with the help of a text editor or some other tool like Barnyard, which will be explained later in this book. With this simple installation you can also send alert data to an SNMP manager, like HP OpenView or OpenNMS, in the form of SNMP traps. Alert data can also be sent to a Microsoft Windows machine in the form of SMB pop-up windows. However, if you install other tools, you can perform more sophisticated operations on the intrusion data, such as logging Snort data to a database and analyzing it through a web interface. Using the web interface, you can view all alerts generated by Snort. The analysis tools allow you to make sense of the captured data instead of spending lots of time with Snort log files.

Other tools that can be used with Snort are listed below. Each of them has a specific task. A comprehensive working Snort system utilizes these tools to provide a web-based user interface with a backend database.

- MySQL is used with Snort to log alert data. Other databases like Oracle can also be used but MySQL is the most popular database with Snort. In fact, any ODBC-compliant database can be used with Snort.

- Apache acts as a web server.
- PHP is used as an interface between the web server and MySQL database.
- ACID is a PHP package that is used to view and analyze Snort data using a web browser.
- GD library is used by ACID to create graphs.
- PHPLOT is used to present data in graphic format on the web pages used in ACID. GD library must be working correctly to use PHPLOT.
- ADODB is used by ACID to connect to MySQL database.

2.1 Snort Installation Scenarios

Typical Snort installations may vary depending upon the environment where you are installing it. Some of the typical installation schemes are listed below for your reference. You can select one of these depending on the type of network you have.

2.1.1 Test Installation

A simple Snort installation consists of a single Snort sensor. Snort logs data to text files. These log files can then be viewed later on by the Snort administrator. This arrangement is suitable only for test environments because the cost of data analysis is very high in the production environment. To install Snort for this purpose, you can get a pre-compiled version from http://www.snort.org and install it on your system. For RedHat Linux, you can download the RPM package. For Microsoft Windows systems, download executables and install on your system.

2.1.2 Single Sensor Production IDS

A production installation of Snort with only one sensor is suitable for small networks with only one Internet connection. Putting the sensor behind a router or firewall will enable you to detect the activity of intruders into the system. However, if you are really interested in scanning all Internet traffic, you can put the sensor outside the firewall as well.

In this installation, you can either download a precompiled version of Snort from its web site (http://www.snort.org) or compile it yourself from the source code. You should compile the source code yourself only if you need some feature which is not available in the precompiled versions. The compilation process for Snort is discussed in detail in this chapter.

In a production installation, you also need to implement startup and shutdown procedures so that Snort automatically starts at boot time. If you are installing a precompiled version for Linux, the installation procedure with RPM will take care of it. On Microsoft Windows systems, you can start Snort as a service or put a batch file in the startup group. Issues related to Microsoft Windows are covered in Chapter 8. The logging is done in text or binary files and tools like SnortSnarf can be used to analyze data. SnortSnarf is discussed in Chapter 6 in detail.

2.1.3   Single Sensor with Network Management System Integration

In a production system, you can configure Snort to send traps to a network management system. There are a variety of network management systems used in the enterprise. The most popular commercial systems are from Hewlett-Packard, IBM and Computer Associates.

Snort integration into these network management systems is done through the use of SNMP traps. When you go through the compilation process of Snort later in this chapter, you will learn how to build SNMP capability into Snort. Chapter 4 provides more information about configuring SNMP trap destinations, community names and so on.

2.1.4   Single Sensor with Database and Web Interface

The most common use of Snort should be with integration to a database. The database is used to log Snort data where it can be viewed and analyzed later on, using a web-based interface. A typical setup of this type consists of three basic components:

1. Snort sensor
2. A database server
3. A web server

Snort logs data into the database. You can view the data using a web browser connected to the sensor. This scheme is shown in Figure 1-1 in Chapter 1. All three components can be present on the same system as shown in Figure 1-2 in Chapter 1.

Different types of database servers like MySQL, PostgresSQL, Oracle, Microsoft SQL server and other ODBC-compliant databases can be used with Snort. PHP is used to get data from the database and to generate web pages.

This setup provides a very good and comprehensive IDS which is easy to manage and user friendly. You have to provide a user name, password, database name and database server address to Snort to enable it to log to the database. In a single-sensor scheme where the database is running on the sensor itself, you can use "localhost" as the host name. You have to build database logging capability into Snort at the compile time, which will be described later in this chapter. Configuring Snort to use the database is discussed in Chapter 4, 5 and 6.

2.1.5   Multiple Snort Sensors with Centralized Database

In a corporate environment, you probably have multiple locations where you would like to install Snort sensors. Managing all of these sensors and analyzing all data collected by these sensors separately is a very difficult job. There are multiple ways to setup and install Snort in the enterprise as a distributed IDS.

One method is shown in Figure 1-3 in Chapter 1 where multiple sensors connect to the same centralized database. All data generated by these sensors is stored in the database. You run a web server like Apache (http://www.apache.org). A user then uses a web browser to view this data and analyze it.

However there are some practical problems with this setup.

- All of the sensors must have access to the database at the time you start Snort. If Snort is not able to connect to the database at the start time, it dies.
- The database must be available all of the time to all sensors. If any of the network links are down, data is lost.
- You have to open up additional ports for database logging in firewalls if a firewall lies between the database server and any of the sensors. Sometime this is not feasible or against security policy.

You can come up with some alternate mechanisms where Snort sensors do not have a direct connection to the database server. The sensors may be configured to log to local files. These files can then be uploaded to a centralized server on a periodic basis using utilities like SCP. The SCP utility is a secure file transfer program that uses Secure Shell (SSH) protocol. Firewall administrators usually allow SSH port (port 22) to pass through. You can run certain utilities like Snort itself,[1] Barnyard or some other tool to extract data from these log files and put it into the database server. You can use the usual web interface to view this data later on. The only problem with this approach is that the data in the database is not strictly "real-time". There is a certain delay which depends upon frequency of uploading data using SCP to the centralized database server. This arrangement is shown in Figure 2-1.

Note that this centralized server must be running SSH server so that SCP utility is able to upload files to this server.

---

1.   Snort can be run to get information from its own log files using a command line parameter.

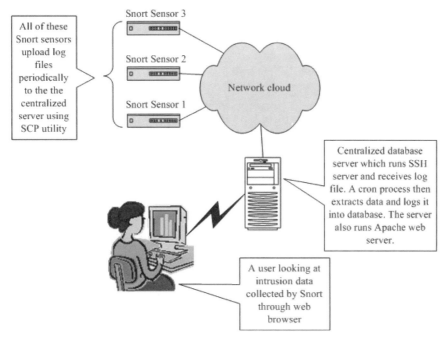

Figure 2-1 Distributed Snort installation with the help of tools like SCP and Barnyard.

As mentioned in Chapter 1, the ultimate objective of this book is to help you install Snort and to make all of these packages work with each other. When you go through this book, you will see how these components act with each other to build a complete working intrusion detection system. The website for this book http://authors.phptr.com/rehman/ contains all of these packages in the source code form. You will also find scripts on the site that are very helpful in installing these packages on a new system with no hassle. In fact, by using the scripts on the site as discussed in this book, you should be able to have a working IDS by just using a few commands as the root user. If you use a version newer than that discussed in this book, the latest versions of the scripts that support new Snort versions can be downloaded from http://www.argusnetsec.com/downloads.

This books details the installation of these components on a RedHat Linux version 7.3 machine. But the process is similar on other platforms and other versions of RedHat Linux. All components are installed under /opt directory for the purpose of this book. However, when a pre-compiled package is used, the location of files may be different. When you use the scripts in the book or from the website, files will be installed under this directory. In this chapter, you will learn how to install Snort as a standalone product. Later chapters will focus on other components.

Snort is available in both source code and binary forms. Pre-compiled binary packages are fine for most installations. As mentioned earlier, if you want to add or remove certain features of Snort, you need to download the source code version and then compile it yourself. For example, someone may be interested in SMB alerts while another may consider it unsecure. If you want to build Snort without support for SMB alerts, you may want to build it yourself. The same is true of other features like SNMP traps, MySQL and so on. Another reason to compile the source code yourself may be when a new version is released but binaries are not yet available. You may also need to compile the Snort package if you take a snapshot of the code under development. This chapter will provide a step-by-step guide to installing Snort.

The basic installation procedure is simple because you have plenty of predefined rules available with Snort that cover most of the known intrusion signatures. However, customization of your installation may require a lot of work.

Version 1.9.0 is used in this chapter, but the installation procedure is similar for other versions of the software. After installation, basic information for getting started with Snort is also provided, including basic Snort concepts, logging and alerting and some information about Snort modes of operation.

2.2 Installing Snort

In this section you will learn how to install precompiled version of Snort as well as how to compile and install it by yourself. Installation of the pre-compiled RPM package is very easy and requires only a few steps. However if you get Snort in source code format, the installation process may take some time and understanding.

2.2.1   Installing Snort from the RPM Package

The installation procedure of Snort from the RPM package involves the following steps.

2.2.1.1   Download

Download the latest version from Snort web site (http://www.snort.org). At the time of writing this book, the latest binary file is snort-1.9.0-1snort.i386.rpm.

2.2.1.2   Install

Run the following command to install Snort binaries:

```
rpm --install  snort-1.9.0-1snort.i386.rpm
```

This command will perform the following actions:

- Create a directory /etc/snort where all Snort rule files and configuration files are stored.
- Create a directory /var/log/snort where Snort log files will be stored.
- Create a directory /usr/share/doc/snort-1.9.0 and store Snort documentation files in that directory. You will see files like FAQ (Frequently Asked Questions), README and other files in this directory.
- Create a file snort-plain in /usr/sbin directory. This is the Snort daemon.
- Create a file /etc/rc.d/init.d/snortd file which is startup and shutdown script. On RedHat Linux, this is equivalent to /etc/init.d/snortd.

Basic installation is complete at this point and you can start using Snort. The version of Snort installed this way is not compiled with database support, so you can use it only for logging to files in the /var/log/snort directory.

2.2.1.3   Starting, Stopping and Restarting Snort

To run Snort manually, use the following command:

```
/etc/init.d/snortd start
```

This command will start Snort and you can run the Snort daemon using the "ps –ef" command. You should see a line like the following in the output of this command:

```
root      15999     1   0 18:31 ?        00:00:01 /usr/sbin/
snort -A fast -b -l /var/log/snort -d -D -i eth0 -c /etc/
snort/snort.conf
```

Note that you have to start Snort manually each time you reboot the machine. You can automate this process by creating links to this file, which will be explained later in this chapter.

To stop Snort, use the following command:

```
/etc/init.d/snortd stop
```

To restart Snort, use this command:

```
/etc/init.d/snortd restart
```

2.2.2   Installing Snort from Source Code

To install Snort from the source code, you have to build it first. You can build the executable snort file using the procedure explained in this section. First, download the latest version of Snort from its web site (http://www.snort.org/). Just look for the "download" link and grab the latest version of the software. At the time of writing this book, the latest version was 1.9.0. The downloadable file name is `snort-1.9.0.tar.gz`, which can be saved in the /opt directory on the Linux box. Note that the installation method is similar for other versions which may be available by the time you read this book.

N O T E   You must have libpcap installed on your UNIX machine or WinPcap if you are using Microsoft Windows. You can get WinPcap from http://winpcap.polito.it/. Libpcap is available from http://www-nrg.ee.lbl.gov/.

2.2.2.1   Unpacking

The first step after downloading is unpacking the source code. Use the following command to unpack it:

```
tar zxvf snort-1.9.0.tar.gz
```

This will create a directory /opt/snort-1.9.0, assuming that you have downloaded the file in /opt directory and have run the `tar` command in this directory. In case of other versions of Snort, the directory name will be different and will reflect the version number. After unpacking you can see the directory tree created by the `tar` command using the `tree` command. The following is a snapshot of directories present under `/opt/snort-1.9.0` directory.

```
[root@conformix opt]# tree -d snort-1.9.0
snort-1.9.0
|-- contrib
|-- doc
|-- etc
|-- rules
|-- src
|   |-- detection-plugins
|   |-- output-plugins
|   |-- preprocessors
|   `-- win32
|       |-- WIN32-Code
|       |-- WIN32-Includes
|       |   |-- NET
|       |   |-- NETINET
|       |   |-- libnet
|       |   |-- mysql
|       |   `-- rpc
|       |-- WIN32-Libraries
|       |   |-- libnet
```

```
|         |    `-- mysql
|         `-- WIN32-Prj
`-- templates

21 directories
[root@conformix opt]#
```

A brief list of the contents of these directories is listed below:

- The `contrib` directory contains utilities which are not strictly part of Snort itself. These utilities include ACID, MySQL database creation scripts and other things.
- The `doc` directory contains documentation files, as is evident from the name of the directory.
- The `etc` directory contains configuration files.
- The `rules` directory contains predefined rule files.
- All source code is present under the `src` directory.
- The `templates` directory is useful only for people who want to write their own plug-ins. It has no significance for general Snort users.

2.2.2.2   Compiling and Installation

The compilation and installation process consists of three steps as listed below:

1. Running the `configure` script.
2. Running the `make` command.
3. Running the `make install` command.

To start the compilation process of Snort, go to `/opt/snort-1.9.0` directory and run the `configure` script. If you are new to GNU style software, the `configure` script is a common utility with open source packages. It is used to set some parameters, create makefiles, and detect development tools and libraries available on your system. Many command line options can be used with the `configure` script. These options determine which Snort components will be compiled with Snort. For example, using these options, you can build support of SNMP, MySQL or SMB alerts, in addition to many other things. You can also determine the directory in which the final Snort files will be installed. Available command line options with the configure script can be listed using the "`./configure -help`" command as shown below:

```
[root@conformix snort-1.9.0]# ./configure --help
Usage: configure [options] [host]
Options: [defaults in brackets after descriptions]
Configuration:
  --cache-file=FILE       cache test results in FILE
  --help                  print this message
  --no-create             do not create output files
  --quiet, --silent       do not print `checking...' messages
  --version               print the version of autoconf that
                          created configure
Directory and file names:
  --prefix=PREFIX         install architecture-independent
                          files in PREFIX
                          [/usr/local]
  --exec-prefix=EPREFIX   install architecture-dependent
                          files in EPREFIX
                          [same as prefix]
  --bindir=DIR            user executables in DIR
                          [EPREFIX/bin]
  --sbindir=DIR           system admin executables in DIR
                          [EPREFIX/sbin]
  --libexecdir=DIR        program executables in DIR
                          [EPREFIX/libexec]
  --datadir=DIR           read-only architecture-independent
                          data in DIR
                          [PREFIX/share]
  --sysconfdir=DIR        read-only single-machine data in
                          DIR [PREFIX/etc]
  --sharedstatedir=DIR    modifiable architecture-independent
                          data in DIR
                          [PREFIX/com]
  --localstatedir=DIR     modifiable single-machine data in
                          DIR [PREFIX/var]
  --libdir=DIR            object code libraries in DIR
                          [EPREFIX/lib]
  --includedir=DIR        C header files in DIR
                          [PREFIX/include]
  --oldincludedir=DIR     C header files for non-gcc in DIR
                          [/usr/include]
  --infodir=DIR           info documentation in DIR
                          [PREFIX/info]
  --mandir=DIR            man documentation in DIR
                          [PREFIX/man]
  --srcdir=DIR            find the sources in DIR
                          [configure dir or ..]
  --program-prefix=PREFIX prepend PREFIX to installed program
                          names
```

```
        --program-suffix=SUFFIX append SUFFIX to installed program
                                names
        --program-transform-name=PROGRAM
                                run sed PROGRAM on installed
                                program names
Host type:
   --build=BUILD                configure for building on BUILD
                                [BUILD=HOST]
   --host=HOST                  configure for HOST [guessed]
   --target=TARGET              configure for TARGET [TARGET=HOST]
Features and packages:
   --disable-FEATURE            do not include FEATURE (same as
                                --enable-FEATURE=no)
   --enable-FEATURE[=ARG]       include FEATURE [ARG=yes]
   --with-PACKAGE[=ARG]         use PACKAGE [ARG=yes]
   --without-PACKAGE            do not use PACKAGE (same as
                                --with-PACKAGE=no)
   --x-includes=DIR             X include files are in DIR
   --x-libraries=DIR            X library files are in DIR
--enable and --with options recognized:
   --enable-debug               enable debugging options
                                (bugreports and developers only)
   --enable-profile             enable profiling options
                                (developers only)
   --with-libpcap-includes=DIR  libcap include directory
   --with-libpcap-libraries=DIR libcap library directory
   --with-mysql=DIR             support for mysql
   --with-odbc=DIR              support for odbc
   --with-postgresql=DIR        support for postgresql
   --with-oracle=DIR            support for oracle
   --with-snmp                  support for snmp
   --with-openssl=DIR           support for openssl
   --enable-sourcefire          Enable Sourcefire specific build
                                options
   --enable-perfmonitor          Enable perfmonitor preprocessor
   --enable-smbalerts           SMB alerting capaility via Samba
   --enable-flexresp            Flexible Responses on hostile
                                connection attempts
[root@conformix snort-1.9.0]#
```

Options values listed in square brackets indicate that if that particular option is not selected, the value mentioned in the square bracket will be used by default. For example, the following three lines show that if the `with-prefix` option is not used on the command line for the configure script, `/usr/local` value will be used as PREFIX by default. Note that PREFIX is the directory under which Snort files are installed when you use the "`make install`" command.

```
--prefix=PREFIX            install architecture-independent
                           files in PREFIX
                           [/usr/local]
```

A typical session with the `configure` scripts may be as follows. Output is truncated after displaying the initial output line to save space. Note the options that have been enabled on the command line.

```
[root@conformix snort-1.9.0]# ./configure --prefix=/opt/snort
--enable-smbalerts --enable-flexresp --with-mysql --with-snmp
--with-openssl
loading cache ./config.cache
checking for a BSD compatible install... (cached) /usr/bin/
install -c
checking whether build environment is sane... yes
checking whether make sets ${MAKE}... (cached) yes
checking for working aclocal... found
checking for working autoconf... found
checking for working automake... found
checking for working autoheader... found
checking for working makeinfo... found
checking for gcc... (cached) gcc
checking whether the C compiler (gcc  ) works... yes
checking whether the C compiler (gcc  ) is a cross-compiler...
no
checking whether we are using GNU C... (cached) yes
checking whether gcc accepts -g... (cached) yes
checking for gcc option to accept ANSI C... (cached) none
needed
checking for ranlib... (cached) ranlib
```

Output is truncated at the end because the `configure` script may create a lot of information. The `prefix` option on the command line is used to tell the `configure` script the location of final installation directory. Other options are used to enable the following components of Snort:

- Support of MySQL database.
- Support of SNMP traps.
- Support of SMB alerts. SMB alerts are used to send pop-up windows to Microsoft Windows machines.
- Enable support of flex response. Flex response is used to terminate network sessions in real time. More information about flex response will be provided in the following chapters. Note that to enable support of this option, you must

have libnet installed. You can download libnet from http://www.securityfocus.net. I have used version 1.0.2a for this installation.[2]

After running the `configure` script, you can run the following two commands to compile and install Snort files.

```
make
make install
```

The first command may take some time to complete depending upon how powerful your machine is. When you run the second command, files are installed in the appropriate directories. The `make install` command installs Snort binaries in `/opt/snort` directory as you selected `--prefix=/opt/snort` on the command line for the `configure` script.

Useful command line parameters that can be used with the `configure` script are shown in Table 2-1

Table 2-1 Command line parameters used with configure scripts

Parameter	Description
`--with-mysql`	Build support of MySQL with Snort.
`--with-snmp`	Build support of SNMP while compiling Snort. You have to use –with-openssl if you use this option.
`--with-openssl`	Enable OpenSSL support. You may need to use this when you use SNMP option.
`--with-oracle`	Enable support for Oracle database.
`--with-odbc`	Build support for ODBC in Snort.
`--enable-flexresp`	Enables use of Flex Response which allows canceling hostile connections. This is still experimental (see README.FLEXRESP file in Snort distribution).
`--enable-smbalerts`	Enable SMB alerts. Be careful using this as this invokes smbclient user space process every time it sends an alert.
`--prefix=DIR`	Set directory for installing Snort files.

2.   The installation procedure for libnet is found in the accompanying README file. Basically it consists of four steps:
     • Untar the file using tar zxvf libnet-1.0.2a.tar.gz
     • Change to directory Libnet-1.0.2a and run the ./configure command.
     • Run make command.
     • Run make install command.

You can also run the "make check" command before running the "make install" command to make sure that Snort is built properly.

After installing, run Snort to see if the executable file is working. Using the above mentioned procedure, Snort binary is installed in the /opt/snort/bin directory. The following command just displays the basic help message of the newly built snort and command line options.

```
[root@conformix snort]# /opt/snort/bin/snort -?
Initializing Output Plugins!

-*> Snort! <*-
Version 1.9.0 (Build 209)
By Martin Roesch (roesch@sourcefire.com, www.snort.org)
USAGE: /opt/snort/bin/snort [-options] <filter options>
Options:
        -A          Set alert mode: fast, full, console,
                    or none  (alert file alerts only)
                    "unsock" enables UNIX socket logging
                    (experimental).
        -a          Display ARP packets
        -b          Log packets in tcpdump format (much
                    faster!)
        -c <rules>  Use Rules File <rules>
        -C          Print out payloads with character data
                    only (no hex)
        -d          Dump the Application Layer
        -D          Run Snort in background (daemon) mode
        -e          Display the second layer header info
        -f          Turn off fflush() calls after binary log
                    writes
        -F <bpf>    Read BPF filters from file <bpf>
        -g <gname>  Run snort gid as <gname> group (or gid)
                    after initialization
        -G <mode>   Add reference ids back into alert msgs
                    (modes: basic, url)
        -h <hn>     Home network = <hn>
        -i <if>     Listen on interface <if>
        -I          Add Interface name to alert output
        -l <ld>     Log to directory <ld>
        -m <umask>  Set umask = <umask>
        -M <wrkst>  Sends SMB message to workstations in file
                    <wrkst>
                    (Requires smbclient to be in PATH)
        -n <cnt>    Exit after receiving <cnt> packets
        -N          Turn off logging (alerts still work)
        -o          Change the rule testing order to
```

```
                        Pass|Alert|Log
        -O              Obfuscate the logged IP addresses
        -p              Disable promiscuous mode sniffing
        -P <snap>       set explicit snaplen of packet
                        (default: 1514)
        -q              Quiet. Don't show banner and status report
        -r <tf>         Read and process tcpdump file <tf>
        -R <id>         Include 'id' in snort_intf<id>.pid file
                        name
        -s              Log alert messages to syslog
        -S <n=v>        Set rules file variable n equal to value v
        -t <dir>        Chroots process to <dir> after
                        initialization
        -T              Test and report on the current Snort
                        configuration
        -u <uname>      Run snort uid as <uname> user (or uid)
                        after initialization
        -U              Use UTC for timestamps
        -v              Be verbose
        -V              Show version number
        -w              Dump 802.11 management and control frames
        -X              Dump the raw packet data starting at the
                        link layer
        -y              Include year in timestamp in the alert and
                        log files
        -z              Set assurance mode, match on established
                        sesions (for TCP)
        -?              Show this information
    <Filter Options> are standard BPF options, as seen in TCPDump
    [root@conformix snort]#
```

If you see this message, you have built Snort properly. In the next section, you will learn how to configure and run Snort.

2.2.2.3 After Installation Processes

Now that you have built Snort binary, you have to do few things before you can start using Snort. These include:

1. Create directory /var/log/snort where Snort creates log files by default.

2. Create a directory to save configuration files. I have created /opt/snort/ etc. You can create a directory of your own.

3. Create or copy the Snort configuration file in /opt/snort/etc directory.

4. Create a directory `/opt/snort/rules` and copy default rule files to `/opt/snort/etc` directory. The path of this directory is mentioned in the main `snort.conf` file and you can create a directory of your own choice if you like.

The steps are explained below in detail.

First, create a directory `/var/log/snort` where Snort will keep its log files. You can use any other directory for this purpose but this is the usual place to store Snort log data files. If you want to use any other directory, you have to use command line option `-l` when starting Snort.

Secondly, you have to create the Snort configuration file. When Snort starts, it can read its configuration, which is `snort.conf`, from the current directory or from `.snortrc` in the home directory of the user who launched Snort. If this file is present in some other directory, you can also use the `-c` option on the command line to specify the name of the rules file. As a starting point, create a directory `/opt/snort/etc` directory and copy the `snort.conf` file that came with the Snort source code files. Copy `classification.config` and `reference.config` files to `/opt/snort/etc` directory. These files are included in the main `snort.conf` file. Also copy all files from the rules directory of the source code tree to `/opt/snort/rules` directory. To perform these actions, you can use the following sequence of commands:[3]

```
mkdir /opt/snort/etc
cp /opt/snort-1.9.0/etc/snort.conf /opt/snort/etc
cp /opt/snort-1.9.0/etc/classification.config /opt/snort/etc
cp /opt/snort-1.9.0/etc/reference.config /opt/snort/etc
mkdir /opt/snort/rules
cp /opt/snort-1.9.0/rules/* /opt/snort/rules
```

Files in the rules directory end with `.rules` and contain different rules. These files are included inside the `snort.conf` file. The location of these rule files is controlled by the RULE_PATH variable defined in `snort.conf` file. A typical definition of this variable in the `snort.conf` file is as follows:

```
var RULE_PATH ../rules
```

This means that rule files are located in a directory named "rules". The path `../rules` is with reference to the location of `snort.conf` file. For example, if `snort.conf` file is located in the `/opt/snort/etc` directory, all rule files should be present in the `/opt/snort/rules` directory. As another example, if `snort.conf` file is present in the `/var/snort` directory, rules files must be

---

3.   Note that you must have root access to run these commands.

present in the /var/rules directory. You can keep all rule files and snort.conf file in the same directory if you set the value of this variable to ./ instead of ../rules in the snort.conf file using the following line:

```
var RULE_PATH ./
```

More information about Snort rules is found in the next chapter where you will learn how to define your own rules as well.

The classification.config file contains information about Snort rules classification and more information about this file is found in the next chapter. Note that /opt/snort-1.9.0 is the directory where all Snort source code files are present. If you are using a different version of Snort, the directory name will be different.

The reference.config file lists URLs for different reference web sites where more information can be found for alerts. These references are used in Snort rules and you will learn more about references in the next chapter. A typical reference.config file is like the following:

```
# $Id: reference.config,v 1.3 2002/08/28 14:19:15 chrisgreen
Exp $
# The following defines URLs for the references found in the
rules
#
# config reference: system URL

config reference: bugtraq    http://www.securityfocus.com/bid/
config reference: cve        http://cve.mitre.org/cgi-bin/
cvename.cgi?name=
config reference: arachNIDS http://www.whitehats.com/info/IDS

# Note, this one needs a suffix as well.... lets add that in a
bit.
config reference: McAfee     http://vil.nai.com/vil/content/v_
config reference: nessus     http://cgi.nessus.org/plugins/
dump.php3?id=
config reference: url        http://
```

Note that both classification.config and reference.config files are included in the main snort.conf file.

N O T E If you used the RPM package, all configuration files are already present in the /etc/snort directory and you don't need to take the above mentioned actions.

Now you can start Snort using the following command. The command displays startup messages and then starts listening to interface eth0. Note the command line option where snort.conf is specified with its full path. I would recommend always using the full path for snort.conf on the command line to avoid any confusion.

```
[root@conformix snort]# /opt/snort/bin/snort -c /opt/snort/
etc/snort.conf
Initializing Output Plugins!
Log directory = /var/log/snort

Initializing Network Interface eth0

        --== Initializing Snort ==--
Decoding Ethernet on interface eth0
Initializing Preprocessors!
Initializing Plug-ins!
Parsing Rules file /opt/snort/etc/snort.conf

+++++++++++++++++++++++++++++++++++++++++++++++++++++
Initializing rule chains...
No arguments to frag2 directive, setting defaults to:
    Fragment timeout: 60 seconds
    Fragment memory cap: 4194304 bytes
    Fragment min_ttl:   0
    Fragment ttl_limit: 5
    Fragment Problems: 0
Stream4 config:
    Stateful inspection: ACTIVE
    Session statistics: INACTIVE
    Session timeout: 30 seconds
    Session memory cap: 8388608 bytes
    State alerts: INACTIVE
    Evasion alerts: INACTIVE
    Scan alerts: ACTIVE
    Log Flushed Streams: INACTIVE
    MinTTL: 1
    TTL Limit: 5
    Async Link: 0
No arguments to stream4_reassemble, setting defaults:
     Reassemble client: ACTIVE
     Reassemble server: INACTIVE
     Reassemble ports: 21 23 25 53 80 143 110 111 513
     Reassembly alerts: ACTIVE
     Reassembly method: FAVOR_OLD
http_decode arguments:
    Unicode decoding
    IIS alternate Unicode decoding
```

```
        IIS double encoding vuln
        Flip backslash to slash
        Include additional whitespace separators
        Ports to decode http on: 80
rpc_decode arguments:
        Ports to decode RPC on: 111 32771
telnet_decode arguments:
        Ports to decode telnet on: 21 23 25 119
Conversation Config:
     KeepStats: 0
     Conv Count: 32000
     Timeout    : 60
     Alert Odd?: 0
     Allowed IP Protocols:   All

Portscan2 config:
     log: /var/log/snort/scan.log
     scanners_max: 3200
     targets_max: 5000
     target_limit: 5
     port_limit: 20
     timeout: 60
1273 Snort rules read...
1273 Option Chains linked into 133 Chain Headers
0 Dynamic rules
+++++++++++++++++++++++++++++++++++++++++++++++++++

Rule application order: ->activation->dynamic->alert->pass-
>log

        --== Initialization Complete ==--

-*> Snort! <*-
Version 1.9.0 (Build 209)
By Martin Roesch (roesch@sourcefire.com, www.snort.org)
```

As you can see from the previous output, Snort has started listening to interface eth0. If any packet matches the rules, Snort will take appropriate action according to that rule and will generate alerts. Alerts may be generated in different forms. Alerts that you will see with this basic setup are logged in /var/log/snort/alerts file. Later on you will see how to generate alerts in other forms and log them to a database. You will also learn about the format of the alert data files generated by Snort later.

You can terminate the Snort session any time by pressing the Ctrl and C keys simultaneously. At this point, Snort will display a summary of its activity and then quit. A typical summary is as follows:

```
============================================================
Snort analyzed 65 out of 65 packets, dropping 0(0.000%)
packets

Breakdown by protocol:                   Action Stats:
      TCP: 55           (84.615%)        ALERTS: 10
      UDP: 10           (15.385%)        LOGGED: 10
     ICMP: 0            (0.000%)         PASSED: 0
      ARP: 0            (0.000%)
    EAPOL: 0            (0.000%)
     IPv6: 0            (0.000%)
      IPX: 0            (0.000%)
    OTHER: 0            (0.000%)
  DISCARD: 0            (0.000%)
============================================================
Wireless Stats:
Breakdown by type:
    Management Packets: 0               (0.000%)
    Control Packets:    0               (0.000%)
    Data Packets:       0               (0.000%)
============================================================
Fragmentation Stats:
Fragmented IP Packets: 0                (0.000%)
    Fragment Trackers: 0
    Rebuilt IP Packets: 0
    Frag elements used: 0
Discarded(incomplete): 0
   Discarded(timeout): 0
   Frag2 memory faults: 0
============================================================
TCP Stream Reassembly Stats:
        TCP Packets Used: 55            (84.615%)
        Stream Trackers: 1
        Stream flushes: 0
        Segments used: 0
    Stream4 Memory Faults: 0
============================================================
Snort received signal 2, exiting
[root@conformix snort]#
```

The above mentioned procedure runs Snort in the foreground and you don't get the command prompt back. To run Snort in the background, you can use the -D command line switch. In this case Snort still logs all of its information in the log directory /var/log/snort and you get the command prompt back. Note that when you installed Snort using the pre-compiled RPM package as explained earlier, you can run Snort using the "/etc/init.d/snortd start" command that starts Snort in the background.

2.2.3 Errors While Starting Snort

At this point, if you have compiled Snort by yourself, you may see the following error when starting Snort:

```
[!] ERROR: Cannot get write access to logging directory "/var/
log/snort".
(directory doesn't exist or permissions are set incorrectly
or it is not a directory at all)

Fatal Error, Quitting..
```

This error is due to the fact that you have not created the /var/log/snort directory. Use the "mkdir /var/log/snort" command and the error will go away.

If you get an error message like the following, you have not specified the Snort configuration file name correctly on the command line or you started Snort without specifying a configuration file name.

```
Initializing rule chains...
ERROR: Unable to open rules file: /root/.snortrc or /root//
root/.snortrc
Fatal Error, Quitting..
```

Note that you can run Snort without specifying a configuration file name if one of the following conditions is true:

1. You are in the same directory where the configuration file exists when you start Snort.

2. You have copied the configuration file in your home directory as .snortrc.

2.2.4 Testing Snort

After starting Snort, you need to know if it is actually capturing data and logging intruder activity. If you started Snort in the foreground with the "-A console" command line option, you will start seeing alerts on the screen when this script is running. However, if you have started Snort in the daemon mode and did not use the command line option mentioned above, alerts will be logged to the /var/log/snort/alert file.

The following command generates some alerts that you can see on the console or in the /var/log/snort/alert file. Generation of alerts indicates that Snort is working properly.

```
ping -n -r -b 255.255.255.255 -p "7569643d3028726f6f74290a" -
c3
```

Alerts displayed on screen will look like the following. Again note that to display
alerts on screen, you have to use the "−A console" command line option.

```
11/19-18:51:04.560952  [**] [1:498:3] ATTACK RESPONSES id
check returned root [**] [Classification: Potentially Bad
Traffic] [Priority: 2] {ICMP} 10.100.1.105 -> 255.255.255.255
```

2.2.4.1   Generating Test Alerts

The following script name is snort-test.sh and it is available on the website (http://
authors.phptr.com/rehman/) that accompanies the book. Basically it uses the same command as
mentioned above but is useful when Snort is running in the daemon mode.

```
 1  #!/bin/sh
 2  #
 3  ################################################################
 4  # You are free to copy and distribute this script under      #
 5  # GNU Public License until this part is not removed           #
 6  # from the script.                                            #
 7  ################################################################
 8  #                         HOW TO USE                          #
 9  #                                                             #
10  # Right after installation of Snort, run this script.        #
11  # It will generate alerts in /var/log/snort/alert file similar#
12  # to the following:                                           #
13  #                                                             #
14  # Note that Snort must be running at the time you run this    #
15  # script.                                                     #
16  #                                                             #
17  # [**] [1:498:3] ATTACK RESPONSES id check returned root [**] #
18  # [Classification: Potentially Bad Traffic] [Priority: 2]     #
19  # 08/31-15:56:48.188882 255.255.255.255 -> 192.168.1.111      #
20  # ICMP TTL:150 TOS:0x0 ID:0 IpLen:20 DgmLen:84                #
21  # Type:0  Code:0  ID:45596  Seq:1024  ECHO REPLY              #
22  #                                                             #
23  # These alerts are displayed at the end of the script.        #
24  ################################################################
25  #
26  clear
27  echo "################################################################"
28  echo "#          Script to test Snort Installation             #"
29  echo "#                     Written By                          #"
30  echo "#                                                         #"
31  echo "#                   Rafeeq Rehman                         #"
32  echo "#                 rr@argusnetsec.com                      #"
33  echo "#         Argus Network Security Services Inc.            #"
34  echo "#              http://www.argusnetsec.com                 #"
35  echo "################################################################"
36  echo
37
```

```
38  echo
39  echo "################################################################"
40  echo "The script generates three alerts in file /var/log/snort/alert"
41  echo "Each alert should start with message like the following:"
42  echo
43  echo "      \"ATTACK RESPONSES id check returned root\" "
44  echo "################################################################"
45  echo
46  echo "Enter IP address of any other host on this network. If you"
47  echo "don't know any IP address, just hit Enter key. By default"
48  echo -n "broacast packets are used [255.255.255.255] : "
49
50  read ADDRESS
51
52  if [ -z $ADDRESS ]
53  then
54      ADDRESS="255.255.255.255"
55  fi
56
57  echo
58  echo "Now generating alerts. If it takes more than 5 seconds, break"
59  echo "the script by pressing Ctrl-C. Probably you entered wrong IP"
60  echo "address. Run the script again and don't enter any IP address"
61
62  ping -i 0.3 -n -r -b $ADDRESS -p "7569643d3028726f6f74290a" -c3 2>/dev/
null >/dev/null
63
64  if [ $? -ne 0 ]
65  then
66      echo "Alerting generation failed."
67      echo "Aborting ..."
68      exit 1
69  else
70      echo
71      echo "Alert generation complete"
72      echo
73  fi
74
75  sleep 2
76
77
78  echo
79  echo "################################################################"
80  echo "Last 18 lines of /var/log/snort/alert file will be displayed now"
81  echo "If snort is working properly, you will see recently generated"
82  echo "alerts with current time"
83  echo "################################################################"
84  echo
85  echo "Hit Enter key to continue ..."
86  read ENTER
87
88  if [ ! -f /var/log/snort/alert ]
```

```
89   then
90      echo "The log file does not exist."
91      echo "Aborting ..."
92      exit 1
93   fi
94
95   tail -n18 /var/log/snort/alert
96
97   echo
98   echo "Done"
99   echo
```

This script generates alerts which you can see in the `/var/log/snort/alert` file (if running in daemon mode) or on the screen where Snort is running. Alerts are generated by sending ICMP echo packets with a predefined pattern in the data part. The echo command is used for this purpose. This pattern triggers the following Snort rule, generating an alert.

```
alert ip any any -> any any (msg:"ATTACK RESPONSES id check
returned root"; content: "uid=0(root)"; classtype:bad-unknown;
sid:498; rev:3;)
```

After generating alerts, the script will display the last eighteen lines of the `/var/log/snort/alert` file.

Now let us examine different parts of this script and how it works. Lines 52 to 55 prompt a user to enter an address to which ping packets should be sent. If no address is entered, a broadcast address (255.255.255.255) is assumed and ping packets are sent as broadcast packets.

Line 62 actually generates the ICMP packets that cause the rule to be triggered. Note that pattern "7569643d3028726f6f74290a" is equal to "uid=0(root)" which is the pattern required to generate alerts.

The `-c3` command line parameter causes three packets to be sent. Note that standard input and standard error are redirected to `/dev/null` to make sure that no messages are displayed on the screen. For a detail of all options used with the ping command, see its man pages using the "man ping" command.

Lines 64 to 73 check the result of the ping command. A message is displayed indicating the success or failure of the ping command. If the command fails, the script aborts at this point and no further processing is done.

If alerts are to be generated successfully, they must be present in the `/var/log/snort/alert` file. Lines 88 to 93 verify that the file exists. If the file does not exist, the script is aborted.

If all goes well, line 95 shows output of alerts generated by displaying the last eighteen lines in the /var/log/snort/alert file.

2.2.4.2 Generating Test Alerts with Automatic Snort Startup

If you installed Snort in the /opt/snort directory, you can also use the following script that will start and stop Snort by itself and verify that it is working properly. Make sure that Snort is NOT already running before starting this script because the script starts Snort by itself. This script is found as snort-test-auto.sh file on the website http://authors.phptr.com/rehman/.

```
 1  #!/bin/sh
 2  #
 3  ##################################################################
 4  # You are free to copy and distribute this script under          #
 5  # GNU Public License until this part is not removed              #
 6  # from the script.                                              #
 7  ##################################################################
 8  #                        HOW TO USE                             #
 9  #                                                               #
10  # Right after installation of Snort, run this script.           #
11  # It is assumed that snort executable is present in the         #
12  # /opt/argus/bin directory and all rules and configuration      #
13  # files are present under /opt/argus/etc/snort directory.       #
14  # If files are in other locations, edit the following location#
15  # of variables. If you used the installation script provided   #
16  # along with this script, the files will be automatically      #
17  # located in appropriate directories.                          #
18  #                                                               #
19  # Note that the script starts and stops Snort by itself and    #
20  # you should make sure that Snort is not running at the time    #
21  # you run this script.                                          #
22  #                                                               #
23  # It will generate alerts in /tmp/alert file similar           #
24  # to the following:                                            #
25  #                                                               #
26  # [**] [1:498:3] ATTACK RESPONSES id check returned root [**] #
27  # [Classification: Potentially Bad Traffic] [Priority: 2]      #
28  # 08/31-15:56:48.188882 255.255.255.255 -> 192.168.1.111       #
29  # ICMP TTL:150 TOS:0x0 ID:0 IpLen:20 DgmLen:84                 #
30  # Type:0  Code:0  ID:45596  Seq:1024   ECHO REPLY              #
31  #                                                               #
32  # These alerts are displayed at the end of the script.         #
33  ##################################################################
34  #
35
36  PREFIX=/opt/snort
37  SNORT=$PREFIX/bin/snort
38  SNORT_CONFIG=$PREFIX/etc/snort.conf
39  LOG_DIR=/tmp
40  ALERT_FILE=$LOG_DIR/alert
```

```
41  ALERT_FILE_OLD=$LOG_DIR/alert.old
42  ADDRESS="255.255.255.255"
43
44  clear
45
46  echo "#############################################################"
47  echo "#            Script to test Snort Installation           #"
48  echo "#                        Written By                      #"
49  echo "#                                                        #"
50  echo "#                     Rafeeq Rehman                      #"
51  echo "#                  rr@argusnetsec.com                    #"
52  echo "#           Argus Network Security Services Inc.         #"
53  echo "#                http://www.argusnetsec.com              #"
54  echo "#############################################################"
55  echo
56
57  echo
58  echo "#############################################################"
59  echo "The script generates three alerts in file /tmp/alert"
60  echo "Each alert should start with message like the following:"
61  echo
62  echo "     \"ATTACK RESPONSES id check returned root\" "
63  echo "#############################################################"
64  echo
65
66  if [ ! -d $LOG_DIR ]
67  then
68     echo "Creating log directory ..."
69     mkdir $LOG_DIR
70
71     if [ $? -ne 0 ]
72     then
73        echo "Directory $LOGDIR creation failed"
74        echo "Aborting ..."
75        exit 1
76     fi
77  fi
78
79  if [ -f $ALERT_FILE ]
80  then
81     mv -f $ALERT_FILE $ALERT_FILE_OLD
82
83     if [ $? -ne 0 ]
84     then
85        echo "Can't rename old alerts file."
86        echo "Aborting ..."
87        exit 1
88     fi
89  fi
90
91  if [ ! -f $SNORT ]
92  then
```

```
 93      echo "Snort executable file $SNORT does not exist."
 94      echo "Aborting ..."
 95      exit 1
 96   fi
 97
 98   if [ ! -f $SNORT_CONFIG ]
 99   then
100      echo "Snort configuration file $SNORT_CONFIG does not exist."
101      echo "Aborting ..."
102      exit 1
103   fi
104
105   if [ ! -x $SNORT ]
106   then
107      echo "Snort file $SNORT is not executable."
108      echo "Aborting ..."
109      exit 1
110   fi
111
112   echo "Starting Snort ..."
113   $SNORT -c $SNORT_CONFIG -D -l /tmp 2>/dev/null
114
115   if [ $? -ne 0 ]
116   then
117      echo "Snort startup failed."
118      echo "Aborting ..."
119      exit 1
120   fi
121
122   echo
123   echo "Now generating alerts."
124
125   ping -i 0.3 -n -r -b $ADDRESS -p "7569643d3028726f6f74290a" -c3 2>/dev/
null >/dev/null
126
127   if [ $? -ne 0 ]
128   then
129      echo "Alerting generation failed."
130      echo "Aborting ..."
131      exit 1
132   else
133      echo
134      echo "Alert generation complete"
135      echo
136   fi
137
138   sleep 2
139
140   tail -n18 $ALERT_FILE 2>/dev/null | grep "ATTACK RESPONSES id check" >/
dev/null
141
142   if [ $? -ne 0 ]
```

```
143  then
144      echo "Snort test failed."
145      echo "Aborting ..."
146      exit 1
147  fi
148
149  echo "Stopping Snort ..."
150  pkill snort >/dev/null 2>&1
151
152  if [ $? -ne 0 ]
153  then
154      echo "Snort stopping failed."
155      echo "Aborting ..."
156      exit 1
157  fi
158
159  echo
160  echo "Done. Snort installation is working properly"
161  echo
```

As you may have noted, this scripts creates alert file in the /tmp directory which is used to find out if the alert creation was successful. When you run the script and everything is working fine, you will see the following output:

```
############################################################
#           Script to test Snort Installation         #
#                      Written By                     #
#                                                     #
#                    Rafeeq Rehman                    #
#                 rr@argusnetsec.com                  #
#          Argus Network Security Services Inc.       #
#              http://www.argusnetsec.com             #
############################################################


############################################################
The script generates three alerts in file /tmp/alert
Each alert should start with message like the following:

    "ATTACK RESPONSES id check returned root"
############################################################

Starting Snort ...

Now generating alerts.

Alert generation complete

Stopping Snort ...

Done. Snort installation is working properly
```

This script does a number of things when you run it. First of all it sets values of some variables using lines from line number 36 to 42.

After setting these variables, the script goes through the following steps:

- Lines 66 to 77 are used to check for the presence of $LOG_DIR directory. The variable LOG_DIR defined in line 39 shows that this directory is /tmp. If the directory does not exist, the script creates it.
- Lines 79 to 89 are used to check for the presence of $ALERT_FILE, which is /tmp/alert. If the file exists, the scripts renames it as /tmp/alert.old.
- Lines 91 to 96 are used to check for the presence of Snort binary file $SNORT, which is /opt/snort/bin/snort. If the file is not present, execution is stopped.
- Lines 98 to 103 are used to check for the presence of $SNORT_CONFIG file, which is /opt/snort/etc/snort.conf. If the file does not exist, execution is stopped.
- Lines 105 to 110 make sure that the Snort binary file is indeed executable.
- Line number 113 starts Snort.
- Lines 115 to 120 check that Snort was started successfully.
- Line 125 generates alerts as described in the previous section. These alerts are sent to broadcast address.
- Lines 127 to 136 are used to make sure that the alert generation process was successful.
- Line 140 checks the last eighteen lines of the alert file to verify that alerts were generated and log entries are created successfully.
- Lines 142 to 147 display an error message if the test in line 140 failed.
- Line 150 stops Snort.
- Line 160 displays a message showing that the test generation process was successful.

2.2.5 Running Snort on a Non-Default Interface

On Linux systems, Snort starts listening to network traffic on Ethernet interface eth0. Many people run Snort on multi-interface machines. If you want Snort to listen to some other interface, you have to specify it on the command line using the -i option. The following command starts Snort so that it listens to network interface eth1.

```
snort -c /opt/snort/etc/snort.conf -i eth1
```

In case of automatic startup and shutdown as explained in the next section, you have to modify /etc/init.d/snortd script so that Snort starts on the desired interface at boot time.

2.2.6   Automatic Startup and Shutdown

You can configure Snort to start at boot time automatically and stop when the system shuts down. On UNIX-type machines, this can be done through a script that starts and stops Snort. The script is usually created in the /etc/init.d directory on Linux. A link to the startup script may be created in /etc/rc3.d directory and shutdown links may be present in /etc/rc2.d, /etc/rc1.d and /etc/rc0.d directories. A typical script file /etc/init.d/snortd that is bundled with Snort RPM is as shown below:[4]

```
[root@conformix]# cat /etc/init.d/snortd
#!/bin/sh
#
# snortd          Start/Stop the snort IDS daemon.
#
# chkconfig: 2345 40 60
# description:  snort is a lightweight network intrusion
# detection tool that
#          currently detects more than 1100 host and network
#          vulnerabilities, portscans, backdoors, and more.
#
# June 10, 2000 -- Dave Wreski <dave@linuxsecurity.com>
#    - initial version
#
# July 08, 2000 Dave Wreski <dave@guardiandigital.com>
#    - added snort user/group
#    - support for 1.6.2
# July 31, 2000 Wim Vandersmissen <wim@bofh.st>
#    - added chroot support

# Source function library.
. /etc/rc.d/init.d/functions

# Specify your network interface here
INTERFACE=eth0

# See how we were called.
case "$1" in
  start)
```

4.   If you are creating a startup/shutdown script when you compile Snort yourself, you have to modify paths to Snort files according to your installation. This script still works very well as a reference starting point.

```
        echo -n "Starting snort: "
           cd /var/log/snort
        daemon /usr/sbin/snort -A fast -b -l /var/log/snort \
           -d -D -i $INTERFACE -c /etc/snort/snort.conf
        touch /var/lock/subsys/snort
        echo
        ;;
    stop)
        echo -n "Stopping snort: "
        killproc snort
        rm -f /var/lock/subsys/snort
        echo
        ;;
    restart)
        $0 stop
        $0 start
        ;;
    status)
        status snort
        ;;
    *)
        echo "Usage: $0 {start|stop|restart|status}"
        exit 1
esac

exit 0
[root@conformix /root]#
```

Note that the same file is used to start and stop Snort. The first character in the name of the link file determines if Snort will be started or stopped in a particular run level. The startup link file starts with the character S. A typical startup file is /etc/rc3.d/S50snort which is actually linked to /etc/init.d/snortd file. Similarly, a typical shutdown script file starts with the letter K. For example, you can create /etc/rc2.d/K50snort file. The init daemon will automatically start Snort when the system moves to run level 3 and will stop it when the system goes to run level 2.

You can start and stop Snort using the script manually as well. The following two lines start and stop Snort respectively.

```
/etc/init.d/snortd start
/etc/init.d/snortd stop
```

Note that the script and its links in the appropriate directories may have different names. Names for links to the script entirely depend upon at what point during the startup/shutdown process you want to start and stop Snort. If you used an RPM file, these links will be created during the installation procedure of the RPM package.

2.3 Running Snort on Multiple Network Interfaces

When you start Snort, it listens to traffic on one interface. Using the command line option −i <interface_name>, you can specify the interface on which you want to run it. If you want to listen to multiple network interfaces, you have to run multiple copies of Snort in parallel. As an example, the following two commands start listening to network interfaces eth0 and eth1 on a Linux machine.

```
/opt/snort/bin/snort -c /opt/snort/etc/snort.conf -i eth0 -l /
var/log/snort0
/opt/snort/bin/snort -c /opt/snort/etc/snort.conf -i eth1 -l /
var/log/snort1
```

Note that you have created two log directories, /var/log/snort0 and /var/log/snort1, so that both of the Snort sessions keep their log files separate. These directories must exist before you start Snort.

If both sessions log to a MySQL database, which is configured through snort.conf file, the same database can be used.

Note that you can also have different configuration files for these two sessions. There may be many reasons for having separate configuration files. The main reason is that HOME_NETWORK is different for the two sessions. Another reason may be that you want to log alert data in log files for one interface and in a database for the second interface. This is shown in Figure 2-2.

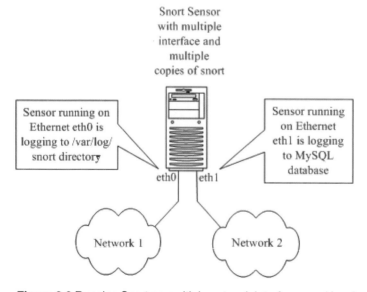

Figure 2-2 Running Snort on multiple network interfaces and logging to different places.

2.4 Snort Command Line Options

Snort has many command line options that are very useful for starting Snort in different situations. As you have already seen, command line options are helpful in running multiple versions of Snort on the same system. You can use "`snort -?`" command to display command line options. Most commonly used and useful command line options are listed in Table 2-2.

Table 2-2 Snort command line options

Options	Description
-A	This options sets alert mode. Alert modes are used to set different levels of detail with the alert data. Options available are fast, full, console or none. You have already seen that the console mode is used to display alert data on the console screen instead of logging to files. The fast mode is useful for high-speed operations of Snort.
-b	This option is used to log packets in `tcpdump` format. Logging is very fast and you can use the `tcpdump` program later on to display the data.
-c	This is the most commonly used option. You specify the location of `snort.conf` file with this option. When specified, Snort does not look into default locations of the configuration file snort.conf. As an example, if the `snort.conf` file is present in `/etc` directory, you will use "`-c /etc/snort.conf`" on the command line while starting Snort.
-D	This option enables Snort to run in the background. In almost all implementations of Snort, this option is used. You don't use this option when you are testing Snort after installation.
-i	This option is used to start Snort so that it listens to a particular network interface. This option is very useful when you have multiple network adapters and want to listen to only one of them. It is also useful when you want to run multiple Snort sessions on multiple network interfaces. For example, if you want Snort to listen to network interface `eth1` only, you will use "`-i eth1`" on the command line while starting Snort.
-l	This option is used to set the directory where Snort logs messages. The default location is `/var/log/snort`. For example, if you want all log files to be generated under `/snort` directory, you will use "`-l /snort`" command line option.
-M	You have to specify a text file as argument to this option. The text file contains a list of Microsoft Windows hosts to which you want to send SMB pop-up windows. Each line should contain only one IP address. Note that you can achieve the same goal through `snort.conf` file as well, which will be explained later.
-T	This option is very useful for testing and reporting on the Snort configuration. You can use this option to find any errors in the configuration files.

There are many other options which are less frequently used. These options will be discussed in related sections later on. The functionality of some command line options can be achieved through `snort.conf` file as well.

2.5 Step-By-Step Procedure to Compile and Install Snort From Source Code

Installing Snort from the RPM package is very easy since you have to use only one command, "`rpm -install <snort_file_name.rpm>`". However, as you have seen, installing from the source code requires much more work. To summarize the process of installing from the source code, here is a step-by-step procedure:

- Download source code file from http://www.snort.org.
- Unpack the `tar` file using "`tar zxvf <filename.tar.gz>`" command.
- Run the configure script. Typical command line is something like "`configure --prefix=/opt/snort --with-mysql -with-snmp -with-opnssl`".
- Run the `make` command.
- Run the "`make install`" command.
- Create a directory `/var/log/snort`.
- Create a directory `/opt/snort/etc`.
- Create a directory `/opt/snort/rules`.
- Copy `snort.conf` to `/opt/snort/etc` directory.
- Copy `classification.config` file to `/opt/snort/etc` directory.
- Copy `reference.config` file to `/opt/snort/etc` directory.
- Copy all rule files to `/opt/snort/rules` directory.
- Create startup script `snortd` and copy it to `/etc/init.d` directory. Create its links in `/etc/rcx` directories, where *x* is a run level number, so that Snort starts at the boot time.
- If you are using MySQL with Snort, it should be started before starting Snort.

2.6 Location of Snort Files

Snort files can be categorized as follows:

- The Snort binary files, which is the actual executable.
- The Snort configuration file, which is typically `snort.conf`.

- Other Snort configuration files like `classification.config` and `reference.config`.
- Rule files.
- Log files.

If you install Snort from the RPM package, the Snort binary file is usually installed in `/usr/sbin` directory. If you compile Snort yourself, the location of this file can be controlled using the `--prefix command line option`.

The main configuration file `snort.conf` is installed in `/etc/snort` directory when you used Snort RPM. However, you can save this file in any directory because you have to specify path to this file on the command line when starting Snort. In the examples used in this book, the file is stored under `/opt/snort/etc` directory.

Other configuration files like `classification.config` and `reference.config` are usually stored in the same location as the `snort.conf` file. The path to the location of these files is found in the `snort.conf` file. By changing that path, you can control the location of these files.

Rules files are referenced in the `snort.conf` file. If you install Snort from the RPM package, rules files are also installed in `/etc/snort` directory. In the examples in this book, when you compile Snort yourself, you have installed these rule files under `/opt/snort/rules` directory. By modifying the `snort.conf` file, you can select a different location for the rule files.

The location of Snort log files can be set with the help of `snort.conf` file or using command line options. Typically the log files are stored in `/var/log/snort` directory. If the log directory does not exist, you have to create it manually. When Snort is logging data from different hosts, it can create a directory for each host under `/var/log/snort` for the log files.

For example, to modify the default location of log files to `/snortlog`, use the following line in `snort.conf` file:

```
config logdir: /snortlog
```

You can also change the location of log files using −l command line option when starting Snort. Chapter 3 contains a more detailed discussion of the `snort.conf` configuration file.

2.7 Snort Modes

Snort operates in two basic modes: packet sniffer mode and NIDS mode. It can be used as a packet sniffer, like tcpdump or snoop. When sniffing packets, Snort can also log these packets to a log file. The file can be viewed later on using Snort or tcpdump. No intrusion detection activity is done by Snort in this mode of operation. Using Snort for this purpose is not very useful as there are many other tools available for packet logging. For example, all Linux distributions come with the tcpdump program which is very efficient.

When you use Snort in network intrusion detection (NIDS) mode, it uses its rules to find out if there is any network intrusion detection activity.

2.7.1 Network Sniffer Mode

In the network sniffer mode, Snort acts like the commonly used program tcpdump. It can capture and display packets from the network with different levels of detail on the console. You don't need a configuration file to run Snort in the packet sniffing mode. The following command displays information about each packet flowing on the network segment:

```
[root@conformix snort]# /opt/snort/bin/snort -v
Initializing Output Plugins!
Log directory = /var/log/snort

Initializing Network Interface eth0

        --== Initializing Snort ==--
Decoding Ethernet on interface eth0

        --== Initialization Complete ==--

-*> Snort! <*-
Version 1.9.0 (Build 209)
By Martin Roesch (roesch@sourcefire.com, www.snort.org)
11/20-15:56:14.632067 192.168.1.100:2474 -> 192.168.1.2:22
TCP TTL:128 TOS:0x0 ID:4206 IpLen:20 DgmLen:40 DF
***A**** Seq: 0x9DAEEE9C  Ack: 0xF5683C3A  Win: 0x43E0  TcpLen: 20
=+=+=+=+=+=+=+=+=+=+=+=+=+=+=+=+=+=+=+=+=+=+=+=+=+=+=+=+=+=+=+=+

11/20-15:56:14.632188 192.168.1.2:22 -> 192.168.1.100:2474
TCP TTL:64 TOS:0x10 ID:57042 IpLen:20 DgmLen:200 DF
***AP*** Seq: 0xF5683C8A  Ack: 0x9DAEEE9C  Win: 0x6330  TcpLen: 20
=+=+=+=+=+=+=+=+=+=+=+=+=+=+=+=+=+=+=+=+=+=+=+=+=+=+=+=+=+=+=+=+
```

```
11/20-15:56:14.632519 192.168.1.2:22 -> 192.168.1.100:2474
TCP TTL:64 TOS:0x10 ID:57043 IpLen:20 DgmLen:120 DF
***AP*** Seq: 0xF5683D2A  Ack: 0x9DAEEE9C  Win: 0x6330  TcpLen: 20
=+=+=+=+=+=+=+=+=+=+=+=+=+=+=+=+=+=+=+=+=+=+=+=+=+=+=+=+=+=+

11/20-15:56:14.633891 192.168.1.2:22 -> 192.168.1.100:2474
TCP TTL:64 TOS:0x10 ID:57044 IpLen:20 DgmLen:184 DF
***AP*** Seq: 0xF5683D7A  Ack: 0x9DAEEE9C  Win: 0x6330  TcpLen: 20
=+=+=+=+=+=+=+=+=+=+=+=+=+=+=+=+=+=+=+=+=+=+=+=+=+=+=+=+=+=+
```

Snort will continue to display captured packets on the screen until you break using Ctrl-C. At the time Snort terminates, it will display statistical information.

Let us now analyze the information displayed on screen when you run Snort in the packet capture mode. The following is a typical output for a TCP packet:

```
11/20-15:56:14.633891 192.168.1.2:22 -> 192.168.1.100:2474
TCP TTL:64 TOS:0x10 ID:57044 IpLen:20 DgmLen:184 DF
***AP*** Seq: 0xF5683D7A  Ack: 0x9DAEEE9C  Win: 0x6330  TcpLen: 20
```

If you analyze the output, you can see the following information about the packet:

- Date and time the packet was captured.
- Source IP address is 192.168.1.2 .
- Source port number is 22.
- Destination IP address is 192.168.1.100.
- Destination port is 2474.
- Transport layer protocol used in this packet is TCP.
- Time To Live or TTL value in the IP header part is 64.
- Type of Service or TOS value is 0x10.
- Packet ID is 57044.
- Length of IP header is 20.
- IP payload is 184 bytes long.
- Don't Fragment or DF bit is set in IP header.
- Two TCP flags A and P are on.
- TCP sequence number is 0xF5683D7A.
- Acknowledgement number in TCP header is 0xDAEEE9C.
- TCP Window field is 0x6330.
- TCP header length is 20.

You can display more information with captured packets using more command line options. The following command displays some information about application data attached to the packet in addition to TCP, UDP and ICMP information. Note that the command still does not display all of the packet data.

```
[root@conformix snort]# /opt/snort/bin/snort -dv
Initializing Output Plugins!
Log directory = /var/log/snort

Initializing Network Interface eth0

        --== Initializing Snort ==--
Decoding Ethernet on interface eth0

        --== Initialization Complete ==--

-*> Snort! <*-
Version 1.9.0 (Build 209)
By Martin Roesch (roesch@sourcefire.com, www.snort.org)
11/20-16:18:11.129548 192.168.1.100:2474 -> 192.168.1.2:22
TCP TTL:128 TOS:0x0 ID:4387 IpLen:20 DgmLen:40 DF
***A**** Seq: 0x9DAEF2FC  Ack: 0xF5688CDA  Win: 0x4190  TcpLen: 20

=+=+=+=+=+=+=+=+=+=+=+=+=+=+=+=+=+=+=+=+=+=+=+=+=+=+=+=+=+=+

11/20-16:18:11.129723 192.168.1.2:22 -> 192.168.1.100:2474
TCP TTL:64 TOS:0x10 ID:57171 IpLen:20 DgmLen:120 DF
***AP*** Seq: 0xF5688D2A  Ack: 0x9DAEF2FC  Win: 0x6330  TcpLen: 20
C5 1D 81 8F 70 B7 12 0B C1 1B 8F 6D A9 8F 1D 05  ....p......m....
40 7D F9 BD 84 21 11 59 05 01 E4 A1 01 20 AC 92  @}...!.Y..... ..
58 50 73 8D 17 EA E2 17 AD 3A AD 54 E2 50 80 CB  XPs......:.T.P..
DA E1 40 30 7B 63 0D 79 5A D8 51 07 93 95 2B A8  ..@0{c.yZ.Q...+.
F8 D4 F5 FA 76 D6 27 35 E8 6E E2 ED 41 2B 01 2D  ....v.'5.n..A+.-

=+=+=+=+=+=+=+=+=+=+=+=+=+=+=+=+=+=+=+=+=+=+=+=+=+=+=+=+=+=+

11/20-16:18:11.130802 192.168.1.2:22 -> 192.168.1.100:2474
TCP TTL:64 TOS:0x10 ID:57172 IpLen:20 DgmLen:120 DF
***AP*** Seq: 0xF5688D7A  Ack: 0x9DAEF2FC  Win: 0x6330  TcpLen: 20
E9 7C 09 E0 E0 5C 3E 17 1C BE 93 1F B0 DA 92 40  .|...\>........@
D1 18 71 52 80 F3 B2 F7 59 CE F7 7C D4 8F FD B4  ..qR....Y..|....
98 08 A9 63 63 23 0D C8 9D A4 4F 68 87 06 0D 16  ...cc#....Oh....
44 61 09 CD FF FE 8B 1A 5B D8 42 43 1D 1A 6F A8  Da......[.BC..o.
14 90 C6 63 4C EE 9D 64 1B 90 CC 3A FB BD 7E E4  ...cL..d...:..~.

=+=+=+=+=+=+=+=+=+=+=+=+=+=+=+=+=+=+=+=+=+=+=+=+=+=+=+=+=+=+

11/20-16:18:11.131701 192.168.1.2:22 -> 192.168.1.100:2474
TCP TTL:64 TOS:0x10 ID:57173 IpLen:20 DgmLen:120 DF
```

```
***AP*** Seq: 0xF5688DCA  Ack: 0x9DAEF2FC  Win: 0x6330  TcpLen: 20
AF CE 60 CB 79 06 BB 3D 58 72 76 F2 51 0F C1 9A  ..`.y..=Xrv.Q...
22 5A E3 27 49 F8 A5 00 1B 5A 4F 24 12 0F BF 70  "Z.'I....ZO$...p
B7 81 A0 0C F9 EB 83 D1 33 EB C1 5A 2A E6 2E 4B  ........3..Z*..K
F1 98 FB 5A A9 C7 C3 92 78 B1 35 FF F7 59 CF B3  ...Z....x.5..Y..
83 D2 E7 FF 37 F8 34 56 CD 0F 61 62 A9 16 A4 9F  ....7.4V..ab....

=+=+=+=+=+=+=+=+=+=+=+=+=+=+=+=+=+=+=+=+=+=+=+=+=+=+=+=+=+=+

11/20-16:18:11.133935 192.168.1.100:2474 -> 192.168.1.2:22
TCP TTL:128 TOS:0x0 ID:4388 IpLen:20 DgmLen:40 DF
***A**** Seq: 0x9DAEF2FC  Ack: 0xF5688D7A  Win: 0x40F0  TcpLen: 20

=+=+=+=+=+=+=+=+=+=+=+=+=+=+=+=+=+=+=+=+=+=+=+=+=+=+=+=+=+=+

11/20-16:18:11.134057 192.168.1.2:22 -> 192.168.1.100:2474
TCP TTL:64 TOS:0x10 ID:57174 IpLen:20 DgmLen:280 DF
***AP*** Seq: 0xF5688E1A  Ack: 0x9DAEF2FC  Win: 0x6330  TcpLen: 20
A6 CF F9 B5 EA 24 E0 48 34 45 4B 57 5D FF CB B5  .....$.H4EKW]...
D6 C9 B3 26 3C 59 66 2C 55 EE C1 CF 09 AD 3A C2  ...&<Yf,U.....:.
74 B6 61 D3 C5 63 ED BD 6F 51 0D 5E 18 44 07 AF  t.a..c..oQ.^.D..
86 D2 8A 3F 82 F0 D2 84 5C A6 7F CC D5 7B 90 56  ...?....\....{.V
93 CF CF 4D DE 03 00 4D E4 4B AD 75 3E 03 71 DC  ...M...M.K.u>.q.
A6 3D 78 DA 01 BF F0 33 46 7D E1 53 B5 62 94 9A  .=x....3F}.S.b..
29 46 56 78 B1 73 C0 3E BB C0 EC 5C 6E D0 E6 BE  )FVx.s.>...\n...
F9 5C 02 90 40 B1 BA 07 F1 96 2F A0 0F 9D E1 3E  .\..@...../....>
8C 3C 40 07 B2 21 28 CA 2D 41 AC 5C 77 C6 D0 3F  .<@..!(.-A.\w..?
73 0B 15 32 47 B5 CE E3 FB 83 B3 72 1A B4 64 9F  s..2G......r..d.
6D C7 55 B8 6B DB FC AF 94 8F F3 58 B0 79 CF 14  m.U.k......X.y..
3F 9A FC 32 1D B6 21 B0 4D C3 64 82 C0 62 A8 8C  ?..2..!.M.d..b..
80 C7 4A C8 BA D9 C3 0D 74 86 76 B8 49 8A 94 D1  ..J.....t.v.I...
4C F3 BF AF 55 3B 57 2B EA C7 48 B7 A4 BD B2 20  L...U;W+..H....
4A 66 B4 4E F3 2A 7E B6 F8 63 A8 61 42 F3 85 3B  Jf.N.*~..c.aB..;

=+=+=+=+=+=+=+=+=+=+=+=+=+=+=+=+=+=+=+=+=+=+=+=+=+=+=+=+=+=+
```

To display all packet information on the console, use the following command. This command displays captured data in hexadecimal as well as ASCII format.

```
[root@conformix snort]# /opt/snort/bin/snort -dev
Initializing Output Plugins!
Log directory = /var/log/snort

Initializing Network Interface eth0

        --== Initializing Snort ==--
Decoding Ethernet on interface eth0
```

```
        --== Initialization Complete ==--

-*> Snort! <*-
Version 1.9.0 (Build 209)
By Martin Roesch (roesch@sourcefire.com, www.snort.org)
05/27-12:11:10.063820 0:D0:59:6C:9:8B -> FF:FF:FF:FF:FF:FF type:0x800
len:0xFC
192.168.1.100:138 -> 192.168.1.255:138 UDP TTL:128 TOS:0x0 ID:48572
IpLen:20 DgmLen:238
Len: 218
11 0E 82 D5 C0 A8 01 64 00 8A 00 C4 00 00 20 46    .......d...... F
43 46 43 43 4E 45 4D 45 42 46 41 46 45 45 50 46    CFCCNEMEBFAFEEPF
41 43 41 43 41 43 41 43 41 43 41 43 41 41 41 00    ACACACACACACAAA.
20 41 42 41 43 46 50 46 50 45 4E 46 44 45 43 46     ABACFPFPENFDECF
43 45 50 46 48 46 44 45 46 46 50 46 50 41 43 41    CEPFHFDEFFPFPACA
42 00 FF 53 4D 42 25 00 00 00 00 00 00 00 00 00    B..SMB%.........
00 00 00 00 00 00 00 00 00 00 00 00 00 00 00 00    ................
00 00 11 00 00 2A 00 00 00 00 00 00 00 00 00 E8    .....*..........
03 00 00 00 00 00 00 00 00 2A 00 56 00 03 00 01    .........*.V....
00 01 00 02 00 3B 00 5C 4D 41 49 4C 53 4C 4F 54    .....;.\MAILSLOT
5C 42 52 4F 57 53 45 00 0C 00 A0 BB 0D 00 42 41    \BROWSE.......BA
54 54 4C 45 43 4F 57 53 00 00 00 00 01 00 03 0A    TTLECOWS........
00 10 00 80 D4 FE 50 03 52 52 2D 4C 41 50 54 4F    ......P.RR-LAPTO
50 00                                              P.

=+=+=+=+=+=+=+=+=+=+=+=+=+=+=+=+=+=+=+=+=+=+=+=+=+=+=+=+=+
11/20-16:20:38.459702 0:D0:59:6C:9:8B -> 0:50:BA:5E:EC:25 type:0x800
len:0x3C
192.168.1.100:2474 -> 192.168.1.2:22 TCP TTL:128 TOS:0x0 ID:4506
IpLen:20 DgmLen:40 DF
***A**** Seq: 0x9DAEFD9C  Ack: 0xF568E2FA  Win: 0x3F20  TcpLen: 20

=+=+=+=+=+=+=+=+=+=+=+=+=+=+=+=+=+=+=+=+=+=+=+=+=+=+=+=+=+

11/20-16:20:38.460728 0:50:BA:5E:EC:25 -> 0:D0:59:6C:9:8B type:0x800
len:0x86
192.168.1.2:22 -> 192.168.1.100:2474 TCP TTL:64 TOS:0x10 ID:57303
IpLen:20 DgmLen:120 DF
***AP*** Seq: 0xF568E34A  Ack: 0x9DAEFD9C  Win: 0x6BD0  TcpLen: 20
F9 7B 4B 96 3F C8 0A BC DF 9E EE 4F DA 27 6F B4    .{K.?......O.'o.
92 BD A7 C5 1D E4 35 AB DB BF 7B 56 B9 F8 BA A1    ......5...{V....
86 BB FE 6E FD 41 55 FF D0 51 04 AF 73 80 13 29    ...n.AU..Q..s..)
D7 62 67 A4 B5 0C 5F 32 30 36 81 C2 9C 31 53 AD    .bg..._206...1S.
3A 65 46 EE F1 52 59 ED 57 C7 6A 85 88 5A 3E D8    :eF..RY.W.j..Z>.

=+=+=+=+=+=+=+=+=+=+=+=+=+=+=+=+=+=+=+=+=+=+=+=+=+=+=+=+=+
```

```
11/20-16:20:38.461631 0:50:BA:5E:EC:25 -> 0:D0:59:6C:9:8B type:0x800
len:0x86
192.168.1.2:22 -> 192.168.1.100:2474 TCP TTL:64 TOS:0x10 ID:57304
IpLen:20 DgmLen:120 DF
***AP*** Seq: 0xF568E39A  Ack: 0x9DAEFD9C  Win: 0x6BD0  TcpLen: 20
81 68 7B F3 7C E7 61 54 F9 6E 4C 24 C6 8B 68 63  .h{.|.aT.nL$..hc
74 A7 BE 99 5C F6 15 01 F7 EB 75 06 26 B7 FA 2C  t...\.....u.&..,
81 A3 27 BD F0 4F CB AD C9 58 D2 9B C7 4F 90 8A  ..'..O...X...O..
1D 15 D2 77 11 DC BC EE BF 05 20 49 BA 72 EA 1F  ...w...... I.r..
12 49 14 B5 6C 6F 66 DC 26 39 84 D9 CE 09 F7 AE  .I..lof.&9......

+=+=+=+=+=+=+=+=+=+=+=+=+=+=+=+=+=+=+=+=+=+=+=+=+=+=+=+=+=+=+

11/20-16:20:38.462524 0:50:BA:5E:EC:25 -> 0:D0:59:6C:9:8B type:0x800
len:0x86
192.168.1.2:22 -> 192.168.1.100:2474 TCP TTL:64 TOS:0x10 ID:57305
IpLen:20 DgmLen:120 DF
***AP*** Seq: 0xF568E3EA  Ack: 0x9DAEFD9C  Win: 0x6BD0  TcpLen: 20
12 92 BE 7B 11 AA E9 DC 09 F9 02 8D B5 8E 08 FB  ...{............
37 48 1D 1E 4B EF DF B2 19 D6 B9 26 F7 6E DF C3  7H..K......&.n..
DD DD 01 A1 93 81 0E 0B 35 4B 6B EA D3 E6 5E BA  ........5Kk...^.
2B 95 78 8A 3D 77 E3 F4 C8 AB 94 E5 A5 7E D7 98  +.x.=w.......~..
00 28 F0 7E 36 14 79 DF 10 B2 C6 13 F5 71 1F F1  .(.~6.y......q..

=+=+=+=+=+=+=+=+=+=+=+=+=+=+=+=+=+=+=+=+=+=+=+=+=+=+=+=+=+=+
```

2.7.1.1   Logging Snort Data in Text Format

You can log Snort data in text mode by adding `-l <directory name>` on the command line. The following command logs all Snort data in `/var/log/snort` directory in addition to displaying it on the console.

```
snort -dev -l /var/log/snort
```

When you go to the `/var/log/snort` directory, you will find multiple directories under it. Each of these directories corresponds to one host and contains multiple files. The name of the directory is usually the same as the IP address of host. These files contain logs for different connections and different types of network data. For example, files containing TCP data will start with TCP. A typical name for a file containing TCP data is `TCP:2489-23`. A typical file containing ICMP data may be `ICMP_ECHO`. The format of data logged in these files is the same as the data displayed on the screen when you run Snort in the network sniffer mode.

2.7.1.2   Logging Snort in Binary Format

On high-speed networks, logging data in ASCII format in many different files may cause high overhead. Snort allows you to log all data in a binary file in tcpdump format and view it later on. In this case, snort logs all data to a single file in raw binary form. A typical command for this type of log is :

```
snort -l /tmp -b
```

Snort will create a file in /tmp directory. A typical file name may be snort.log.1037840339. The last part of the file name is dependent on the clock on your machine. Each time you start Snort in this mode, a new file will be created in the log directory. Sometimes this mode of logging data is also called a *quick mode*.

To view this raw binary data, you can use Snort. The -r command line switch is used to specify a file name with Snort. The following command will display the captured data from file snort.log.1037840339.

```
snort -dev -r /tmp/snort.log.1037840339| more
```

The output of this command will show data in exactly the same way if you are looking at it on the console in real time. You can use different switches to display different levels of detail with this data.

You can also display a particular type of data from the log file. The following command displays all TCP type data from the log file:

```
snort -dev -r / tmp/snort.log.1037840339 tcp
```

Similarly, ICMP and UDP types of data can also be displayed.

You can also use the tcpdump program to read files generated by Snort when logging in this mode. The following command reads the Snort files and displays captured packets in the file:

```
[root@conformix snort]# tcpdump -r /tmp/snort.log.1037840514
20:01:54.984286 192.168.1.100.2474 > 192.168.1.2.ssh: . ack 4119588794
win 16960 (DF)
20:01:54.984407 192.168.1.2.ssh > 192.168.1.100.2474: P 81:161(80) ack
0 win 32016 (DF) [tos 0x10]
20:01:54.985428 192.168.1.2.ssh > 192.168.1.100.2474: P 161:241(80) ack
0 win 32016 (DF) [tos 0x10]
20:01:54.986325 192.168.1.2.ssh > 192.168.1.100.2474: P 241:321(80) ack
0 win 32016 (DF) [tos 0x10]
20:01:54.988508 192.168.1.100.2474 > 192.168.1.2.ssh: . ack 161 win
16800 (DF)
20:01:54.988627 192.168.1.2.ssh > 192.168.1.100.2474: P 321:465(144)
ack 0 win 32016 (DF) [tos 0x10]
20:01:54.990771 192.168.1.100.2474 > 192.168.1.2.ssh: . ack 321 win
16640 (DF)
20:01:55.117890 192.168.1.100.2474 > 192.168.1.2.ssh: . ack 465 win
16496 (DF)
20:01:55.746665 192.168.1.1.1901 > 239.255.255.250.1900:  udp 269
```

```
20:01:55.749466 192.168.1.1.1901 > 239.255.255.250.1900:   udp 325
20:01:55.751968 192.168.1.1.1901 > 239.255.255.250.1900:   udp 253
20:01:55.754145 192.168.1.1.1901 > 239.255.255.250.1900:   udp 245
20:01:55.756781 192.168.1.1.1901 > 239.255.255.250.1900:   udp 289
20:01:55.759258 192.168.1.1.1901 > 239.255.255.250.1900:   udp 265
20:01:55.761763 192.168.1.1.1901 > 239.255.255.250.1900:   udp 319
20:01:55.764365 192.168.1.1.1901 > 239.255.255.250.1900:   udp 317
20:01:55.767103 192.168.1.1.1901 > 239.255.255.250.1900:   udp 321
20:01:55.769557 192.168.1.1.1901 > 239.255.255.250.1900:   udp 313
20:01:56.336697 192.168.1.100.2474 > 192.168.1.2.ssh: P 0:80(80) ack
465 win 16496 (DF)
[root@conformix snort]#
```

You can use different command line options with tcpdump to manipulate the display of data. For more information about tcpdump, use the "man tcpdump" command or see Appendix A.

2.7.2   Network Intrusion Detection Mode

In intrusion detection mode, Snort does not log each captured packet as it does in the network sniffer mode. Instead, it applies rules on all captured packets. If a packet matches a rule, only then is it logged or an alert is generated. If a packet does not match any rule, the packet is dropped silently and no log entry is created. When you use Snort in intrusion detection mode, typically you provide a configuration file on the command line. This configuration file contains Snort rules or reference to other files that contain Snort rules. In addition to rules, the configuration file also contains information about input and output plug-ins, which are discussed in Chapter 4. The typical name of the Snort configuration file is `snort.conf`. We have previously saved `snort.conf` configuration file in `/opt/snort/etc` directory along with other files. This was done during the installation procedure.[5] The following command starts Snort in the Network Intrusion Detection (NID) mode:

```
snort -c /opt/snort/etc/snort.conf
```

When you start this command, Snort will read the configuration file `/opt/snort/etc/snort.conf` and all other files included in this file. Typically these files contain Snort rules and configuration data. After reading these files, Snort will build its internal data structures and rule chains. All captured packets will then be matched against these rules and appropriate action will be taken, if configured to do so.

---

5.   If you used the RPM package to install Snort, the typical location of the Snort configuration file is `/etc/snort/snort.conf`.

If you modify the snort.conf file, or any other file included in this file, you have to restart Snort for the changes to take effect.

Other command line options and switches can be used when Snort is working in IDS mode. For example, you can log data into files as well as display data on the command line. However if Snort is being used for long-term monitoring, the more data you log, the more disk space you need. Logging data to the console also requires some processing power and the processing power of the host where Snort is running becomes a consideration. The following command will log data to `/var/log/snort` directory and will display it on the console screen in addition to acting as NIDS:

```
snort -dev -l /var/log/snort -c /etc/snort/snort.conf
```

However in most real-life situations, you will use `-D` command line switch with Snort so that it does not log on the console but runs as a daemon.

In a typical scenario, you will also want to log Snort data into a database. Logging data into MySQL database is discussed in Chapter 5.

2.8 Snort Alert Modes

When Snort is running in the Network Intrusion Detection (NID) mode, it generates alerts when a captured packet matches a rule. Snort can send alerts in many modes. These modes are configurable through the command line as well as through `snort.conf` file. Common alert modes are explained in this section. To explain the alert modes, I have used a rule that creates an alert when Snort detects an ICMP packet with TTL 100. This rule is listed below.

```
alert icmp any any -> any any (msg: "Ping with TTL=100"; \
    ttl:100;)
```

Rules will be explained in the next chapter in detail. For this discussion, it is sufficient to understand that this rule will create an alert with the text message "Ping with TTL=100" whenever such an ICMP packet is captured. The rule does not care about source or destination address in the packet. I have used the following command on my Windows PC to send one ICMP echo packet with TTL=100.

```
C:\rrehman>ping -n 1 -i 100 192.168.1.3

Pinging 192.168.1.3 with 32 bytes of data:

Reply from 192.168.1.3: bytes=32 time=3ms TTL=255

Ping statistics for 192.168.1.3:
    Packets: Sent = 1, Received = 1, Lost = 0 (0% loss),
```

```
Approximate round trip times in milli-seconds:
    Minimum = 3ms, Maximum = 3ms, Average = 3ms
```

```
C:\rrehman>
```

The "-n 1" command line option is used to send only one ICMP packet. The "-i 100" option is used to set the TTL value equal to 100 in the ICMP packet. For details on the format of ICMP packet headers, refer to RFC 792 at ftp://ftp.isi.edu/in-notes/rfc792.txt or Appendix C.

Whenever this command is executed, Snort captures the ICMP packet and creates an alert. The amount of information logged with the alert depends on the particular alerting mode. Now let us see how different alerting modes work on a packet.

2.8.1 Fast Mode

The fast alert mode logs the alert with following information:

- Timestamp
- Alert message (configurable through rules)
- Source and destination IP addresses
- Source and destination ports

To configure fast alert mode, you have to use "-A fast" command line option. This alert mode causes less overhead for the system. The following command starts Snort in fast alert mode:

```
/opt/snort/bin/snort -c /opt/snort/etc/snort.conf -q -A fast
```

The –q option used on the command line stops the initial messages and final statistical summary from being displayed on the screen. Now when you create an alert, it will be logged in /var/log/snort/alert file. However, you can change the location of this file using -l command line option. The alert message is similar to the following:

```
05/28-22:16:25.126150  [**] [1:0:0] Ping with TTL=100 [**]
{ICMP} 192.168.1.100 -> 192.168.1.3
```

This alert message shows the following information:

- Date and time the alert occurred.
- Message present in the rule that generated this alert. In this example, the message is "Ping with TTL=100".
- Source address which is 192.168.1.100.

- Destination address which is 192.168.1.3.
- Type of packet; in the above example, type of packet is ICMP.

Note that the actual packet is not logged in this file when using this alert mode.

2.8.2 Full Mode

This is the default alert mode. It prints the alert message in addition to the packet header. Let us start Snort with full alerting enabled with the following command:

```
/opt/snort/bin/snort -c /opt/snort/etc/snort.conf -q -A full
```

When Snort generates an alert in this mode, the message logged in /var/log/ snort/alert file is similar to the following:

```
[**] [1:0:0] Ping with TTL=100 [**]
05/28-22:14:37.766150 192.168.1.100 -> 192.168.1.3
ICMP TTL:100 TOS:0x0 ID:40172 IpLen:20 DgmLen:60
Type:8  Code:0  ID:768   Seq:20224   ECHO
```

As you can see, additional information is logged with the alert message. This additional information shows different values in the packet header, including:

- Time to Live (TTL) value in the IP packet header. For details on TTL value, refer to RFC 791 at ftp://ftp.isi.edu/in-notes/rfc791.txt
- The Type Of Service (TOS) value in the IP packet header. For details on TOS value, refer to RFC 791 at at ftp://ftp.isi.edu/in-notes/rfc791.txt and Appendix C.
- Length of IP packet header shown as IpLen:20.
- Total length of IP packet shown as DgmLen:60.
- ICMP Type field. For details on ICMP type field refer to RFC 792.
- ICMP code value. For details on ICMP type field refer to RFC 792.
- IP packet ID.
- Sequence number.
- ICMP packet type which is ECHO.

2.8.3 UNIX Socket Mode

If you use "-a unsock" command line option with Snort, you can send alerts to another program through UNIX sockets. This is useful when you want to process alerts using a custom application with Snort. For more information on socket, use the "man socket" command.

2.8.4   No Alert Mode

You can also completely disable Snort alerts using "-A none" command line option. This option is very useful for high speed intrusion detection using unified logging. You can disable normal logging using this option while using the unified option. Unified output plug-in is discussed in Chapter 4.

2.8.5   Sending Alerts to Syslog

This command allows Snort to send alerts to Syslog daemon. Syslog is a system logger daemon and it generates log files for system events. It reads its configuration file /etc/syslog.conf where the location of these log files is configured. The usual location of syslog files is /var/log directory. On Linux systems, usually /var/log/messages is the main logging file. For more information, use the "man syslog" command. The "man syslog.conf" command shows the format of the syslog.conf file.

Depending on the configuration of the Syslog using /etc/syslog.conf file, the alerts can be saved into a particular file. The following command enables Snort to log to the Syslog daemon:

```
/opt/snort/bin/snort -c /opt/snort/etc/snort.conf -s
```

Using the default configuration on my RedHat 7.1 computer, the messages are logged to /var/log/messages file. When you cause an alert message by sending the special ICMP packet with TTL=100, the following line will be logged to the /var/log/messages file.

```
May 28 22:21:02 snort snort[1750]: [1:0:0] Ping with TTL=100
{ICMP} 192.168.1.100 -> 192.168.1.3
```

Using Syslog facility will be discussed in Chapter 4 later on in this book. You will also learn how to enable logging to Syslog using the output plug-in.

2.8.6   Sending Alerts to SNMP

One very useful feature of Snort is SNMP traps. You can configure an output plug-in to send messages in the form of SNMP traps to a network management system. Using this feature you can integrate your intrusion detection sensors into any centralized NMS like HP OpenView, OpenNMS, MRTG and so on. Snort can generate SNMP version 2 and version 3 traps. The configuration process for SNMP traps will be discussed later on in detail.

2.8.7   Sending Alerts to Windows

Snort can send alerts to Microsoft Windows machines in the form of pop-up windows. These pop-up windows are controlled by Windows Messenger Service. Windows Messenger Service must be running on your Windows machine for pop-up windows to work. You can go to Control Panel and start the *Services* applet to find out if Windows Messenger Service is running. The *Services* applet is found in the Administrative Tools menu on your Windows system. Depending on your version of Microsoft Windows, it may be found in Control Panel or some other place.

The SAMBA client package must be installed on your UNIX machine. SAMBA is an open source software suite that allows UNIX file and printer sharing with Microsoft Windows machines. SAMBA software runs on UNIX platforms. It can work with any other operating system that understands Common Internet File System (CIFS) or Server Message Block (SMB) protocol. More information about SAMBA is available from http://www.samba.org.

The Snort alert mechanism uses smbclient program on the UNIX machine to connect to the Windows machines and send the alerts. Make sure that the SAMBA client is working properly before trying to use this service. SAMBA operations are dependent upon its configuration file /etc/samba/smb.conf on a RedHat system. This file may be located at a different place on other UNIX systems. Although detailed discussion on SAMBA is beyond the scope of this book, a sample SAMBA configuration file is listed below. This file can be used to jump start SAMBA. The file creates a workgroup REHMAN which you can view from "Network Neighborhood" part of your Windows machines.

2.8.7.1   Sample Samba Configuration File

A sample `/etc/samba/smb.conf` file is as follows:

```
[global]
    workgroup = REHMAN
    server string = REHMAN file server
    log file = /var/log/samba/log.%m
    max log size = 50
    security = user
    encrypt passwords = yes
    socket options = TCP_NODELAY SO_RCVBUF=8192 SO_SNDBUF=8192
    dns proxy = no
    domain logons = no
    unix password sync = no
    map to guest = never
    password level = 0
    null passwords = no
    os level = 0
    preferred master = yes
    domain master = yes
    wins support = yes
    dead time = 0
```

```
        debug level = 0
        load printers = yes
[homes]
        comment = Home Directories
        browseable = yes
        writable = yes
        available = yes
        public = yes
        only user = no
[htmldir]
        comment = html stuff
        path = /home/httpd/html
        public = yes
        writable = yes
        printable = no
        write list = rehman
[virtualhosting]
        comment = html stuff
        path = /usr/virt_web
        public = yes
        writable = yes
        printable = no
        write list = rehman
[printers]
[netlogon]
        available = no
```

More information about SMB alerts will be presented in later chapters. Note that you should compile Snort with `--with-smbalerts` option in the configure script if you want to use this option. Without this option in the configure script, SAMBA services can't be used with Snort.

2.9 Running Snort in Stealth Mode

Sometimes you may want to run Snort in stealth mode. In stealth mode, other hosts are not able to detect the presence of the Snort machine. In other words, the Snort machine is not visible to intruders or other people. There are multiple ways to run Snort in stealth mode. One of these methods is to run Snort on a network interface where no IP address is assigned. Running Snort on a network interface without an IP address is feasible in the following two cases:

1. A stand-alone Snort sensor with only one network adapter.
2. A Snort sensor with two network adapters: one to access the sensor from an isolated network and the other one connected to the public network and running

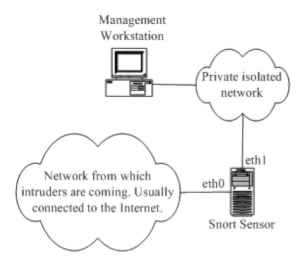

Figure 2-3 Running Snort in stealth mode on a system with two network adapters.

in stealth mode. This arrangement is shown in Figure 2-3 where network interface eth1 is connected to a private isolated network and eth0 is connected to a public network.

When you want to access the sensor itself, you go through network interface eth1 which has an IP address configured to it. The management workstation shown in the figure may be used to connect to the sensor either to collect data or to log information to a centralized database. If many sensors are present in an organization, all of these are connected to this isolated network so that they can log information to the central database running on the management workstation or to some other database server connected to this isolated network.

No IP address is configured on network interface eth0 which has connectivity to the Internet. Interface eth0 remains in stealth mode but can still listen to the network traffic from this side of the network.

Before starting Snort on eth0, you have to bring it up. On Linux systems, you can do it by using the following command:

```
ifconfig eth0 up
```

The command makes the interface usable without allocating an IP address. After that, you can start Snort on this interface by using "-i eth0" command line option as follows:

```
snort -c /opt/snort/etc/snort.conf -i eth0 -D
```

2.10 References

1. Snort web site at http://www.snort.org
2. SNMP information at http://www.simpletimes.com
3. Winpcap Library at http://winpcap.polito.it/
4. Apache web server at http://www.apache.org
5. Argus Network Security Services Inc. at http://www.argusnetsec.com
6. Libpcap is available from http://www-nrg.ee.lbl.gov/
7. Libnet at http://www.packetfactory.net
8. RFC 792 at ftp://ftp.isi.edu/in-notes/rfc792.txt
9. RFC 791 at at ftp://ftp.isi.edu/in-notes/rfc791.txt
10. SAMBA at http://www.samba.org

## CHAPTER 3

Working with Snort Rules

Like viruses, most intruder activity has some sort of signature. Information about these signatures is used to create Snort rules. As mentioned in Chapter 1, you can use honey pots to find out what intruders are doing and information about their tools and techniques. In addition to that, there are databases of known vulnerabilities that intruders want to exploit. These known attacks are also used as signatures to find out if someone is trying to exploit them. These signatures may be present in the header parts of a packet or in the payload. Snort's detection system is based on rules. These rules in turn are based on intruder signatures. Snort rules can be used to check various parts of a data packet. Snort 1.x versions can analyze layer 3 and 4 headers but are not able to analyze application layer protocols. Upcoming Snort version 2 is expected to add support of application layer headers as well. Rules are applied in an orderly fashion to all packets depending on their types.

A rule may be used to generate an alert message, log a message, or, in terms of Snort, *pass* the data packet, i.e., drop it silently. The word *pass* here is not equivalent to the traditional meaning of *pass* as used in firewalls and routers. In firewalls and routers, *pass* and *drop* are opposite to each other. Snort rules are written in an easy to understand syntax. Most of the rules are written in a single line. However you can also extend rules to multiple lines by using a backslash character at the end of lines. Rules are usually placed in a configuration file, typically `snort.conf`. You can also use multiple files by including them in a main configuration file.

This chapter provides information about different types of rules as well as the basic structure of a rule. You will find many examples of common rules for intrusion detection activity at the end of this chapter. After reading this chapter, along with the two preceding chapters, you should have enough information to set up Snort as a basic intrusion detection system.

3.1 TCP/IP Network Layers

Before you move to writing rules, let us have a brief discussion about TCP/IP layers. This is important because Snort rules are applied on different protocols in these layers.

TCP/IP is a five layer protocol. These layers interact with each other to make the communication process work. The names of these layers are:

1. The physical layer.
2. The data link layer. In some literature this is also called the network interface layer. The physical and data link layers consist of physical media, the network interface adapter, and the driver for the network interface adapter. Ethernet addresses are assigned in the data link layer.
3. The network layer, which is actually IP (Internet Protocol) layer. This layer is responsible for point-to-point data communication and data integrity. All hosts on this layer are distinguished by IP addresses. In addition to IP protocol, ICMP (Internet Control Message Protocol) is another major protocol in this layer. Information about IP protocol is available in RFC 791 available at http://www.rfc-editor.org/rfc/rfc791.txt. Information about ICMP protocol is available at http://www.rfc-editor.org/rfc/rfc792.txt.
4. The transport layer, which is actually TCP/UDP layer in the TCP/IP protocol. TCP (Transmission Control Protocol) is used for connection-oriented and reliable data transfer from source to destination. UDP (User Datagram Protocol), on the other hand, is used for connectionless data transfer. There is no assurance that data sent through UDP protocol will actually reach its destination. UDP is used where data loss can be tolerated. Information about UDP protocol is available in RFC 768 at http://www.rfc-editor.org/rfc/rfc768.txt. Information about TCP protocol is available in RFC 793 at http://www.rfc-editor.org/rfc/rfc793.txt.

5. The application layer consists of applications to provide user interface to the
network. Examples of network applications are Telnet, Web browsers, and FTP
clients. These applications usually have their own application layer protocol for
data communication.

Snort rules operate on network (IP) layer and transport (TCP/UDP) layer protocols. However there are methods to detect anomalies in data link layer and application
layer protocols. The second part of each Snort rule shows the protocol and you will
learn shortly how to write these rules.

3.2 The First Bad Rule

Here is the first (very) bad rule. In fact, this may be the worst rule ever written, but it
does a very good job of testing if Snort is working well and is able to generate alerts.

```
alert ip any any -> any any (msg: "IP Packet detected";)
```

You can use this rule at the end of the `snort.conf` file the first time you install
Snort. The rule will generate an alert message for *every* captured IP packet. It will soon
fill up your disk space if you leave it there! This rule is bad because it does not convey
any information. What is the point of using a rule on a permanent basis that tells you
nothing other than the fact that Snort is working? This should be your first test to make
sure that Snort is installed properly. In the next section, you will find information about
the different parts of a Snort rule. However for the sake of completeness, the following
is a brief explanation of different words used in this rule:

- The word "alert" shows that this rule will generate an alert message when the
  criteria are met for a captured packet. The criteria are defined by the words that
  follow.
- The "ip" part shows that this rule will be applied on all IP packets.
- The first "any" is used for source IP address and shows that the rule will be
  applied to all packets.
- The second "any" is used for the port number. Since port numbers are irrelevant
  at the IP layer, the rule will be applied to all packets.
- The -> sign shows the direction of the packet.
- The third "any" is used for destination IP address and shows that the rule will
  be applied to all packets irrespective of destination IP address.
- The fourth "any" is used for destination port. Again it is irrelevant because this
  rule is for IP packets and port numbers are irrelevant.

• The last part is the rule options and contains a message that will be logged along with the alert.

The next rule isn't quite as bad. It generates alerts for all captured ICMP packets. Again, this rule is useful to find out if Snort is working.

```
alert icmp any any -> any any (msg: "ICMP Packet found";)
```

If you want to test the Snort machine, send a ping packet (which is basically ICMP ECHO REQUEST packet on UNIX machines). Again, you can use this rule when you install Snort to make sure that it is working well. As an example, send an ICMP packet to your gateway address or some other host on the network using the following command:

```
ping 192.168.2.1
```

Note that 192.168.2.1 is the IP address of gateway/router or some other host on the same network where the Snort machine is present. This command should be executed on the machine where you installed Snort. The command can be used both on UNIX and Microsoft Windows machines.

T I P   I use a slightly modified version of this rule to continuously monitor multiple Snort sensors just to make sure everybody is up and running. This rule is as follows:

```
alert icmp 192.168.1.4 any -> 192.168.1.1 any (msg: "HEARTBEAT";)
```

My Snort sensor IP address is 192.168.1.4 and gateway address is 192.168.1.1. I run the following command through cron daemon on the Linux machine to trigger this rule every 10 minutes.

```
ping -n 1 192.168.1.1
```

The command sends exactly one ICMP packet to the gateway machine. This packet causes an alert entry to be created. If there is no alert every 10 minutes, there is something wrong with the sensor.

3.3 CIDR

Classless Inter-Domain Routing or CIDR is defined in RFC 1519. It was intended to make better use of available Internet addresses by eliminating different classes (like class A and class B). With the CIDR, you can define any number of bits in the netmask field, which was not possible with class-based networking where the number of bits was fixed. Using CIDR, network addresses are written using the number of bits in the netmask at the end of the IP address. For example, 192.168.1.0/24 defines a network with network address 192.168.1.0 with 24 bits in the netmask. A netmask with 24 bits is equal to 255.255.255.0. An individual host can be written using all of the netmask bits, i.e., 32. The following rule shows that only those packets that go to a single host with IP address192.168.2.113 will generate an alert:

```
alert icmp any any -> 192.168.1.113/32 any \
    (msg: "Ping with TTL=100"; ttl:100;)
```

All addresses in Snort are written using the CIDR notation, which makes it very convenient to monitor any subset of hosts.

3.4 Structure of a Rule

Now that you have seen some rules which are not-so-good but helpful in a way, let us see the structure of a Snort rule. All Snort rules have two logical parts: rule *header* and rule *options*. This is shown in Figure 3-1.

Rule Header	Rule Options

Figure 3-1 Basic structure of Snort rules.

The rule header contains information about what action a rule takes. It also contains criteria for matching a rule against data packets. The options part usually contains an alert message and information about which part of the packet should be used to generate the alert message. The options part contains additional criteria for matching a rule against data packets. A rule may detect one type or multiple types of intrusion activity. Intelligent rules should be able to apply to multiple intrusion signatures.

The general structure of a Snort rule header is shown in Figure 3-2.

Action	Protocol	Address	Port	Direction	Address	Port

Figure 3-2 Structure of Snort rule header.

The *action* part of the rule determines the type of action taken when criteria are met and a rule is exactly matched against a data packet. Typical actions are generating an alert or log message or invoking another rule. You will learn more about actions later in this chapter.

The *protocol* part is used to apply the rule on packets for a particular protocol only. This is the first criterion mentioned in the rule. Some examples of protocols used are IP, ICMP, UDP etc.

The *address* parts define source and destination addresses. Addresses may be a single host, multiple hosts or network addresses. You can also use these parts to exclude some addresses from a complete network. More about addresses will be discussed later. Note that there are two address fields in the rule. Source and destination addresses are determined based on direction field. As an example, if the direction field is "->", the Address on the left side is source and the Address on the right side is destination.

In case of TCP or UDP protocol, the *port* parts determine the source and destination ports of a packet on which the rule is applied. In case of network layer protocols like IP and ICMP, port numbers have no significance.

The *direction* part of the rule actually determines which address and port number is used as source and which as destination.

For example, consider the following rule that generates an alert message whenever it detects an ICMP[1] ping packet (ICMP ECHO REQUEST) with TTL equal to 100, as you have seen in Chapter 2.

```
alert icmp any any -> any any (msg: "Ping with TTL=100"; \
ttl: 100;)
```

The part of the rule before the starting parenthesis is called the rule header. The part of the rule that is enclosed by the parentheses is the options part. The header contains the following parts, in order:

- A rule action. In this rule the action is "alert", which means that an alert will be generated when conditions are met. Remember that packets are logged by default when an alert is generated. Depending on the action field, the rule options part may contain additional criteria for the rules.
- Protocol. In this rule the protocol is ICMP, which means that the rule will be applied only on ICMP-type packets. In the Snort detection engine, if the protocol of a packet is not ICMP, the rest of the rule is not considered in order to save CPU time. The protocol part plays an important role when you want to apply Snort rules only to packets of a particular type.

---

1.   ICMP or Internet Control Message Protocol is defined in RFC 792. ICMP packets are used to convey different types of information in the network. ICMP ECHO REQUEST is one type of ICMP packet. There are many other types of ICMP packets as defined in the RFC 792. The references at the end of this chapter contains a URL to download the RFC document.

- Source address and source port. In this example both of them are set to "any", which means that the rule will be applied on all packets coming from any source. Of course port numbers have no relevance to ICMP packets. Port numbers are relevant only when protocol is either TCP or UDP.
- Direction. In this case the direction is set from left to right using the -> symbol. This shows that the address and port number on the left hand side of the symbol are source and those on the right hand side are destination. It also means that the rule will be applied on packets traveling from source to destination. You can also use a <- symbol to reverse the meaning of source and destination address of the packet. Note that a symbol <> can also be used to apply the rule on packets going in either direction.
- Destination address and port address. In this example both are set to "any", meaning the rule will be applied to all packets irrespective of their destination address. The direction in this rule does not play any role because the rule is applied to all ICMP packets moving in either direction, due to the use of the keyword "any" in both source and destination address parts.

The options part enclosed in parentheses shows that an alert message will be generated containing the text string "Ping with TTL=100" whenever the condition of TTL=100 is met. Note that TTL or *Time To Live* is a field in the IP packet header. Refer to RFC 791 at http://www.rfc-editor.org/rfc/rfc791.txt or Appendix C for information on IP packet headers.

3.5 Rule Headers

As mentioned earlier, a rule header consists of the section of the rule before starting parentheses and has many parts. Let us take a detailed look at different parts used in the rule header, starting with rule actions.

3.5.1 Rule Actions

The action is the first part of a Snort rule. It shows what action will be taken when rule conditions are met. An action is taken only when all of the conditions mentioned in a rule are true. There are five predefined actions. However, you can also define your own actions as needed. As a precaution, keep in mind that Snort versions 1.x and 2.x apply rules in different ways. In Snort 1.x, if multiple rules match a given packet, only the first one is applied. After applying the first rule, no further action is taken on the packet. However in Snort version 2, all rules are applied before generating an alert message. The most severe alert message is then generated.

3.5.1.1   Pass

This action tells Snort to ignore the packet. This action plays an important role in speeding up Snort operation in cases where you don't want to apply checks on certain packets. For example, if you have a vulnerability assessment host on your own network that you use to find possible security holes in your network, you may want Snort to ignore any attacks from that host. The pass rule plays an important part in such a case.

3.5.1.2   Log

The log action is used to log a packet. Packets can be logged in different ways, as discussed later in this book. For example, a message can be logged to log files or in a database. Packets can be logged with different levels of detail depending on the command line arguments and configuration file. To find available command line arguments with your version of Snort, use "`snort -?`" command.

3.5.1.3   Alert

The alert action is used to send an alert message when rule conditions are true for a particular packet. An alert can be sent in multiple ways. For example, you can send an alert to a file or to a console. The functional difference between Log and Alert actions is that Alert actions send an alert message and then log the packet. The Log action only logs the packet.

3.5.1.4   Activate

The activate action is used to create an alert and then to activate another rule for checking more conditions. Dynamic rules, as explained next, are used for this purpose. The activate action is used when you need further testing of a captured packet.

3.5.1.5   Dynamic

Dynamic action rules are invoked by other rules using the "activate" action. In normal circumstances, they are not applied on a packet. A dynamic rule can be activated only by an "activate" action defined in another role.

3.5.1.6   User Defined Actions

In addition to these actions, you can define your own actions. These rule actions can be used for different purposes, such as:

- Sending messages to syslog. Syslog is system logger daemon and creates log file in `/var/log` directory. Location of these files can be changed using `/etc/syslog.conf` file. For more information, use "`man syslog`" and "`man syslog.conf`" commands on a UNIX system. Syslog may be compared to the event logger on Microsoft Windows systems.

- Sending SNMP traps. SNMP traps are sent to a network management system like HP OpenView or Open NMS at http://www.opennms.org.
- Taking multiple actions on a packet. As you have seen earlier in the structure of Snort rules, a rule only takes one action. User defined rules can be used to take multiple actions. For example, a user defined rule can be used to send an SNMP trap as well as to log the alert data to the syslog daemon.
- Logging data to XML files.

Logging messages into a database. Snort is able to log messages to MySQL, Postgress SQL, Oracle and Microsoft SQL server.

These new action types are defined in the configuration file `snort.conf`. A new action is defined in the following general structure:

```
ruletype action_name
{
    action definition
}
```

The `ruletype` keyword is followed by the action name. Two braces enclose the actual definition of the action, just like a function in C programming. For example, an action named `smb_db_alert` that is used to send SMB pop-up window alert messages to hosts listed in `workstation.list` file and to MySQL database named "snort" is defined below:

```
ruletype smb_db_alert
{
    type alert
    output alert_smb: workstation.list
    output database: log, mysql, user=rr password=rr \
       dbname=snort host=localhost
}
```

Theses types of rules will be discussed in the next chapter in detail. Usually they are related to configuration of output plug-ins.

3.5.2 Protocols

Protocol is the second part of a Snort rule. The protocol part of a Snort rule shows on which type of packet the rule will be applied. Currently Snort understands the following protocols:

- IP
- ICMP

- TCP
- UDP

If the protocol is IP, Snort checks the link layer header to determine the packet type. If any other type of protocol is used, Snort uses the IP header to determine the protocol type. Different packet headers are discussed in Appendix C.

The protocols only play a role in specifying criteria in the header part of the rule. The options part of the rule can have additional criteria unrelated to the specified protocol. For example, consider the following rule where the protocol is ICMP.

```
alert icmp any any -> any any (msg: "Ping with TTL=100"; \
    ttl: 100;)
```

The options part checks the TTL (Time To Live) value, which is not part of the ICMP header. TTL is part of IP header instead. This means that the options part can check parameters in other protocol fields as well. Header fields for common protocols and their explanation is found in Appendix C.

3.5.3 Address

There are two address parts in a Snort rule. These addresses are used to check the source from which the packet originated and the destination of the packet. The address may be a single IP address or a network address. You can use *any* keyword to apply a rule on all addresses. The address is followed by a slash character and number of bits in the netmask. For example, an address 192.168.2.0/24 represents C class network 192.168.2.0 with 24 bits in the network mask. A network mask with 24 bits is 255.255.255.0. Keep the following in mind about number of bits in the netmask:

- If the netmask consists of 24 bits, it is a C class network.
- If the netmask consists of 16 bits, it is a B class network.
- If the netmask consists of 8 bits, it is an A class network.
- For a single host, use 32 bits in the netmask field.

You can also use any number of bits in the address part allowed by Classless Inter-Domain Routing or CIDR. Refer to RFC 791 at http://www.rfc-editor.org/rfc/rfc791.txt for structure of IP addresses and netmasks and to RFC 1519 at http://www.rfc-editor.org/rfc/rfc1519.txt for more information on CIDR.

As mentioned earlier, there are two address fields in the Snort rule. One of them is the source address and the other one is the destination address. The direction part of the rule determines which address is source and which one is destination. Refer to the explanation of the direction part to find more information about how this selection is made.

Following are some examples of how addresses are mentioned in Snort rules:

- An address 192.168.1.3/32 defines a single host with IP address 192.168.1.3.
- An address 192.168.1.0/24 defines a class C network with addresses ranging from 192.168.1.0 to 192.168.1.255. There are 24 bits in the netmask, which is equal to 255.255.255.0.
- An address 152.168.0.0/16 defines a class B network with addresses ranging from 152.168.0.0 to 152.168.255.255. There are 16 bits in the netmask, which is equal to 255.255.0.0.
- An address 10.0.0.0/8 defines a class A network with addresses ranging from 10.0.0.0 to 10.255.255.255. There are 8 bits in the netmask, which is equal to 255.0.0.0.
- An address 192.168.1.16/28 defines an address range of 192.168.1.16 to 192.168.1.31. There are 28 bits in the netmask field, which is equal to 255.255.255.240, and the network consists of 16 addresses. You can place only 14 hosts in this type of network because two of the total 16 addresses are used up in defining the network address and the broadcast address. Note that the first address in each network is always the network address and the last address is the broadcast address. For this network 192.168.1.16 is the network address and 192.168.1.31 is the broadcast address.

For example, if you want to generate alerts for all TCP packets with TTL=100 going to web server 192.168.1.10 at port 80 from any source, you can use the following rule:

```
alert tcp any any -> 192.168.1.10/32 80 (msg: "TTL=100"; \
ttl: 100;)
```

This rule is just an example to provide information about how IP addresses are used in Snort rules.

3.5.3.1   Address Exclusion

Snort provides a mechanism to exclude addresses by the use of the negation symbol !, an exclamation point. This symbol is used with the address to direct Snort not to test packets coming from or going to that address. For example, the following rule is applied to all packets except those that originate from class C network 192.168.2.0.

```
alert icmp ![192.168.2.0/24] any -> any any \
    (msg: "Ping with TTL=100";  ttl: 100;)
```

This rule is useful, for instance, when you want to test packets that don't originate from your home network (which means you trust everyone in your home network!).

3.5.3.2   Address Lists

You can also specify list of addresses in a Snort rule. For example, if your home network consists of two C class IP networks 192.168.2.0 and 192.168.8.0 and you want to apply the above rule to all addresses but hosts in these two, you can use the following modified rule where the two addresses are separated by a comma.

```
alert icmp ![192.168.2.0/24,192.168.8.0/24] any -> any \
    any (msg: "Ping with TTL=100";  ttl: 100;)
```

Note that a square bracket is used with the negation symbol. You don't need to use brackets if you are not using the negation symbol.

3.5.4 Port Number

The port number is used to apply a rule on packets that originate from or go to a particular port or a range of ports. For example, you can use source port number 23 to apply a rule to those packets that originate from a Telnet server. You can use the keyword *any* to apply the rule on all packets irrespective of the port number. Port number is meaningful only for TCP and UDP protocols. If you have selected IP or ICMP as the protocol in the rule, port number does not play any role. The following rule is applied to all packets that originate from a Telnet server in 192.168.2.0/24, which is a class C network and contains the word "confidential":

```
alert tcp 192.168.2.0/24 23 -> any any \
    (content: "confidential"; msg: "Detected confidential";)
```

The same rule can be applied to traffic either going to or originating from any Telnet server in the network by modifying the direction to either side as shown below:

```
alert tcp 192.168.2.0/24 23 <> any any \
    (content: "confidential"; msg: "Detected confidential";)
```

Port numbers are useful when you want to apply a rule only for a particular type of data packet. For example, if a vulnerability is related to only a HTTP (Hyper Text Transfer Protocol) web server, you can use port 80 in the rule to detect anybody trying to exploit it. This way Snort will apply that rule only to web server traffic and not to any other TCP packets. Writing good rules always improves the performance of IDS.

3.5.4.1 Port Ranges

You can also use a range of ports instead of only one port in the port field. Use a colon to separate starting and ending port numbers. For example, the following rule will create an alert for all UDP traffic coming from ports 1024 to 2048 from all hosts.

```
alert udp any 1024:2048 -> any any (msg: "UDP ports";)
```

3.5.4.2 Upper and Lower Boundaries

While listing port numbers, you can also use only the starting port number or the ending port number in the range. For example, a range specified as :1024 includes all port numbers up to and including port 1024. A port range specified as 1000: will include all ports numbers including and above port 1000.

3.5.4.3 Negation Symbol

As with addresses, you can also use the negation symbol with port numbers to exclude a port or a range of ports from the scope of the Snort rule. The following rule logs all UDP traffic except for source port number 53.

```
log udp any !53 -> any any log udp
```

You can't use comma character in the port filed to specify multiple ports. For example, specifying 53,54 is not allowed. However you can use 53:54 to specify a port range.

3.5.4.4 Well-Known Port Numbers

Well-known port numbers are used for commonly used applications. Some of these port numbers and their applications are listed in Table 3-1.

Table 3-1 Well-Known Port Numbers

Port Number	Description
20	FTP data
21	FTP
22	SSH or Secure shell
23	Telnet
25	SMTP, used for e-mail server like Sendmail
37	NTP (Network Time Protocol) used for synchronizing time on network hosts
53	DNS server
67	BootP/DHCP client
68	BootP/DHCP server
69	TFTP
80	HTTP, used for all web servers

Table 3-1 Well-Known Port Numbers (continued)

Port Number	Description
110	POP3, used for e-mail clients like Microsoft Outlook
161	SNMP
162	SNMP traps
443	HTTPS or Secure HTTP
514	Syslog
3306	MySQL

You can also look into /etc/services file on the UNIX platform to see more port numbers. Refer to RFC 1700 for a detailed list at http://www.rfc-editor.org/rfc/rfc1700.txt. The Internet Corporation for Assigned Names and Numbers (ICANN) now keeps track of all port numbers and names. You can find more information at http://www.icann.org.

3.5.5 Direction

The direction field determines the source and destination addresses and port numbers in a rule. The following rules apply to the direction field:

- A -> symbol shows that address and port numbers on the left hand side of the direction field are the source of the packet while the address and port number on the right hand side of the field are the destination.
- A <- symbol in the direction field shows that the packet is traveling from the address and port number on the right hand side of the symbol to the address and port number on the left hand side.
- A <> symbol shows that the rule will be applied to packets traveling on either direction. This symbol is useful when you want to monitor data packets for both client and server. For example, using this symbol, you can monitor all traffic coming from and going to a POP or Telnet server.

3.6 Rule Options

Rule options follow the rule header and are enclosed inside a pair of parentheses. There may be one option or many and the options are separated with a semicolon. If you use multiple options, these options form a logical AND. The action in the rule header is invoked only when all criteria in the options are true. You have already used options like *msg* and *ttl* in previous rule examples. All options are defined by keywords. Some rule options also contain arguments. In general, an option may have two parts: a keyword and an argument. Arguments are separated from the option keyword by a colon. Consider the following rule options that you have already seen:

```
msg: "Detected confidential";
```

In this option *msg* is the keyword and "*Detected confidential*" is the argument to this keyword.

The remainder of this section describes keywords used in the options part of Snort rules.

3.6.1 The ack Keyword

The TCP header contains an Acknowledgement Number field which is 32 bits long. The field shows the next sequence number the sender of the TCP packet is expecting to receive. This field is significant only when the ACK flag in the TCP header is set. Refer to Appendix C and RFC 793 for more information about the TCP header.

Tools like nmap (http://www.nmap.org) use this feature of the TCP header to ping a machine. For example, among other techniques used by nmap, it can send a TCP packet to port 80 with ACK flag set and sequence number 0. Since this packet is not acceptable by the receiving side according to TCP rules, it sends back a RST packet. When nmap receives this RST packet, it learns that the host is alive. This method works on hosts that don't respond to ICMP ECHO REQUEST ping packets.

To detect this type of TCP ping, you can have a rule like the following that sends an alert message:

```
alert tcp any any -> 192.168.1.0/24  any (flags: A; \
    ack: 0; msg: "TCP ping detected";)
```

This rule shows that an alert message will be generated when you receive a TCP packet with the A flag set and the acknowledgement contains a value of 0. Other TCP flags are listed in Table 3-2. The destination of this packet must be a host in network 192.168.1.0/24. You can use any value with the ACK keyword in a rule, however it is added to Snort only to detect this type of attack. Generally when the A flag is set, the ACK value is not zero.

3.6.2 The classtype Keyword

Rules can be assigned classifications and priority numbers to group and distinguish them. To fully understand the classtype keyword, first look at the file classi-fication.config which is included in the snort.conf file using the *include* keyword. Each line in the classification.config file has the following syntax:

```
config classification: name,description,priority
```

The *name* is a name used for the classification. The name is used with the *classtype* keyword in Snort rules. The *description* is a short description of the class type. *Priority* is a number that shows the default priority of the classification, which can be modified using a *priority* keyword inside the rule options. You can also place these lines in `snort.conf` file as well. An example of this configuration parameter is as follows:

```
config classification: DoS,Denial of Service Attack,2
```

In the above line the classification is DoS and the priority is 2. In Chapter 6, you will see that classifications are used in ACID,[2] which is a web-based tool to analyze Snort alert data. Now let us use this classification in a rule. The following rule uses default priority with the classification DoS:

```
alert udp any any -> 192.168.1.0/24 6838 (msg:"DoS"; \
    content: "server";  classtype:DoS;)
```

The following is the same rule but we override the default priority used for the classification.

```
alert udp any any -> 192.168.1.0/24 6838 (msg:"DoS"; \
    content: "server";  classtype:DoS; priority:1)
```

Using classifications and priorities for rules and alerts, you can distinguish between high- and low-risk alerts. This feature is very useful when you want to escalate high-risk alerts or want to pay attention to them first.

N O T E   Low priority numbers show high priority alerts.

If you look at the ACID browser window, as discussed in Chapter 6, you will see the classification screens as shown in Figure 3-3. The second column in the middle part of the screen displays different classifications for captured data.

Other tools also use the classification keyword to prioritize intrusion detection data. A typical `classification.config` file is shown below. This file is distributed with the Snort 1.9.0. You can add your own classifications to this file and use them in your own rules.

---

2.   ACID stands for Analysis Control for Intrusion Detection. It provides a web-based user interface to analyze data generated by Snort.

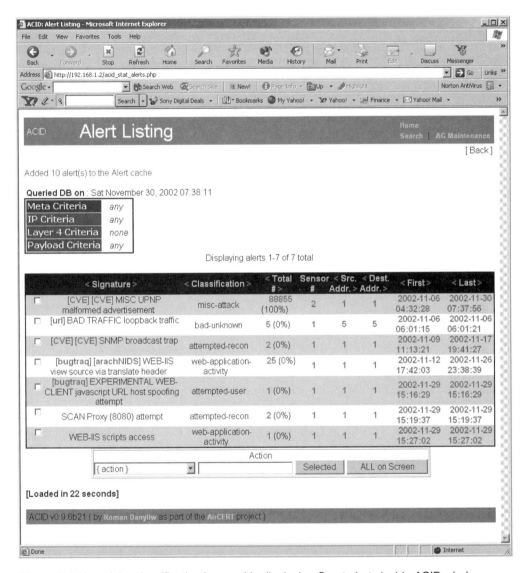

Figure 3-3 Use of the classification keyword in displaying Snort alerts inside ACID window.

```
# $Id: classification.config,v 1.10 2002/08/11 23:37:18 cazz Exp $
# The following includes information for prioritizing rules
#
# Each classification includes a shortname, a description, and a
  default
# priority for that classification.
```

```
#
# This allows alerts to be classified and prioritized.  You can specify
# what priority each classification has.  Any rule can override the
  default
# priority for that rule.
#
# Here are a few example rules:
#
#   alert TCP any any -> any 80 (msg: "EXPLOIT ntpdx overflow";
#       dsize: > 128; classtype:attempted-admin; priority:10;
#
#   alert TCP any any -> any 25 (msg:"SMTP expn root"; flags:A+; \
#           content:"expn root"; nocase; classtype:attempted-recon;)
#
# The first rule will set its type to "attempted-admin" and override
# the default priority for that type to 10.
#
# The second rule set its type to "attempted-recon" and set its
# priority to the default for that type.
#


#
# config classification:shortname,short description,priority
#

config classification: not-suspicious,Not Suspicious Traffic,3
config classification: unknown,Unknown Traffic,3
config classification: bad-unknown,Potentially Bad Traffic, 2
config classification: attempted-recon,Attempted Information Leak,2
config classification: successful-recon-limited,Information Leak,2
config classification: successful-recon-largescale,Large Scale
  Information Leak,2
config classification: attempted-dos,Attempted Denial of Service,2
config classification: successful-dos,Denial of Service,2
config classification: attempted-user,Attempted User Privilege Gain,1
config classification: unsuccessful-user,Unsuccessful User Privilege
  Gain,1
config classification: successful-user,Successful User Privilege Gain,1
config classification: attempted-admin,Attempted Administrator
  Privilege Gain,1
config classification: successful-admin,Successful Administrator
  Privilege Gain,1


# NEW CLASSIFICATIONS
config classification: rpc-portmap-decode,Decode of an RPC Query,2
config classification: shellcode-detect,Executable code was detected,1
```

```
config classification: string-detect,A suspicious string was detected,3
config classification: suspicious-filename-detect,A suspicious filename
   was detected,2
config classification: suspicious-login,An attempted login using a
   suspicious username was detected,2
config classification: system-call-detect,A system call was detected,2
config classification: tcp-connection,A TCP connection was detected,4
config classification: trojan-activity,A Network Trojan was detected, 1
config classification: unusual-client-port-connection,A client was
   using an unusual port,2
config classification: network-scan,Detection of a Network Scan,3
config classification: denial-of-service,Detection of a Denial of
   Service Attack,2
config classification: non-standard-protocol,Detection of a non-
   standard protocol or event,2
config classification: protocol-command-decode,Generic Protocol Command
   Decode,3
config classification: web-application-activity,access to a potentially
   vulnerable web application,2
config classification: web-application-attack,Web Application Attack,1
config classification: misc-activity,Misc activity,3
config classification: misc-attack,Misc Attack,2
config classification: icmp-event,Generic ICMP event,3
config classification: kickass-porn,SCORE! Get the lotion!,1
config classification: policy-violation,Potential Corporate Privacy
   Violation,1
config classification: default-login-attempt,Attempt to login by a
   default username and password,2
```

3.6.3 The content Keyword

One important feature of Snort is its ability to find a data pattern inside a packet. The pattern may be presented in the form of an ASCII string or as binary data in the form of hexadecimal characters. Like viruses, intruders also have signatures and the content keyword is used to find these signatures in the packet. Since Snort version 1.x does not support application layer protocols, this keyword, in conjunction with the off-set keyword, can also be used to look into the application layer header.

The following rule detects a pattern "GET" in the data part of all TCP packets that are leaving 192.168.1.0 network and going to an address that is not part of that network. The GET keyword is used in many HTTP related attacks; however, this rule is only using it to help you understand how the content keyword works.

```
alert tcp 192.168.1.0/24 any -> ![192.168.1.0/24] any \
   (content: "GET"; msg: "GET matched";)
```

The following rule does the same thing but the pattern is listed in hexadecimal.

```
alert tcp 192.168.1.0/24 any -> ![192.168.1.0/24] any \
    (content: "|47 45 54|"; msg: "GET matched";)
```

Hexadecimal number 47 is equal to ASCII character G, 45 is equal to E, and 54 is equal to T. You can also match both ASCII strings and binary patterns in hexadecimal form inside one rule. Just enclose the hexadecimal characters inside a pair of bar symbols: ||.

When using the content keyword, keep the following in mind:

- Content matching is a computationally expensive process and you should be careful of using too many rules for content matching.
- If you provide content as an ASCII string, you should escape the double quote, colon and bar symbols.
- You can use multiple content keywords in one rule to find multiple signatures in the data packet.
- Content matching is case sensitive.

There are three other keywords that are used with the content keyword. These keywords add additional criteria while finding a pattern inside a packet. These are:

- The offset keyword
- The depth keyword
- The nocase keyword

These keywords are discussed later in this chapter. The first two keywords are used to confine the search within a certain range of the data packet. The nocase keyword is used to make the search case-insensitive.

3.6.4   The offset Keyword

The offset keyword is used in combination with the content keyword. Using this keyword, you can start your search at a certain offset from the start of the data part of the packet. Use a number as argument to this keyword. The following rule starts searching for the word "HTTP" after 4 bytes from the start of the data.

```
alert tcp 192.168.1.0/24 any -> any any \
    (content: "HTTP"; offset: 4; msg: "HTTP matched";)
```

You can use the depth keyword to define the point after which Snort should stop searching the pattern in the data packets.

3.6.5 The depth Keyword

The depth keyword is also used in combination with the content keyword to specify an upper limit to the pattern matching. Using the depth keyword, you can specify an offset from the start of the data part. Data after that offset is not searched for pattern matching. If you use both offset and depth keywords with the content keyword, you can specify the range of data within which pattern matching should be done. The following rule tries to find the word "HTTP" between characters 4 and 40 of the data part of the TCP packet.

```
alert tcp 192.168.1.0/24 any -> any any (content: \
    "HTTP"; offset: 4; depth: 40; msg: "HTTP matched";)
```

This keyword is very important since you can use it to limit searching inside the packet. For example, information about HTTP GET requests is found in the start of the packet. There is no need to search the entire packet for such strings. Since many packets you capture are very long in size, it wastes a lot of time to search for these strings in the entire packet. The same is true for many other Snort signatures.

3.6.6 The content-list Keyword

The content-list keyword is used with a file name. The file name, which is used as an argument to this keyword, is a text file that contains a list of strings to be searched inside a packet. Each string is located on a separate line of the file. For example, a file named "porn" may contain the following three lines:

"porn"

"hardcore"

"under 18"

The following rule will search these strings in the data portion of all packets matching the rule criteria.

```
alert ip any any -> 192.168.1.0/24 any (content-list: \
    "porn"; msg: "Porn word matched";)
```

You can also use the negation sign ! with the file name if you want to generate an alert for a packet where no strings match.

3.6.7 The dsize Keyword

The dsize keyword is used to find the length of the data part of a packet. Many attacks use buffer overflow vulnerabilities by sending large size packets. Using this keyword, you can find out if a packet contains data of a length larger than, smaller than, or equal to a certain number. The following rule generates an alert if the data size of an IP packet is larger than 6000 bytes.

```
alert ip any any -> 192.168.1.0/24 any (dsize: > 6000; \
    msg: "Large size IP packet detected";)
```

3.6.8   The flags Keyword

The flags keyword is used to find out which flag bits are set inside the TCP header of a packet. Each flag can be used as an argument to flags keyword in Snort rules. A detailed description of the TCP flag bits is present in RFC 793 at http://www.rfc-editor.org/rfc/rfc793.txt. These flag bits are used by many security related tools for different purposes including port scanning tools like nmap (http://www.nmap.org). Snort supports checking of these flags listed in Table 3-2.

Table 3-2 TCP flag bits

Flag	Argument character used in Snort rules
FIN or Finish Flag	F
SYN or Sync Flag	S
RST or Reset Flag	R
PSH or Push Flag	P
ACK or Acknowledge Flag	A
URG or Urgent Flag	U
Reserved Bit 1	1
Reserved Bit 2	2
No Flag set	0

You can also use !, +, and * symbols just like IP header flag bits (discussed under the fragbits keyword) for AND, OR and NOT logical operations on flag bits being tested. The following rule detects any scan attempt using SYN-FIN TCP packets.

```
alert tcp any any -> 192.168.1.0/24 any (flags: SF; \
    msg: "SYNC-FIN packet detected";)
```

Note that ! symbol is used for NOT, + is used for AND, and * is used for OR operation.

3.6.9 The fragbits Keyword

The IP header contains three flag bits that are used for fragmentation and re-assembly of IP packets. These bits are listed below:

- Reserved Bit (RB), which is reserved for future use.
- Don't Fragment Bit (DF). If this bit is set, it shows that the IP packet should not be fragmented.
- More Fragments Bit (MF). If this bit is set, it shows that more fragments of this IP packet are on the way. If this bit is not set, it shows that this is the last fragment (or the only fragment) of the IP packet. The sending host fragments IP packets into smaller packets depending on the maximum size packet that can be transmitted through a communication medium. For example, the Maximum Transfer Units or MTU defines the maximum length of a packet on the Ethernet networks. This bit is used at the destination host to reassemble IP fragments.

For more information on Flag bits refer to RFC 791 at http://www.rfc-editor.org/rfc/rfc791.txt. Sometimes these bits are used by hackers for attacks and to find out information related to your network. For example, the DF bit can be used to find the minimum and maximum MTU for a path from source to destination. Using the fragbits keyword, you can find out if a packet contains these bits set or cleared. The following rule is used to detect if the DF bit is set in an ICMP packet.

```
alert icmp any any -> 192.168.1.0/24 any (fragbits: D; \
    msg: "Don't Fragment bit set";)
```

In this rule, D is used for DF bit. You can use R for reserved bit and M for MF bit. You can also use the negation symbol ! in the rule. The following rule detects if the DF bit is not set, although this rule is of little use.

```
alert icmp any any -> 192.168.1.0/24 any (fragbits: !D; \
    msg: "Don't Fragment bit not set";)
```

The AND and OR logical operators can also be used to check multiple bits. The + symbol specifies all bits be matched (AND operation) while the * symbol specifies any of the specified bits be matched (OR operation).

3.6.10 The icmp_id Keyword

The icmp_id option is used to detect a particular ID used with ICMP packet. Refer to Appendix C for ICMP header information. The general format for using this keyword is as follows:

```
icmp_id: <ICMP_id_number>
```

An ICMP identified field is found in ICMP ECHO REQUEST and ICMP ECHO REPLY messages as discussed in RFC 792. This field is used to match ECHO REQUEST and ECHO REPLY messages. Usually when you use the ping command, both of these types of ICMP packets are exchanged between sending and receiving hosts. The sending host sends ECHO REQUEST packets and the destination host replies with ECHO REPLY-type ICMP packets. This field is useful for discovering which packet is the reply to a particular request. The following rule checks if the ICMP ID field in the ICMP header is equal to 100. It generates an alert if this criterion is met.

```
alert icmp any any -> any any (icmp_id: 100; \
    msg: "ICMP ID=100";)
```

3.6.11 The icmp_seq Keyword

The icmp_seq option is similar to the icmp_id keyword The general format for using this keyword is as follows:

```
icmp_seq: <ICMP_seq_number>
```

The sequence number is also a field in the ICMP header and is also useful in matching ICMP ECHO REQUEST and ECHO REPLY matches as mentioned in RFC 792. The keyword helps to find a particular sequence number. However, the practical use of this keyword is very limited. The following rule checks a sequence number of 100 and generates an alert:

```
alert icmp any any -> any any (icmp_seq: 100; \
    msg: "ICMP Sequence=100";)
```

3.6.12 The itype Keyword

The ICMP header comes after the IP header and contains a type field. Appendix C explains the IP header and the different codes that are used in the type field. A detailed discussion is found in RFC 792 at http://www.rfc-editor.org/rfc/rfc792.txt. The itype keyword is used to detect attacks that use the type field in the ICMP packet header. The argument to this field is a number and the general format is as follows:

```
itype: "ICMP_type_number"
```

The type field in the ICMP header of a data packet is used to determine the type of the ICMP packet. Table 3-3 lists different ICMP types and values of the type field in the ICMP header.

Table 3-3 ICMP type filed values

Value	Type of ICMP Packet
0	Echo reply
3	Destination unreachable
4	Source quench
5	Redirect
8	Echo request
11	Time exceed
12	Parameter problem
13	Timestamp request
14	Timestamp reply
15	Information request
16	Information reply

For example, if you want to generate an alert for each source quench message, use the following rule:

```
alert icmp any any -> any any (itype: 4; \
    msg: "ICMP Source Quench Message received";)
```

The ICMP code field is used to further classify ICMP packets.

3.6.13 The icode Keyword

In ICMP packets, the ICMP header comes after the IP header. It contains a code field, as shown in Appendix C and RFC 792 at http://www.rfc-editor.org/rfc/rfc792.txt. The icode keyword is used to detect the code field in the ICMP packet header. The argument to this field is a number and the general format is as follows:

```
icode: "ICMP_codee_number"
```

The type field in the ICMP header shows the type of ICMP message. The code field is used to explain the type in detail. For example, if the type field value is 5, the ICMP packet type is "ICMP redirect" packet. There may be many reasons for the generation of an ICMP redirect packet. These reasons are defined by the code field as listed below:

- If code field is 0, it is a network redirect ICMP packet.
- If code field is 1, it is a host redirect packet.
- If code is 2, the redirect is due to the type of service and network.
- If code is 2, the redirect is due to type of service and host.

The icode keyword in Snort rule options is used to find the code field value in the ICMP header. The following rule generates an alert for host redirect ICMP packets.

```
alert icmp any any -> any any (itype: 5; \
    icode: 1; msg: "ICMP ID=100";)
```

Both itype and icode keywords are used. Using the icode keyword alone will not do the job because other ICMP types may also use the same code value.

3.6.14 The id Keyword

The id keyword is used to match the fragment ID field of the IP packet header. Its purpose is to detect attacks that use a fixed ID number in the IP header of a packet. Its format is as follows:

```
id: "id_number"
```

If the value of the id field in the IP packet header is zero, it shows that this is the last fragment of an IP packet (if the packet was fragmented). The value 0 also shows that it is the only fragment if the packet was not fragmented. The id keyword in the Snort rule can be used to determine the last fragment in an IP packet.

3.6.15 The ipopts Keyword

A basic IPv4 header is 20 bytes long as described in Appendix C. You can add options to this IP header at the end. The length of the options part may be up to 40 bytes. IP options are used for different purposes, including:

- Record Route (rr)
- Time Stamps (ts)

- Loose Source Routing (lsrr)
- Strict Source Routing (ssrr)

For a complete list of IP options see RFC 791 at http://www.rfc-editor.org/rfc/rfc791.txt. In Snort rules, the most commonly used options are listed above. These options can be used by some hackers to find information about your network. For example, loose and strict source routing can help a hacker discover if a particular network path exists or not.

Using Snort rules, you can detect such attempts with the ipopts keyword. The following rule detects any attempt made using Loose Source Routing:

```
alert ip any any -> any any (ipopts: lsrr; \
    msg: "Loose source routing attempt";)
```

You can also use a logto keyword to log the messages to a file. However, you can't specify multiple IP options keywords in one rule.

3.6.16 The ip_proto Keyword

The ip_proto keyword uses IP Proto plug-in to determine protocol number in the IP header. The keyword requires a protocol number as argument. You can also use a name for the protocol if it can be resolved using /etc/protocols file. Sample entries in this file look like the following:

```
ax.25    93      AX.25         # AX.25 Frames
ipip     94      IPIP          # Yet Another IP encapsulation
micp     95      MICP          # Mobile Internetworking
Control Pro.
scc-sp   96      SCC-SP        # Semaphore Communications
Sec. Pro.
etherip  97      ETHERIP       # Ethernet-within-IP
Encapsulation
encap    98      ENCAP         # Yet Another IP encapsulation
#        99                    # any private encryption
scheme
gmtp     100     GMTP          # GMTP
ifmp     101     IFMP          # Ipsilon Flow Management
Protocol
pnni     102     PNNI          # PNNI over IP
```

The following rule checks if IPIP protocol is being used by data packets:

```
alert ip any any -> any any (ip_proto: ipip; \
    msg: "IP-IP tunneling detected";)
```

The next rule is the same except that it uses protocol number instead of name (more efficient).

```
alert ip any any -> any any (ip_proto: 94; \
    msg: "IP-IP tunneling detected";)
```

Protocol numbers are defined in RFC 1700 at http://www.rfc-editor.org/rfc/rfc1700.txt. The latest numbers can be found from the ICANN web site at http://www.icann.org or at IANA web site http://www.iana.org.

3.6.17 The logto Keyword

The logto keyword is used to log packets to a special file. The general syntax is as follows:

```
logto:logto_log
```

Consider the following rule:

```
alert icmp any any -> any any (logto:logto_log; ttl: 100;)
```

This rule will log all ICMP packets having TTL value equal to 100 to file logto_log. A typical logged packet in this file is as follows:

```
[root@conformix]# cat logto_log
07/03-03:57:56.496845 192.168.1.101 -> 192.168.1.2
ICMP TTL:100 TOS:0x0 ID:33822 IpLen:20 DgmLen:60
Type:8  Code:0  ID:768    Seq:9217  ECHO
61 62 63 64 65 66 67 68 69 6A 6B 6C 6D 6E 6F 70
abcdefghijklmnop
71 72 73 74 75 76 77 61 62 63 64 65 66 67 68 69
qrstuvwabcdefghi

=+=+=+=+=+=+=+=+=+=+=+=+=+=+=+=+=+=+=+=+=+=+=+=+

[root@conformix]#
```

Information logged in the above example is as follows:

- Data and time the packet was logged.
- Source IP address is 192.168.1.101.
- Destination IP address is 192.168.1.2.
- Protocol used in the packet is ICMP.
- The TTL (Time To Live) field value in the IP header is 100.
- The TOS (Type Of Service) field value in IP header is 0. This value shows that this is a normal packet. For details of other TOS values, refer to RFC 791.

- IP packet ID is 33822.
- Length of IP header is 20 bytes.
- Length of the packet is 60 bytes.
- ICMP type filed value is 8.
- ICMP code value is 0.
- ICMP ID value is 768.
- ICMP Sequence field value is 9217.
- The ECHO part shows that this is an ICMP ECHO packet.
- The remaining part of the log shows the data that follows the ICMP header.

There are a few things to remember when you use this option:

- Don't use the full path with the file name. The file will automatically be created in the log directory which is `/var/log/snort` by default.
- Don't use a space character after the colon character used with logto keyword. If you use a space character, it is considered part of the file name. If you use a space character for clarity, enclose the file name in double quotation marks.

3.6.18 The msg Keyword

The msg keyword in the rule options is used to add a text string to logs and alerts. You can add a message inside double quotations after this keyword. The msg keyword is a common and useful keyword and is part of most of the rules. The general form for using this keyword is as follows:

```
msg: "Your message text here";
```

If you want to use some special character inside the message, you can escape them by a backslash character.

3.6.19 The nocase Keyword

The nocase keyword is used in combination with the content keyword. It has no arguments. Its only purpose is to make a case insensitive search of a pattern within the data part of a packet.

3.6.20 The priority Keyword

The priority keyword assigns a priority to a rule. Priority is a number argument to this keyword. Number 1 is the highest priority. The keyword is often used with the classtype keyword. The following rule has a priority 10:

```
alert ip any any -> any any (ipopts: lsrr; \
   msg: "Loose source routing attempt"; priority: 10;)
```

The priority keyword can be used to differentiate high priority and low priority alerts.

3.6.21 The react Keyword

The react keyword is used with a rule to terminate a session to block some sites or services. Not all options with this keyword are operational. The following rule will block all HTTP connections originating from your home network 192.168.1.0/24. To block the HTTP access, it will send a TCP FIN and/or FIN packet to both sending and receiving hosts every time it detects a packet that matches these criteria. The rule causes a connection to be closed.

```
alert tcp 192.168.1.0/24 any -> any 80 (msg: "Outgoing \
   HTTP connection"; react: block;)
```

In the above rule, *block* is the basic modifier. You can also use the *warn* modifier to send a visual notice to the source. You can also use the additional modifier *msg* which will include the msg string in the visual notification on the browser. The following is an example of this additional modifier.

```
alert tcp 192.168.1.0/24 any -> any 80 (msg: "Outgoing \
   HTTP connection"; react: warn, msg;)
```

In order to use the react keyword, you should compile Snort with --enable-flexresp command line option in the configure script. For a discussion of the compilation process, refer to Chapter 2.

The react should be the last keyword in the options field. The warn modifier still does not work properly in the version of Snort I am using.

3.6.22 The reference Keyword

The reference keyword can add a reference to information present on other systems available on the Internet. It does not play any role in the detection mechanism itself and you can safely ignore it as far as writing Snort rules is concerned. There are many reference systems available, such as CVE and Bugtraq. These systems keep additional information about known attacks. By using this keyword, you can link to this additional information in the alert message. For example, look at the following rule in the misc.rules file distributed with Snort:

```
alert udp $EXTERNAL_NET any -> $HOME_NET 1900 \
(msg:"MISC UPNP malformed advertisement"; \
content:"NOTIFY * "; nocase; classtype:misc-attack; \
reference:cve,CAN-2001-0876; reference:cve, \
CAN-2001-0877; sid:1384; rev:2;)
```

This rule generates the following entry in /var/log/snort/alert file:

```
[**] [1:1384:2] MISC UPNP malformed advertisement [**]
[Classification: Misc Attack] [Priority: 2]
12/01-15:25:21.792758 192.168.1.1:1901 -> 239.255.255.250:1900
UDP TTL:150 TOS:0x0 ID:9 IpLen:20 DgmLen:341
Len: 321
[Xref => cve CAN-2001-0877][Xref => cve CAN-2001-0876]
```

The last line of this alert shows a reference where more information about this alert can be found. The reference.config file plays an important role because it contains the actual URL to reach a particular reference. For example, the following line in reference.config file will reach the actual URL using the last line of the alert message.

```
config reference: cve  http://cve.mitre.org/cgi-bin/
cvename.cgi?name=
```

When you add CAN-2001-0876 at the end of this URL, you will reach the web site containing information about this alert. So the actual URL for information about this alert is http://cve.mitre.org/cgi-bin/cvename.cgi?name= CAN-2001-0876.

Multiple references can be placed in a rule. References are also used by tools like ACID[3] to provide additional information about a particular vulnerability. The same log message, when displayed in an ACID window, will look like Figure 3-4. In this figure, the URL is already inserted under the "Triggered Signature" heading. You can click on it to go to the CVE web site for more information.

3.6.23 The resp Keyword

The resp keyword is a very important keyword. It can be used to knock down hacker activity by sending response packets to the host that originates a packet matching the rule. The keyword is also known as Flexible Response or simply FlexResp and is based on the FlexResp plug-in. The plug-in should be compiled into Snort, as explained in Chapter 2, using the command line option (--with-flexresp) in the

---

3.   ACID is discussed in Chapter 6.

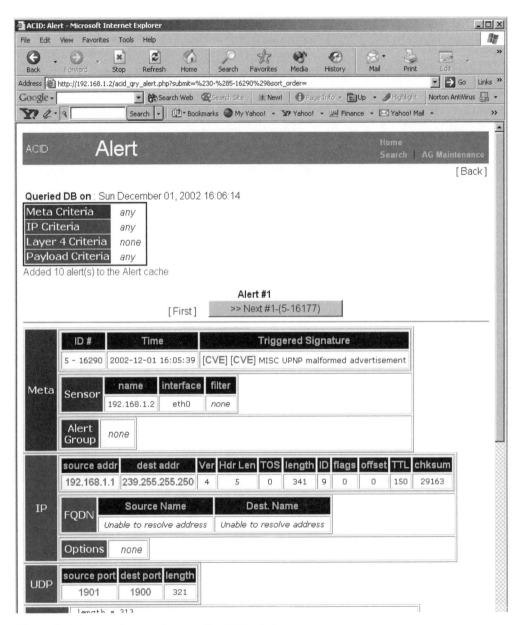

Figure 3-4 Use of reference keyword in ACID window.

configure script. The following rule will send a TCP Reset packet to the sender whenever an attempt to reach TCP port 8080 on the local network is made.

```
alert tcp any any -> 192.168.1.0/24 8080 (resp: rst_snd;)
```

You can send multiple response packets to either sender or receiver by specifying multiple responses to the resp keyword. The arguments are separated by a comma. The list of arguments that can be used with this keyword is found in Table 3-4.

Table 3-4 Arguments to resp keyword

Argument	Description
rst_snd	Sends a TCP Reset packet to the sender of the packet
rst_rcv	Sends a TCP Reset packet to the receiver of the packet
rst_all	Sends a TCP Reset packet to both sender and receiver
icmp_net	Sends an ICMP Network Unreachable packet to sender
icmp_host	Sends an ICMP Host Unreachable packet to sender
icmp_port	Sends an ICMP Port Unreachable packet to sender
icmp_all	Sends all of the above mentioned packets to sender

3.6.24 The rev Keyword

The rev keyword is added to Snort rule options to show a revision number for the rule. If you are updating rules, you can use this keyword to distinguish among different revision. Output modules can also use this number to identify the revision number. The following rule shows that the revision number is 2 for this rule:

```
alert ip any any -> any any (ipopts: lsrr; \
    msg: "Loose source routing attempt"; rev: 2;)
```

For more information, refer to the sid keyword, which is related to the rev keyword.

3.6.25 The rpc Keyword

The rpc keyword is used to detect RPC based requests. The keyword accepts three numbers as arguments:

• Application number

- Procedure number
- Version number

These arguments are separated by a comma. You can also use an asterisk to match all numbers in a particular location of the arguments. The following rule detects RPC requests for TPC number 10000, all procedures and version number 3.

```
alert ip any any -> 192.168.1.0/24 any (rpc: 10000,*,3; \
    msg: "RPC request to local network";)
```

3.6.26 The sameip Keyword

The sameip keyword is used to check if source and destination IP addresses are the same in an IP packet. It has no arguments. Some people try to spoof IP packets to get information or attack a server. The following rule can be used to detect these attempts.

```
alert ip any any -> 192.168.1.0/24 any (msg: "Same IP"; \
    sameip;)
```

3.6.27 The seq Keyword

The seq keyword in Snort rule options can be used to test the sequence number of a TCP packet. The argument to this keyword is a sequence number. The general format is as follows:

```
seq: "sequence_number";
```

Sequence numbers are a part of the TCP header. More explanation of sequence number is found in Appendix C where the TCP header is discussed.

3.6.28 The flow[4] Keyword

The flow keyword is used to apply a rule on TCP sessions to packets flowing in a particular direction. You can use options with the keyword to determine direction. The following options can be used with this keyword determine direction:

- to_client
- to_server
- from_client
- from_server

---

4.   This is available in Snort 1.9 and above.

These options may be confusing the first time you look at them. Just keep in mind that options starting with "to" are used for responses and options starting with "from" are used for requests.

Other options are also available which are used to apply the rule to different states of a TCP connection.

- The *stateless* option is used to apply the rule without considering the state of a TCP session.
- The *established* option is used to apply the rule to established TCP sessions only.
- The *no_stream* option enables rules to be applied to packets that are not built from a stream.
- The *stream_only* option is used to apply the rules to only those packets that are built from a stream.

TCP streams are handled by the stream4 preprocessor discussed in the next chapter. TCP streams are also discussed in RFC 793. A TCP session is established and finished with a defined sequence of TCP packet exchanges as defined in RFC 793. The *stateless* and *established* options are related to TCP session state.

3.6.29 The session Keyword

The session keyword can be used to dump all data from a TCP session. It can dump all session data or just printable characters. The following rule dumps all printable data from POP3 sessions:

```
log tcp any any -> 192.168.1.0/24 110 (session: printable;)
```

If you use "all" as argument to this keyword, everything will be dumped. Use the logto keyword to log the traffic to a particular file.

A TCP session is a sequence of data packets exchanged between two hosts. The session is usually initiated and closed by the client using the three-way handshake method discussed in RFC 793. For example, when your e-mail client software starts collecting e-mail from a POP3 server, it first starts the communication by exchanging TCP packets. The mail is then downloaded. After downloading the e-mail, the client closes the connection. All communication taking place during this process is a TCP session.

3.6.30 The sid Keyword

The sid keyword is used to add a "Snort ID" to rules. Output modules or log scanners can use SID to identify rules. Authors have reserved SID ranges for rules as shown below:

- Range 0-99 is reserved for future use.
- Range 100-1,000,000 is reserved for rules that come with Snort distribution.
- All numbers above 1,000,000 can be used for local rules.

Refer to the list of rules that came with your Snort distribution for examples. The only argument to this keyword is a number. The following rule adds SID equal to 1000001.

```
alert ip any any -> any any (ipopts: lsrr; \
    msg: "Loose source routing attempt"; sid: 1000001;)
```

Using SID, tools like ACID can display the actual rule that generated a particular alert.

3.6.31 The tag Keyword

The tag keyword is another very important keyword that can be used for logging additional data from/to the intruder host when a rule is triggered. The additional data can then be analyzed later on for detailed intruder activity. The general syntax of the keyword is as follows:

```
tag: <type>, <count>, <metric>[, direction]
```

The arguments are explained in Table 3-5.

Table 3-5 Arguments used with tag keyword

Argument	Description
Type	You can use either "session" or "host" as the type argument. Using session, packets are logged from the particular session that triggered the rule. Using host, all packets from the host are logged.
Count	This indicates either the number of packets logged or the number of seconds during which packets will be logged. The distinction between the two is made by the metric argument.
Metric	You can use either "packets" or "seconds" as mentioned above.
Direction	This argument is optional. You can use either "src" to log packets from source or "dst" to log packets from the destination.

The following rule logs 100 packets on the session after it is triggered.

```
alert tcp 192.168.2.0/24 23 -> any any \
    (content: "boota"; msg: "Detected boota"; \
    tag: session, 100, packets;)
```

3.6.32 The tos Keyword

The tos keyword is used to detect a specific value in the Type of Service (TOS) field of the IP header. The format for using this keyword is as follows:

```
tos: 1;
```

For more information on the TOS field, refer to RFC 791 and Appendix C, where the IP packet header is discussed.

3.6.33 The ttl Keyword

The ttl keyword is used to detect Time to Live value in the IP header of the packet. The keyword has a value which should be an exact match to determine the TTL value. This keyword can be used with all types of protocols built on the IP protocol, including ICMP, UDP and TCP. The general format of the keyword is as follows:

```
ttl: 100;
```

The traceroute utility uses TTL values to find the next hop in the path. The traceroute sends UDP packets with increasing TTL values. The TTL value is decremented at every hop. When it reaches zero, the router generates an ICMP packet to the source. Using this ICMP packet, the utility finds the IP address of the router. For example, to find the fifth hop router, the traceroute utility will send UDP packets with TTL value set to 5. When the packet reaches the router at the fifth hop, its value becomes zero and an ICMP packet is generated.

Using the ttl keyword, you can find out if someone is trying to traceroute through your network. The only problem is that the keyword needs an exact match of the TTL value.

For more information on the TTL field, refer to RFC 791 and Appendix C where the IP packet header is discussed.

3.6.34 The uricontent Keyword

The uricontent keyword is similar to the content keyword except that it is used to look for a string only in the URI part of a packet.

3.7 The Snort Configuration File

Snort uses a configuration file at startup time. A sample configuration file
snort.conf is included in the Snort distribution. You can use any name for the configuration file, however snort.conf is the conventional name. You use the -c command line switch to specify the name of the configuration file. The following command
uses /opt/snort/snort.conf as the configuration file.

```
/opt/snort/snort -c /opt/snort/snort.conf
```

You can also save the configuration file in your home directory as .snortrc, but
specifying it on the command line is the most widely used method. There are other
advantages to using the configuration file name as a command line argument to Snort.
For example, it is possible to invoke multiple Snort instances on different network interfaces with different configuration. This file contains six basic sections:

- Variable definitions, where you define different variables. These variables are
  used in Snort rules as well as for other purposes, like specifying the location of
  rule files.
- Config parameters. These parameters specify different Snort configuration
  options. Some of them can also be used on the command line.
- Preprocessor configuration. Preprocessors are used to perform certain actions
  before a packet is operated by the main Snort detection engine.
- Output module configuration. Output modules control how Snort data will be
  logged.
- Defining new action types. If the predefined action types are not sufficient for
  your environment, you can define custom action types in the Snort
  configuration file.
- Rules configuration and include files. Although you can add any rules in the
  main snort.conf file, the convention is to use separate files for rules. These
  files are then included inside the main configuration file using the *include*
  keyword. This keyword will be discussed later in this chapter.

Although the out-of-the-box configuration file works, you need to modify it to
adapt it to your environment. A sample configuration file is presented later on.

3.7.1 Using Variables in Rules

In the configuration file, you can use variables. This is a very convenient way of creating rules. For example, you can define a variable HOME_NET in the configuration file.

```
var HOME_NET 192.168.1.0/24
```

Later on you can use this variable HOME_NET in your rules:

```
alert ip any any -> $HOME_NET any (ipopts: lsrr; \
    msg: "Loose source routing attempt"; sid: 1000001;)
```

As you can see, using variables makes it very convenient to adapt the configuration file and rules to any environment. For example, you don't need to modify all rules when you copy rules from one network to another; you just need to modify a single variable.

3.7.1.1   Using a List of Networks in Variables

You can also define variables that contain multiple items. Consider that you have multiple networks in the company. Your intrusion detection system is right behind the company firewall connecting to the Internet. You can define a variable as a list of all of these networks. The following variable shows that HOME_NETWORK consists of two networks, 192.168.1.0/24 and 192.168.10.0/24.

```
var HOME_NET [192.168.1.0/24,192.168.10.0/24]
```

All networks in the variable name are separated by a comma.

3.7.1.2   Using Interface Names in Variables

You can also use interface names in defining variables. The following two statements define HOME_NET and EXTERNAL_NET variables on a Linux machine.

```
var HOME_NET $eth0_ADDRESS
var EXTERNAL_NET $eth1_ADDRESS
```

The HOME_NET variable uses the IP address and network mask value assigned to interface eth0 and EXTERNAL_NET uses the IP address and network mask assigned to network interface eth1. This arrangement is more convenient since you can change IP addresses on the interfaces without modifying rules or even variables themselves.

3.7.1.3   Using the any Keyword

The any keyword can also be a variable. It matches to everything, just as it does in rules (such as addresses and port numbers). For example, if you want to test packets regardless of their source, you can define a variable like the following for EXTERNAL_NET.

```
var EXTERNAL_NET any
```

There are many variables defined in the snort.conf file that come with the Snort distribution. While installing Snort, you need to modify these variables according to your network.

3.7.2   The config Directives

The config directives in the `snort.conf` file allow a user to configure many general settings for Snort. Examples include the location of log files, the order of applying rules and so on. These directives can be used to replace many command line options as well. The general format of applying a config directive is as follows:

```
config directive_name[: value]
```

Table 3-6 shows a list of directives used in the `snort.conf` file.

Table 3-6 Snort config directives

Directive	Description
order	Changes the order in which rules are applied. It is equivalent to the –o command line option.
alertfile	Used to set the name of the alert file. Alert file is created in log directory (see logdir directive).
classification	Builds classification for rules. See explanation of the classtype keyword used in rules.
decode_arp	Equivalent to –a command line option. It turns ON arp decoding.
dump_chars_only	Equivalent –C command line option.
dump_payload	Equivalent to –d command line option. It is used to dump the data part of the packet.
decode_data_link	Equivalent to –e command line option. Using this directive you can decode data link layer headers (Ethernet header, for example).
bpf_file	Equivalent to –F command line option.
set_gid	Equivalent to –g command line option. Using this directive you can set the group ID under which Snort runs. For example, you can use "config set_gid: mygroup"
daemon	Equivalent to –D command line option. It invokes Snort as daemon instead of foreground process.
reference_net	Equivalent to –h command line option. It sets the home network address.
interface	Equivalent to –i command line option. It sets the interface for Snort.
alert_with_interface_name	Equivalent to –T command line option. This directive is used to append the interface name to the alert message. This is sometimes useful if you are monitoring multiple interfaces on the same sensor.
logdir	Equivalent to –l command line option. It sets the directory where Snort logs data. The default location of the log directory is `/var/log/snort`.

Table 3-6 Snort config directives (continued)

Directive	Description
umask	Equivalent to –m command line option. Using this option you can set the UMASK while running Snort.
pkt_count	Equivalent to –n command line option. Using this directive you can exit from Snort after a defined number of packets.
nolog	Equivalent to –N command line option. Logging is disabled except alerts. Remember, alerts are really both alerts and logs.
obfuscate	Equivalent to –O command line option. It is used to obfuscate IP addresses so that you are able to send the logs for analysis to someone without disclosing the identity of your network.
no_promisc	Equivalent to –p command line option and is used to disable promiscuous mode.
quiet	Equivalent to –q command line option. This will disable banner information at Snort startup time and prevent statistical information from being displayed.
chroot	Equivalent to –t command line option. It is used to change root directory for Snort to a specific directory.
checksum_mode	Used to checksum for particular types of packets. It takes arguments such as none, noip, notcp, noicmp, noudp, and all.
set_uid	Equivalent to –u command line option and is used to set user ID for the Snort process.
utc	Equivalent to –U command line option and is used to use UTC instead of local time in alerts and logs.
verbose	Equivalent to –v command line option. It is used to log messages to standard output in addition to standard logging.
dump_payload_verbose	Equivalent to –X command line option. This dumps the received raw packet on the standard output.
show_year	Equivalent to –y command line option and is used to display year in the timestamp.
stateful	Used to set assurance mode for stream4 preprocessor. Preprocessors are discussed in detail in Chapter 4.

You have already seen how the classification directive is used in the `classification.config` file. As another example, the following line is used to start Snort in the daemon mode.

```
config daemon
```

You can also use –D command line option to start Snort in the daemon mode.

3.7.3   Preprocessor Configuration

Preprocessors or input plug-ins operate on received packets before Snort rules are applied to them. The preprocessor configuration is the second major part of the configuration file. This section provides basic information about adding or removing Snort preprocessors. Detailed information about each preprocessor is found in the next chapter.

The general format of configuring a preprocessor is as follows:

```
preprocessor <preprocessor_name>[: <configuration_options>]
```

The first part of the line is the keyword *preprocessor*. The name of the preprocessor follows this keyword. If the preprocessor can accept some options or arguments, you can list these options after a colon character at the end of the name of preprocessor, which is optional.

The following is an example of a line in the configuration file for IP defragmentation preprocessor frag2.

```
preprocessor frag2
```

The following is an example of a stream4 preprocessor with an argument to detect port scans. The stream4 preprocessor has many other arguments as well, as described in Chapter 4.

```
preprocessor stream4: detect_scans
```

Both frag2 and stream4 are predefined preprocessors. You can also write your own preprocessors if you are a programmer. Guidelines for writing preprocessors are provided with the Snort source code.

3.7.4   Output Module Configuration

Output modules, also called output plug-ins, manipulate output from Snort rules. For example, if you want to log information to a database or send SNMP traps, you need output modules. The following is the general format for specifying an output module in the configuration file.

```
output <output_module_name>[: <configuration_options>]
```

For example, if you want to store log messages to a MySQL database, you can configure an output module that contains the database name, database server address, user name and password.

```
output database: alert, mysql, user=rr password=boota \
    dbname=snort host=localhost
```

There may be additional steps to make the output module work properly. In the case of MySQL database, you need to setup a database, create tables, create user, set permissions and so on. More information on configuring output modules is found in Chapter 4.

3.7.5   Defining New Action Types

You already know that the first part of each Snort rule is the action item. Snort has predefined action types; however, you can also define your own action types in the configuration file. A new action type may use multiple output modules. The following action type creates alert messages that are logged into the database as well as in a file in the tcpdump format.

```
ruletype dump_database
{
  type alert
  output database: alert, mysql, user=rr dbname=snort \
    host=localhost
  output log_tcpdump: tcpdump_log_file
}
```

This new action type can be used in rules just like other action types.

```
dump_database icmp any any -> 192.168.1.0/24 any \
  (fragbits: D; msg: "Don't Fragment bit set";)
```

When a packet matches the criteria in this rule, the alert will be logged to the database as well as to the tcpdump_log_file.

3.7.6   Rules Configuration

The rules configuration is usually the last part of the configuration file. You can create as many rules as you like using variables already defined in the configuration file. All of the previous discussion in this chapter was about writing new rules. The rules configuration is the place in the configuration file where you can put your rules. However the convention is to put all Snort rules in different text files. You can include these text files in the `snort.conf` file using the "include" keyword. Snort comes with many predefined rule files. The names of these rule files end with `.rule`. You have already seen in the last chapter how to put these rule files in the proper place during the installation process.

3.7.7   Include Files

You can include other files inside the main configuration file using the *include* keyword. You can think of including a file as equivalent to inserting the contents of the included file into the main configuration file at the point where it is included. In fact, most of the predefined rules that come with the Snort distribution are found in include files. All files in the Snort distribution whose name ends with `.rules` contain rules and they are included in the `snort.conf` file. These rule files are included in the main `snort.conf` file using the "include" keyword. The following is an example of including `myrules.rules` file in the main configuration file.

```
include myrules.rules
```

It is not necessary that the name of the rules file must end with `.rule`. You can use a name of your choice for your rule file.

3.7.8 Sample snort.conf File

The following is a sample configuration file for Snort. All lines starting with the # character are comment lines. Whenever you modify the configuration file, you have to restart Snort for the changes to take effect.

```
# Variable Definitions
var HOME_NET 192.168.1.0/24
var EXTERNAL_NET any
var HTTP_SERVERS $HOME_NET
var DNS_SERVERS $HOME_NET
var RULE_PATH ./

# preprocessors
preprocessor frag2
preprocessor stream4: detect_scans
preprocessor stream4_reassemble
preprocessor http_decode: 80 -unicode -cginull
preprocessor unidecode: 80 -unicode -cginull
preprocessor bo: -nobrute
preprocessor telnet_decode
preprocessor portscan: $HOME_NET 4 3 portscan.log
preprocessor arpspoof

# output modules
output alert_syslog: LOG_AUTH LOG_ALERT
output log_tcpdump: snort.log
output database: log, mysql, user=rr password=boota \
   dbname=snort host=localhost
output xml: log, file=/var/log/snortxml

# Rules and include files
include $RULE_PATH/bad-traffic.rules
include $RULE_PATH/exploit.rules
```

```
include $RULE_PATH/scan.rules
include $RULE_PATH/finger.rules
include $RULE_PATH/ftp.rules
include $RULE_PATH/telnet.rules
include $RULE_PATH/smtp.rules
include $RULE_PATH/rpc.rules
include $RULE_PATH/dos.rules
include $RULE_PATH/ddos.rules
include $RULE_PATH/dns.rules
include $RULE_PATH/tftp.rules
include $RULE_PATH/web-cgi.rules
include $RULE_PATH/web-coldfusion.rules
include $RULE_PATH/web-iis.rules
include $RULE_PATH/web-frontpage.rules
include $RULE_PATH/web-misc.rules
include $RULE_PATH/web-attacks.rules
include $RULE_PATH/sql.rules
include $RULE_PATH/x11.rules
include $RULE_PATH/icmp.rules
include $RULE_PATH/netbios.rules
include $RULE_PATH/misc.rules
include $RULE_PATH/attack-responses.rules
include $RULE_PATH/myrules.rules
```

3.8 Order of Rules Based upon Action

The five types of the rules can be categorized into three basic types.

1. Alert rules
2. Pass rules
3. Log rules

When a packet is received by Snort, it is checked in this order. Each packet has to go through all Alert rule checks before it is allowed to pass. This scheme is the most secure since no packet passes through without being checked against all alert types. However most of the packets are normal traffic and do not show any intruder activity. Testing all of the packets against all alert rules requires a lot of processing power. Snort provides a way to change this testing order to one which is more efficient, but more dangerous.

1. Pass rules
2. Alert rules
3. Log rules

You must be careful when choosing this order because just one badly written pass rule may allow many alert packets to pass through without being checked. If you really know what you are doing, you can use the –o command line switch to disable the default order and enable the new order of applying rules. You can also use "config order" in the configuration file for this purpose. Again, this is dangerous and you have been warned twice now! If you are sure of what you are doing, add this line in the snort.conf file:

```
config order
```

If you define your own rule types, they are checked last in the sequence. For example, if you have defined a rule type snmp_alerts, the order of rule application will be:

```
Alert -> Pass -> Log ->snmp_alerts
```

3.9 Automatically Updating Snort Rules

There are multiple tools available to update Snort signatures. When using any of these tools you must be careful because you may accidentally modify or delete your customized rules. I shall discuss two methods of updating rules.

3.9.1   The Simple Method

This method consists of a simple shell script. It requires that you have wget program installed on your system. The wget program is used to retrieve any file using HTTP protocol. In essence, it is just like a web browser, but it retrieves one file from a command line argument.

```
#!/bin/sh
# Place of storing your Snort rules. Change these variables
# according to your installation.

RULESDIR=/etc/snort
RULESDIRBAK=/etc/snort/bak

# Path to wget program. Modify for your system if needed.
WGETPATH=/usr/bin

# URI for Snort rules
RULESURI=http://www.snort.org/downloads/snortrules.tar.gz

# Get and untar rules.
cd /tmp
rm -rf rules
$WGETPATH/wget $RULESURI
```

```
tar -zxf snortrules.tar.gz
rm -f snortrules.tar.gz

# Make a backup copy of existing rules
mv $RULESDIR/*.rules $RULESDIRBAK

# Copy new rules to the location
mv /tmp/rules/*.rules $RULESDIR
```

Let us explore how this script works. The following lines simply set some variables.

```
RULESDIR=/etc/snort
RULESDIRBAK=/etc/snort/bak
WGETPATH=/usr/bin
RULESURI=http://www.snort.org/downloads/snortrules.tar.gz
```

The following three lines are used to go to /tmp directory, remove any existing directory /tmp/rules and download the snortrules.tar.gz file from the URI specified by the $RULESURI variable.

```
cd /tmp
rm -rf rules
$WGETPATH/wget $RULESURI
```

After downloading, you extract the rules files from snortrules.tar.gz file and then delete it using the following two lines. The files extracted are placed in /tmp/rules directory.

```
tar -zxf snortrules.tar.gz
rm -f snortrules.tar.gz
```

The following line makes a backup copy of existing rules files, just in case you need the old copy later on.

```
mv $RULESDIR/*.rules $RULESDIRBAK
```

The last line in the script moves new rules from /tmp/rules directory to the actual rules directory /etc/snort where Snort can read them.

```
mv /tmp/rules/*.rules $RULESDIR
```

Make sure to restart Snort after running this script. If you have a start script like the one described in Chapter 2, you can add a line at the end of the shell script to restart Snort.

```
/etc/init.d/snortd restart
```

You may also restart Snort using the command line.

3.9.2 The Sophisticated and Complex Method

This section provides information about the use of Oinkmaster found at http://www.algonet.se/~nitzer/oinkmaster/. Oinkmaster is a tool to update Snort rule files. It is written in Perl, so you must have Perl installed on your Snort machine to make this tool work. It can be configured to download new rule files from the Internet, find out what rules need to be updated and then updates them. If you have modified some standard rules according to your own requirements, you can configure Oinkmaster not to update these customized rules. At the time of writing this book, version 0.6 of this tool is available. By now updated versions may be available. Oinkmaster is a Perl script and uses a configuration file to update the rules.

It is recommended that you use a temporary directory the first time you use this Perl script. I have used /tmp/rules directory. When you use the following command, it will download all rules, untar them and save all files in /tmp/rules directory.

```
[rr@conformix]$ ./oinkmaster.pl -o /tmp/rules/
Downloading rules archive from http://www.snort.org/dl/signatures/
   snortrules.tar.gz...
12:27:09 URL:http://www.snort.org/dl/signatures/snortrules.tar.gz [79487/79487]
   -> "/tmp/oinkmaster.9875/snortrules.tar.gz" [1]
Archive successfully downloaded, unpacking... tar: rules/attack-responses.rules:
   time stamp 2002-07-14 13:10:24 is 348194 s in the future
tar: rules/classification.config: time stamp 2002-07-14 13:10:24 is 348194 s in
   the future
tar: rules/sid-msg.map: time stamp 2002-07-14 13:10:24 is 348194 s in the future
tar: rules/x11.rules: time stamp 2002-07-14 13:10:24 is 348194 s in the future
tar: rules/web-misc.rules: time stamp 2002-07-14 13:10:24 is 348194 s in the
   future
tar: rules/web-iis.rules: time stamp 2002-07-14 13:10:24 is 348194 s in the
   future
tar: rules/web-frontpage.rules: time stamp 2002-07-14 13:10:24 is 348194 s in
   the future
tar: rules/web-coldfusion.rules: time stamp 2002-07-14 13:10:24 is 348194 s in
   the future
tar: rules/web-cgi.rules: time stamp 2002-07-14 13:10:24 is 348194 s in the
   future
tar: rules/web-attacks.rules: time stamp 2002-07-14 13:10:24 is 348194 s in the
   future
tar: rules/virus.rules: time stamp 2002-07-14 13:10:24 is 348194 s in the future
tar: rules/tftp.rules: time stamp 2002-07-14 13:10:24 is 348194 s in the future
tar: rules/telnet.rules: time stamp 2002-07-14 13:10:24 is 348194 s in the
   future
tar: rules/sql.rules: time stamp 2002-07-14 13:10:24 is 348194 s in the future
tar: rules/smtp.rules: time stamp 2002-07-14 13:10:24 is 348194 s in the future
tar: rules/shellcode.rules: time stamp 2002-07-14 13:10:24 is 348194 s in the
   future
tar: rules/scan.rules: time stamp 2002-07-14 13:10:24 is 348194 s in the future
```

```
tar: rules/rservices.rules: time stamp 2002-07-14 13:10:24 is 348194 s in the
   future
tar: rules/rpc.rules: time stamp 2002-07-14 13:10:24 is 348194 s in the future
tar: rules/porn.rules: time stamp 2002-07-14 13:10:24 is 348194 s in the future
tar: rules/policy.rules: time stamp 2002-07-14 13:10:24 is 348194 s in the
   future
tar: rules/netbios.rules: time stamp 2002-07-14 13:10:24 is 348194 s in the
   future
tar: rules/misc.rules: time stamp 2002-07-14 13:10:24 is 348194 s in the future
tar: rules/local.rules: time stamp 2002-07-14 13:10:24 is 348194 s in the future
tar: rules/info.rules: time stamp 2002-07-14 13:10:24 is 348194 s in the future
tar: rules/icmp.rules: time stamp 2002-07-14 13:10:24 is 348194 s in the future
tar: rules/icmp-info.rules: time stamp 2002-07-14 13:10:24 is 348194 s in the
   future
tar: rules/ftp.rules: time stamp 2002-07-14 13:10:24 is 348194 s in the future
tar: rules/finger.rules: time stamp 2002-07-14 13:10:24 is 348194 s in the
   future
tar: rules/exploit.rules: time stamp 2002-07-14 13:10:24 is 348194 s in the
   future
tar: rules/dos.rules: time stamp 2002-07-14 13:10:24 is 348194 s in the future
tar: rules/dns.rules: time stamp 2002-07-14 13:10:24 is 348194 s in the future
tar: rules/ddos.rules: time stamp 2002-07-14 13:10:24 is 348194 s in the future
tar: rules/bad-traffic.rules: time stamp 2002-07-14 13:10:24 is 348194 s in the
   future
tar: rules/backdoor.rules: time stamp 2002-07-14 13:10:24 is 348194 s in the
   future
tar: rules/snort.conf: time stamp 2002-07-14 13:10:24 is 348194 s in the future
tar: rules: time stamp 2002-07-14 13:10:24 is 348194 s in the future
done.
Disabling rules according to ./oinkmaster.conf... 0 rules disabled.
Comparing new files to the old ones... done.

[***] Results from Oinkmaster started Wed Jul 10 12:25:37 2002 [***]

[*] Rules added/removed/modified: [*]

  [+++]          Added:            [+++]

    -> File "tftp.rules":
       alert udp any any -> any 69 (msg:"TFTP GET shadow"; content: "|0001|";
offset:0; depth:2; content:"shadow"; nocase; classtype:successful-admin;
sid:1442; rev:1;)
       alert udp any any -> any 69 (msg:"TFTP GET passwd"; content: "|0001|";
offset:0; depth:2; content:"passwd"; nocase; classtype:successful-admin;
sid:1443; rev:1;)
       alert udp $EXTERNAL_NET any -> $HOME_NET 69 (msg:"TFTP parent directory";
content:".."; reference:arachnids,137; reference:cve,CVE-1999-0183;
classtype:bad-unknown; sid:519; rev:1;)

  [///]        Modified active:      [///]

    -> File "tftp.rules":
```

```
    Old: alert udp $EXTERNAL_NET any -> $HOME_NET 64 (msg:"TFTP Put";
content:"|00 02|"; offset:0; depth:2; reference:cve,CVE-1999-0183;
reference:arachnids,148; classtype:bad-unknown; sid:518; rev:3;)
    New: alert udp $EXTERNAL_NET any -> $HOME_NET 69 (msg:"TFTP Put";
content:"|00 02|"; offset:0; depth:2; reference:cve,CVE-1999-0183;
reference:arachnids,148; classtype:bad-unknown; sid:518; rev:3;)


[*] Non-rule lines added/removed: [*]
    None.

[*] Added files: [*]
    None.
```

The tool gives you a detailed report of actions taken during the update process. You can test this by deleting and modifying some rules and running the tool again. The following is a partial output seen when Oinkmaster adds and updates some rules.

```
Comparing new files to the old ones... done.

[***] Results from Oinkmaster started Wed Jul 10 12:25:37 2002 [***]

[*] Rules added/removed/modified: [*]

  [+++]              Added:             [+++]

   -> File "tftp.rules":
      alert udp any any -> any 69 (msg:"TFTP GET shadow"; content: "|0001|";
offset:0; depth:2; content:"shadow"; nocase; classtype:successful-admin;
sid:1442; rev:1;)
      alert udp any any -> any 69 (msg:"TFTP GET passwd"; content: "|0001|";
offset:0; depth:2; content:"passwd"; nocase; classtype:successful-admin;
sid:1443; rev:1;)
      alert udp $EXTERNAL_NET any -> $HOME_NET 69 (msg:"TFTP parent directory";
content:".."; reference:arachnids,137; reference:cve,CVE-1999-0183;
classtype:bad-unknown; sid:519; rev:1;)

  [///]        Modified active:     [///]

   -> File "tftp.rules":
      Old: alert udp $EXTERNAL_NET any -> $HOME_NET 64 (msg:"TFTP Put";
content:"|00 02|"; offset:0; depth:2; reference:cve,CVE-1999-0183;
reference:arachnids,148; classtype:bad-unknown; sid:518; rev:3;)
      New: alert udp $EXTERNAL_NET any -> $HOME_NET 69 (msg:"TFTP Put";
content:"|00 02|"; offset:0; depth:2; reference:cve,CVE-1999-0183;
reference:arachnids,148; classtype:bad-unknown; sid:518; rev:3;)


[*] Non-rule lines added/removed: [*]
    None.

[*] Added files: [*]
    None.
```

The script uses a configuration file where many options can be configured. Specifically you can configure the following in the configuration file `oinkmaster.conf`:

- URL of the location from where it downloads the Snort rules. By default this URL is http://www.snort.org/downloads/signatures/snortrules.tar.gz or http://www.snort.org/downloads/snortrules.tar.gz. This is configured using the url keyword in the configuration file.
- Files to be updated. By default files ending with `.rules`, `.config`, `.conf`, `.txt` and `.map` are updated and all other files are ignored. This is done using the `update_files` keyword.
- Files to be skipped when updating rules. This is done using the skipfile keyword. You can use as many skipfiles lines as you like. This option is useful when you have customized rules in some files. When you skip these files, your customized rules will not be overwritten during the update process.
- You can disable certain rules permanently using the disablesid keyword in the configuration file. The tool will not update these rules during the update.

Please use the README and INSTALL files that come with the tool. You can use this tool from a cron script to periodically update your rule set.

3.10 Default Snort Rules and Classes

Snort comes with a rich set of rules. These rules are divided into different files. Each file represents one class of rules. In the source code distribution of Snort, these files are present under the `rules` directory in the source code tree. The following is a list of the rule files in Snort 1.9.0 distribution:

```
attack-responses.rules
backdoor.rules
bad-traffic.rules
chat.rules
ddos.rules
deleted.rules
dns.rules
dos.rules
experimental.rules
exploit.rules
finger.rules
ftp.rules
icmp-info.rules
icmp.rules
```

```
imap.rules
info.rules
local.rules
Makefile
Makefile.am
Makefile.in
misc.rules
multimedia.rules
mysql.rules
netbios.rules
nntp.rules
oracle.rules
other-ids.rules
p2p.rules
policy.rules
pop3.rules
porn.rules
rpc.rules
rservices.rules
scan.rules
shellcode.rules
smtp.rules
snmp.rules
sql.rules
telnet.rules
tftp.rules
virus.rules
web-attacks.rules
web-cgi.rules
web-client.rules
web-coldfusion.rules
web-frontpage.rules
web-iis.rules
web-misc.rules
web-php.rules
x11.rules
```

For example, all rules related to X-Windows attacks are combined in x11.rules file.

```
# (C) Copyright 2001,2002, Martin Roesch, Brian Caswell, et al.
#    All rights reserved.
# $Id: x11.rules,v 1.12 2002/08/18 20:28:43 cazz Exp $
#----------
# X11 RULES
#----------
```

```
alert tcp $EXTERNAL_NET any -> $HOME_NET 6000 (msg:"X11 MIT Magic
  Cookie detected"; flow:established
; content: "MIT-MAGIC-COOKIE-1"; reference:arachnids,396;
  classtype:attempted-user; sid:1225; rev:3;
)
alert tcp $EXTERNAL_NET any -> $HOME_NET 6000 (msg:"X11 xopen";
  flow:established; content: "|6c00 0b
00 0000 0000 0000 0000|"; reference:arachnids,395; classtype:unknown;
  sid:1226; rev:2;)
```

Similarly, each file contains rules specific to a particular class. The `dns.rules` file contains all rules related to attacks on DNS servers, the `telnet.rules` file contains all rules related to attacks on the telnet port, and so on.

3.10.1 The local.rules File

The `local.rules` file has no rules. This is meant to be used by Snort administrator for customized rules. However, you can use any file name for your own customized rules and include it in the main `snort.conf` file.

3.11 Sample Default Rules

You have learned the structure of Snort rules and how to write your own rules. This section lists some predefined rules that come with Snort. All of the rules in this section are taken from the `telnet.rules` file. Let us discuss each of these to give you an idea about rules that are used in production systems.

3.11.1 Checking su Attempts from a Telnet Session

The first rule generates an alert when a user tries to su to root through a telnet session. The rule is as shown below:

```
alert tcp $TELNET_SERVERS 23 -> $EXTERNAL_NET any (msg:"TELNET
  Attempted SU from wrong group"; flow:
from_server,established; content:"to su root"; nocase;
  classtype:attempted-admin; sid:715; rev:6;)
```

There are a number of things to note about this rule. The rule generates an alert and applies to TCP packets. Major points are listed below:

- The variable $TELNET_SERVERS is defined in `snort.conf` file and shows a list of Telnet servers.
- Port number 23 is used in the rule, which means that the rule will be applied to TCP traffic going from port 23. The rule checks only response from Telnet servers, not the requests.

- The variable $EXTERNAL_NET is defined in the `snort.conf` file and shows all addresses which are outside the private network. The rule will apply to those telnet sessions which originate from outside of the private network. If someone from the internal network starts a Telnet session, the rule will not detect that traffic.
- The flow keyword is used to apply this rule only to an established connection and traffic flowing from the server.
- The content keyword shows that an alert will be generated when a packet contains "to su root".
- The nocase keyword allows the rule to ignore case of letters while matching the content.
- The classtype keyword is used to assign a class to the rule. The attempted-admin class is defined with a default priority in classification.config file.
- The rule ID is 715.
- The rev keyword is used to show version of the rule.

3.11.2 Checking for Incorrect Login on Telnet Sessions

The following rule is similar to the rule for checking su attempts. It checks incorrect login attempts on the Telnet server port.

```
alert tcp $TELNET_SERVERS 23 -> $EXTERNAL_NET any (msg:"TELNET login
   incorrect"; content:"Login inco
rrect"; flow:from_server,established; reference:arachnids,127;
   classtype:bad-unknown; sid:718; rev:6;)
```

There is one additional keyword used in this rule which is "reference: arachnids, 127". This is a reference to a web site where you can find more information about this vulnerability. The URLs for external web sites are placed in the `reference.config` file in the Snort distribution. Using the information in `reference.config`, the URL for more information about this rule is http://www.whitehats.com/info/IDS=127. 127 is the ID used for searching the database at the arachnids web site.

3.12 Writing Good Rules

There is a large list of predefined rules that are part of Snort distribution. Looking at these rules gives you a fairly good idea of how to write good rules. Although it is not mandatory, you should use the following parts in the options for each rule:

- A message part using the msg keyword.
- Rule classification, using the classification keyword.

- Use a number to identify a rule with the help of the sid keyword.
- If the vulnerability is known, always use a reference to a URL where more information can be found using the reference keyword.
- Always use the rev keyword in rules to keep a record of different rule versions.

In addition, you should always try to write rules that are generalized and are able to detect multiple variations of an attack. Usually bad guys use the same tools with little modifications for different purposes. Good rules can and should be able to detect these variations.

3.13 References

1. Classless Inter-Domain Routing or CIDR. RFC 1519 at http://www.rfc-editor.org/rfc/rfc1519.txt
2. Transmission Control Protocol RFC 793 at http://www.rfc-editor.org/rfc/rfc793.txt
3. User Datagram Protocol RFC 768 at http://www.rfc-editor.org/rfc/rfc768.txt
4. The nmap at it web site http://www.nmap.org
5. The Internet Protocol RFC 791 at http://www.rfc-editor.org/rfc/rfc791.txt
6. The Internet Control Message Protocol at http://www.rfc-editor.org/rfc/rfc792.txt
7. Assigned Numbers RFC 1700 at http://www.rfc-editor.org/rfc/rfc1700.txt
8. Oinkmaster at http://www.algonet.se/~nitzer/oinkmaster/
9. Open NMS at http://www.opennms.org
10. Internet Corporation for Assigned Names and Numbers (ICANN) at http://www.icann.org
11. The arachnids web site at http://www.whitehats.com/info/IDS
12. The securityfocus mailing list archive at http://online.securityfocus.com/archive/1

## CHAPTER 4

Plugins, Preprocessors and Output Modules

Preprocessors and output modules are two important parts of Snort architecture. Preprocessors process received data packets before rules are applied to them. Output modules control output generated from Snort's detection mechanism. The flow of a packet through Snort is shown in Figure 4-1 where a packet is captured and then passed through preprocessors first. After that, the packet goes to the Snort detection engine where Snort rules are applied on the packet. As a result of application of Snort rules, if an alert or log message is generated, output processors or plug-ins operate on that output. The output of configured output modules is then used by the security administrators.

Snort allows you to select which preprocessors and output modules should be enabled. From a user standpoint, this is done through the Snort configuration file `snort.conf`. Preprocessors and Output modules are also called plug-ins in some literature. So for the sake of this book "input plug-in", "input module" and "preprocessor" mean the same thing. Similarly, "output plug-in" and "output module" mean the same thing. This chapter provides information about these components and their internal working. This information will help you write good rules for Snort.

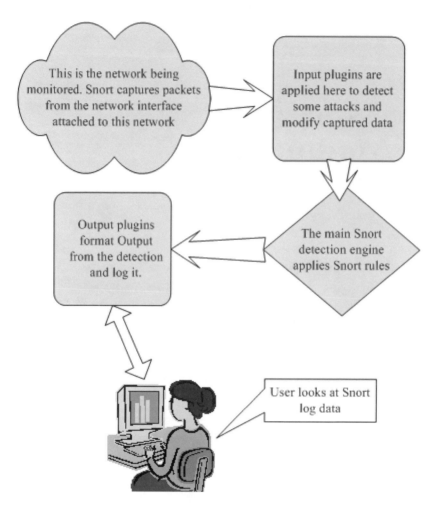

Figure 4-1 Simplified block diagram for Snort.

4.1 Preprocessors

When a packet is received by Snort, it may not be ready for processing by the main Snort detection engine and application of Snort rules. For example, a packet may be fragmented. Before you can search a string within the packet or determine its exact size, you need to defragment it by assembling all fragments of the data packet. The job of a preprocessor is to make a packet suitable for the detection engine to apply different rules to it. In addition, some preprocessors are used for other tasks such as detection of anomalies and obvious errors in data packets. A detailed description of available pre-processors will show how they work.

During the installation process, you can compile support of different preprocessors into Snort. Configuration parameters for different preprocessors (also called *input plug-ins* and *input modules*) are present in the `snort.conf` file. Using the file, you can enable or disable different preprocessors.

All enabled preprocessors operate on each packet. There is no way to bypass some of the preprocessors based upon some criteria. If you have enabled a large number of preprocessors, you may slow down Snort detection process. Therefore you should be careful when enabling preprocessors.

All preprocessors are enabled in the Snort configuration file using the preprocessor keyword. The general format of enabling a preprocessor is as follows:

```
preprocessor <name of preprocessor>[: parameters]
```

The name of the preprocessor follows the *preprocessor* keyword. For example, the following line in `snort.conf` file enables frag2 preprocessor:

```
preprocessor frag2
```

Usually preprocessors also accept parameters to configure different options for the preprocessors. These parameters are usually optional. Mandatory parameters will be specified explicitly in this text. Widely used preprocessors are discussed next.

You can write your own preprocessors. The information is available in README.PLUGINS in the doc directory of Snort source code. You can also find sample code in the templates directory of the source code tree.

4.1.1   HTTP Decode

The Hyper Text Transfer Protocol (HTTP) allows intrusion detection systems to use hexadecimal characters in URI to defeat known attacks. For example, this can be done by inserting something like %3A%2F%2F in the URI to replace :// characters. The HTTP decode preprocessor normalizes the HTTP requests so that they can be processed properly by the detection engine. You can use a list of ports used by HTTP servers or proxy servers as an argument to the preprocessor. The following line in the configuration file will apply HTTP decode for packets coming to ports 80, 8080, 443.

```
preprocessor http_decode: 80 8080 443
```

A large number of attacks on web servers are carried by obfuscating URI characters using hexadecimal numbers in the URI. The HTTP decode blocks any such attempts by converting them to the actual URI. For example, if you have written a Snort rule to attempt access to "/wwwboard/passwd.txt", an attacker can defeat the rule by using hexadecimal characters in the request. So if the attacker sends a request to get URI "%2Fwwwboard%2Fpasswd.txt", the Snort rule will not detect the attack because the rule is looking for "/wwwboard/passwd.txt". However, if you are using HTTP decode preprocessor, this attempt can detected.

4.1.2 Port Scanning

Port scanning is a process of finding out which ports are open on a particular host or all hosts on a network. The first step in any intruder activity is usually to find out what services are running on a network. Once an intruder has found this information, attacks for known vulnerabilities for these services are tried. The portscan preprocessor is designed to detect port scanning activities. The preprocessor can be used to log the port scanning activities to a particular location in addition to standard logging. Hackers can use multiple port scanning methods. Refer to man pages or documentation of the nmap utility (http://www.nmap.org/) to learn more about port scanning methods. The nmap utility is a widely used tool for port scanning.

The following is the general format of the preprocessor used in the `snort.conf` file.

```
preprocessor portscan: <address> <ports> <time period> <file>
```

There are four arguments to the preprocessor.

- The address range of IP addresses to monitor is a single IP address or a network address. The range is specified using the CIDR block.
- The number of ports accessed within a certain time period can be specified. For example, a number 5 means that if five ports are scanned within the time period specified, an alert is generated.
- The time period is the number of seconds that defines the time period used for threshold.
- The path of the file name where the activity should be logged.

The following line in the Snort configuration file is used to detect port scanning on network 192.168.1.0/24 and to log activity in `/var/log/snort/portscan.log` file.

```
preprocessor portscan: 192.168.1.0/24 5 10 \
    /var/log/snort/portscan.log
```

In the example, number 5 is the number of scanning attempts and number 10 is the time period. If five port scan attempts are detected within ten seconds, the preprocessor will generate an alert.

The port scanning activity is detected both for TCP and UDP ports. The preprocessor is able to detect both normal and stealth port scans. For information on stealth port scans, please see the nmap web site. A brief description of port scanning methods is presented below:

- TCP connect port scanning. In this method, the attack tries to connect to a number of ports using standard TCP connect methods. If connection is established, it shows the port is open.
- The SYN scan method sends a TCP packet to a port with SYN flag set. In response the attacker looks for a TCP packet with both SYN and ACK flags set. If the packet is received, the port is open. However if a TCP packet with RST flag set is received, it shows the port is closed.
- NULL port scanning method, FIN port scanning, and XMAS port scanning methods are almost similar. A TCP packet is sent and either a RST packet is received or no packet is received. If a RST packet is received, the port is closed. If no packet is received, there is a probability that the port is open.
- In the UDP port scanning method, UDP packets are sent. If an ICMP port unreachable packet is received, the port is closed. Otherwise there is a probability that the port is open.

You can also use another preprocessor in conjunction with this preprocessor. This preprocessor is portscan-ignorehosts, which can be used to ignore some hosts if any port scanning activity is detected from them. The following line in the configuration file will ignore two hosts, 192.168.1.10 and 192.168.1.13.

```
preprocessor portscan-ignorehosts: 192.168.1.10/32 \
    192.168.1.13/32
```

We have used 32 in the CIDR block number to specify a single host. The portscan-ignorehosts preprocessor is useful when you use some host on your own network for periodic vulnerability assessment.

4.1.3 The frag2 Module

This preprocessor does IP packet defragmentation. Old versions of Snort used another preprocessor named defrag. The frag2 preprocessor uses a splay tree algorithm, which is a self-organizing data structure. For configuration, use and administration of Snort, you need not understand this algorithm.

With frag2, you can configure timeout and memory limits for packet defragmentation. By default, the preprocessor uses 4 MB of memory and a 60-second timeout period. If a packet assembly is not successful within this time period, previously collected fragments are discarded. The following command enables the preprocessor with default values.

```
preprocessor frag2
```

The following command configures the preprocessor with 2MB memory and a timeout period of 30 seconds.

```
preprocessor frag2: 2097152, 30
```

On high-speed networks, you should use large amounts of memory since a large number of data packets may be fragmented. RFC 791 describes the fragmentation and reassembly process in detail. The link to this RFC is found at the end of the chapter.

4.1.4 The stream4 Module

Stream4 is a replacement for the Stream module used in older versions of Snort. It provides two basic functions:

1. TCP stream reassembly
2. Stateful inspection

You must configure two preprocessors in the `snort.conf` file for Stream4 to work properly. These modules are "`stream4`" and "`stream4_reassemble`." Both of these take a number of arguments. If you don't specify an argument, a default value is used instead. The general format of stream4 preprocessor is as follows:

```
preprocessor stream4: [noinspect], [keepstats], \
    [timeout <seconds>], [memcap <bytes>], [detect_scan], \
    [detect_state]
```

Here is a brief explanation of the arguments to the preprocessor and their default values:

noinspect	Turns off stateful inspection (default: ACTIVE)
keepstats	Records session summary in `session.log` file (default: INACTIVE)
timeout	Timeout for keeping a stream in active state (default: 30 seconds)

memcap   Maximum amount of memory used by the module
                           (default: 8 MB)

detect_scan   Detects port scan activity (default: INACTIVE)

detect_state_problems   Detects miscellaneous problems related to TCP streams
                           (default: INACTIVE)

The general format of the stream4_reassemble preprocessor is as follows:

```
preprocessor stream4_reassemble: [clientonly],
     [serveronly],[noalerts],[ports<portlist>]
```

Here is a brief explanation of arguments to stream4_reassemble preprocessor:

clientonly   Reassembles client side stream data packets.

serveronly   Reassembles server side stream data packets.

noalerts   Don't alert for insertion or evasion type attacks.

ports   List of ports for which streams will be assembled. The
                           port numbers should be separated by a space character.
                           The keyword "all" will enable reassembly on port num-
                           bers 21 (FTP), 23 (Telnet), 25 (SMTP), 53 (DNS), 80
                           (HTTP), 110 (POP3), 111, 143, and 513. The port feature
                           is very useful if you want to enable reassembly for only a
                           few services. It saves CPU time.

Snort-type attacks can be detected and/or ignored with this preprocessor. For more information, see http://www.sec33.com/sniph/.

4.1.5 The spade Module

Detailed information about Statistical Packet Anomaly Detection Engine (SPADE) is available at http://www.silicondefense.com/software/spice/index.htm. It is used to detect general packet anomalies in IP packets and a number of preprocessor keywords are associated with it. They are listed in commented form in the default snort.conf configuration file that comes with Snort distribution. SPADE keeps a record of history data and uses threshold values to report anomalies. For a detailed discussion, please see the README and Usage links on the web site mentioned above.

You should keep in mind some efficiency and memory requirements for SPADE. It can take a lot of memory to keep SPADE's statistical data and significant processing power may be required on high-load networks.

4.1.6 ARP Spoofing

Address Resolution Protocol (ARP) is used to find a MAC address when an IP address is known. ARP is needed when a host wants to send an IP packet to another host on the local network. The sending host broadcasts an ARP packet on the network asking, "Who has this IP address?" The host who has that IP address will respond with its MAC address. After that, the sending host will send the data packet (usually called a frame at the link layer level) to the destination host.

The ARP protocol is used by many people for various attacks, sniffing and spoofing. For example, see the dsniff package at http://www.monkey.org/~dugsong/dsniff/ which exploits the ARP. By spoofing, someone can redirect network traffic for a host to some other location.

The arpspoof preprocessor detects anomalies in ARP packets. Specifically it does the following:

- For all ARP requests, if source MAC address and sender's MAC address are different, an alert is generated. If the source MAC address in the packet does not match the MAC address associated with source IP address, then an alert is generated. For details on ARP packet header, refer to Appendix C.
- For ARP replies, source MAC address is compared to sender's MAC address. Similarly, destination MAC address is compared to receiver's MAC address. An alert is generated if these entries mismatch.
- For unicast ARP requests, if destination MAC address is not the broadcast address (FF:FF:FF:FF:FF:FF), an alert is generated. To check this anomaly, you need to place a line in `snort.conf` file as "`preprocessor arpspoof: -unicast`".
- You can pre-populate MAC Address/IP Address pairs in Snort internal cache. The preprocessor will compare these pre-populated entries with information in the received ARP packets. In case of mismatch, an alert will be generated. For example, if the MAC address for a particular IP address in ARP replies does not match the pre-populated pair, an alert is generated.

The following entry in the Snort configuration file (`snort.conf`) will configure this preprocessor and will detect unicast anomalies:

```
preprocessor arpspoof: -unicast
```

The following line adds an IP address and MAC address pair which can be used later on to detect ARP spoofing attempts.

```
preprocessor arpspoof_detect_host: 192.168.1.13 \
    34:45:fd:3e:a2:01
```

If in any ARP packet these two addresses don't match, an alert will be generated. You can use multiple lines in the configuration file to create many similar pairs.

4.2 Output Modules

Output modules are used to control the output from Snort detection engine. By default, the output from alerts and logs go into files in the /var/log/snort directory. Using output modules, you can process output and send output messages a number of other destinations. Commonly used output modules are:

- The database module is used to store Snort output data in databases.
- The SNMP module can be used to send Snort alerts in the form of traps to a management server.
- The SMB alerts module can send alerts to Microsoft Windows machines in the form of pop-up SMB alert windows.
- The syslog module logs messages to the syslog utility. Using this module you can log messages to a centralized logging server.
- You can also use XML or CSV modules to save data in XML or comma separated files. The CSV files can then be imported into databases or spreadsheet software for further processing or analysis.

Output modules can be defined in the Snort configuration file and some of them can also be configured on the command line as well. The general format for defining the output module inside the configuration file is as follows:

```
output <module_name>[: arguments]
```

For example, if you want to log messages to MySQL database called "snort" using database user name "rr" and password "rr" located on the same machine where Snort is running, you use the following line in snort.conf file.

```
output database: log, mysql, user=rr password=rr \
    dbname=snort host=localhost
```

However when you use an output module in the configuration file, alerts will not go into the alert file. Once you place this line in the snort.conf file, all alerts will go into the MySQL database. There are ways to send alerts to multiple destinations.

N O T E In addition to the above line, you also need to configure MySQL database and create tables. Discussion about this process is the subject of the next chapter.

Another example of using output modules is as follows. This line in the `snort.conf` file will cause alerts to be sent as SMB pop-up windows to a list of hosts located in the `workstation.list` file.

```
output alert_smb: workstation.list
```

Sometimes you may want to send alerts to multiple locations. Defining your own action using the ruletype keyword is a good idea. For example, the following lines in the `snort.conf` file will define an action type called "smb_db_alert" that will cause alerts to be sent to both the database and SMB pop-up windows for rules that use this action type.

```
ruletype smb_db_alert
{
   type alert
   output alert_smb: workstation.list
   output database: log, mysql, user=rr password=rr \
     dbname=snort host=localhost
}
```

The following rule uses this new action type. Alerts generated by this rule will go to MySQL database as well as to the Windows machine in the form of pop-up windows.

```
smb_db_alert icmp any any -> 192.168.1.0/24 any \
   (fragbits: D; msg: "Dont Fragment bit set";)
```

You can also use command line options with some output modules. For example, you can use `-s` option to log alerts to Syslog.

4.2.1   The alert_syslog Output Module

Syslog is a system logging daemon available on almost all UNIX systems. It uses a configuration file `/etc/syslog.conf` where you can define different parameters to determine what happens when a message for a defined facility is received. A detailed discussion of Syslog is beyond the scope of this book and you should refer to the manual pages of `syslogd` and `syslog.conf`.

The `alert_syslog` module allows you to send alerts to the syslog facility. The Syslog daemon can also be used to forward alerts to some other host as well if you need centralized logging. The following is the general format for using this module.

```
output alert_syslog: <facility> <priority> <options>
```

Facility names that can be used with this module are:

- LOG_AUTH
- LOG_AUTHPRIV
- LOG_DAEMON
- LOG_LOCAL0
- LOG_LOCAL1
- LOG_LOCAL2
- LOG_LOCAL3
- LOG_LOCAL4
- LOG_LOCAL5
- LOG_LOCAL6
- LOG_LOCAL7
- LOG_USER

Priorities that are available with this module are:

- LOG_EMERG
- LOG_ALERT
- LOG_CRIT
- LOG_ERR
- LOG_WARNING
- LOG_NOTICE
- LOG_INFO
- LOG_DEBUG

Note that LOG_EMERG is the highest priority and LOG_DEBUG is the lowest priority. Options that you can use with this module are:

- LOG_CONS
- LOG_NDELAY
- LOG_PERROR
- LOG_PID

Note that you have to configure Syslog daemon on your host to properly utilize this module. On Linux systems, read the manual pages for sysklogd for a detailed discussion of how to configure and use the daemon. The configuration is done through the

use of /etc/syslog.conf file on UNIX systems. A typical syslog.conf file on
RedHat Linux 7.3 system follows. As you can see from this file, a log file is defined for
each type of facility. Most of the messages go into /var/log/messages files.

```
# Log all kernel messages to the console.
# Logging much else clutters up the screen.
kern.*                  /dev/console

# Log anything (except mail) of level info or higher.
# Don't log private authentication messages!
*.info;mail.none;news.none;authpriv.none;cron.none          /var/
   log/messages

# The authpriv file has restricted access.
authpriv.*           /var/log/secure

# Log all the mail messages in one place.
mail.*               /var/log/maillog


# Log cron stuff
cron.*               /var/log/cron

# Everybody gets emergency messages
*.emerg              *

# Save news errors of level crit and higher in a special file.
uucp,news.crit     /var/log/spooler

# Save boot messages also to boot.log
local7.*             /var/log/boot.log

#
# INN
#
news.=crit           /var/log/news/news.crit
news.=err            /var/log/news/news.err
news.notice          /var/log/news/news.notice
```

If you want to send different types of alerts using different facilities or priorities,
you can define your own actions using the ruletype keyword as mentioned earlier. After
defining these rule types, you can use them in your rules as actions. As you will remember from previous discussions, the first word in each rule is the action part.

4.2.2   The alert_full Output Module

The `alert_full` module logs full alert messages in a file. The following line will log all alert messages to `alert_detailed` file under the Snort logging directory.

```
output alert_full: alert_detailed
```

However keep in mind that full logging has its own disadvantages as well. Especially in high-speed networks, enabling full alerts consumes a significant amount of time to log data into a file, causing some packets to be ignored by the detection engine.

Note that as mentioned earlier, you can log messages to multiple destinations using a new action type. The following lines in `snort.conf` file define an action type "multi". When this action type is used in any rule, the message will be sent as SMB pop-up window on hosts listed in `workstation.list` file as well as to a file `alert_detailed`.

```
ruletype multi
{
    type alert
    output alert_smb: workstation.list
    output alert_full: alert_detailed
}
```

4.2.3   The alert_fast Output Module

Like alert_full, alert_fast also takes as an argument a file name for storing data. It is fast compared to full alerting. Packet headers are not saved in the alert file. The following line in the `snort.conf` file enables one-line alert messages to be stored in `alert_quick` file.

```
output alert_fast: alert_quick
```

This mode is useful for high-speed intrusion detection applications of Snort.

4.2.4   The alert_smb Module

SMB alerts are sent to Microsoft Windows-based workstations using the `smbclient` program which is part of the SAMBA client package on Linux machines. To send these alerts, the `smbclient` must be present in the PATH variable.

SMB alerts are displayed on Windows machines as pop-up windows as shown in Figure 4-2. A list of workstations should be present in a file that is provided as an argument to the output module. The following line in `snort.conf` file will cause alert messages to be sent to workstations listed in file `workstation.list`.

```
output alert_smb: workstation.list
```

Figure 4-2 SMB alert display window.

Each workstation name should be listed in `workstation.list` file on a separate line. Note that these are the SMB names, not IP addresses or DNS hostnames. The SMB names of workstations are configured in Control Panel on Windows machines. The smbclient program resolves these SMB names by itself.

You have to compile the SMB alert support when building Snort using the configure script. A typical line to build this support is:

```
./configure --prefix=/opt/snort --enable-smbalerts
```

Refer to Chapter 2 for more information about how to compile Snort. The messenger service must be enabled on the Windows system for pop-up windows to be displayed.

4.2.5   The log_tcpdump Output Module

This module is used to store alert data in a tcpdump format file that can be viewed later on using `tcpdump` or some other tool. This method is quick for heavily loaded networks where you want to offload processing from the Snort system and analyze data using some other mechanism. Following is the general format for using this module in `snort.conf` file.

```
output log_tcpdump: <filename>
```

Typical entries in the `snort.conf` file may look like the following:

```
output log_tcpdump: /var/log/snort/snort_tcpdump.log
```

In Snort 1.8 and older, Month, Data and Time are pre-pended to the file name so that you can have multiple files every time you restart Snort. In Snort 1.9, the seconds counter[1] is appended to the file name. Each time you start Snort, a new file is created.

---

1.   In fact, the time() function is used in Snort 1.9.0 to determine this number. For more information, use the "man 2 time" command in Linux.

Some typical names of files created by using this line in `snort.conf` file in Snort 1.9 are:

```
snort_tcpdump.log.1039971287
snort_tcpdump.log.1039971389
```

If you use the file command to determine the type of the files created by Snort, an output like the following will be displayed.

```
[root@conformix]# file /var/log/snort/
snort_tcpdump.log.1039971287
/var/log/snort/snort_tcpdump.log.1039971287: tcpdump capture
file (little-endian) - version 2.4 (Ethernet, capture length
1514)
[root@conformix]#
```

This output shows that this file is in rcpdump format. Now you can display the contents of this file (the captured data) using the tcpdump command as follows:

```
[root@conformix]# tcpdump -v -r  /var/log/snort/
  snort_tcpdump.log.1039971287
11:55:03.163301 192.168.1.1.1901 > 239.255.255.250.1900:  [udp sum ok]
  udp 269 (ttl 150, id 0, len 297)
11:55:03.166078 192.168.1.1.1901 > 239.255.255.250.1900:  [udp sum ok]
  udp 325 (ttl 150, id 1, len 353)
11:55:03.168592 192.168.1.1.1901 > 239.255.255.250.1900:  [udp sum ok]
  udp 253 (ttl 150, id 2, len 281)
11:55:03.170912 192.168.1.1.1901 > 239.255.255.250.1900:  [udp sum ok]
  udp 245 (ttl 150, id 3, len 273)
11:55:03.173415 192.168.1.1.1901 > 239.255.255.250.1900:  [udp sum ok]
  udp 289 (ttl 150, id 4, len 317)
11:55:03.175796 192.168.1.1.1901 > 239.255.255.250.1900:  [udp sum ok]
  udp 265 (ttl 150, id 5, len 293)
11:55:03.178429 192.168.1.1.1901 > 239.255.255.250.1900:  [udp sum ok]
  udp 319 (ttl 150, id 6, len 347)
11:55:03.181288 192.168.1.1.1901 > 239.255.255.250.1900:  [udp sum ok]
  udp 317 (ttl 150, id 7, len 345)
11:55:03.183845 192.168.1.1.1901 > 239.255.255.250.1900:  [udp sum ok]
  udp 321 (ttl 150, id 8, len 349)
11:55:03.186581 192.168.1.1.1901 > 239.255.255.250.1900:  [udp sum ok]
  udp 313 (ttl 150, id 9, len 341)
[root@conformix]#
```

This is especially useful if you want to create log files in binary format and then use tcpdump to analyze the log files later.

4.2.6 The XML Output Module

The Simple Network Modeling Language (SNML) is available for exporting Snort alerts so they can be read and interpreted by any XML-based interpreter or browser. Information about Snort XML plug-in is available at http://www.cert.org/kb/snortxml/. At the time of writing this book, version 0.2 of SNML DTD is available from this web site and is also available in Appendix E.

Using this plug-in, you can save XML data in a file on the local machine or send it to a web server using HTTP or HTTPS protocols.

General format of using XML output plug-in is as follows:

```
output xml: [log | alert], [parameter list]
```

You can use either log or alert option with XML module. In case of alert, only alert messages will be logged. Other parameters that can be used with this plug-in are listed in Table 4-1.

Table 4-1 Parameters Used with XML Module

Parameter	Description
File	Stores data to an XML file.
Protocol	Logs message to some other host using that protocol. Important protocols are HTTP, HTTPS, and TCP. When you use HTTP protocol, you also need to specify a file parameter. Data will be logged to the HTTP server using the POST method in the specified file. If you want to use HTTPS protocol, you also need to provide file, cert, and key parameters for secure logging. If you use TCP protocol, a server must be listening to a parrot specified with port parameter.
Host	Defines remote host where data will be logged.
Port	Defines the port number on the remote host where data will be logged. Default port numbers for HTTP, HTTPS, and TCP are 80, 443, and 9000 respectively.
Cert	This is the certificate to be used with HTTPS protocol. It is X.509 client certificate.
Key	The client private key.
Ca	The server certificate used for authentication.
Server	The Common Name or CN for X.509 certificate.

Note that XML output is important for much web application development and for integrating Snort into such systems. Some Snort XML parsers exist, including ACID-XML at http://www.maximumunix.org, although these are still in their infancy.

4.2.6.1   Examples

Logging to a file "xmlout" on the local host:

```
output xml: log,   file=xmlout
```

The date and time will be appended to the name of the file so that data can be saved for multiple Snort sessions.

Logging to a file "xmlout" on host snort.conformix.com using HTTP protocol:

```
output xml: alert, protocol=http  \
    host=snort.conformix.com file=xmlout
```

Logging to a file "xmlout" on host snort.conformix.com using HTTPS protocol:

```
output xml: alert, protocol=https \
   host=snort.conformix.com file=xmlout cert=conformix.crt \
   key=conformix.pem ca=ca.crt server=Conformix_server
```

Logging to a TCP server running on host snort.conformix.com and listening to port number 5555:

```
output xml: alert, protocol=tcp \
    host=snort.conformix.com port=5555
```

Typical entries present in the output XML file:

```
<?xml version="1.0" encoding="UTF-8"?>
<!DOCTYPE snort-message-version-0.2>

<file>

  <event version="1.0">
    <sensor encoding="hex" detail="full">
      <interface>eth0</interface>
      <ipaddr version="4">192.168.1.2</ipaddr>
      <hostname>conformix.conformix.net</hostname>
    </sensor>
    <signature>ICMP Packet with TTL=100</signature>
    <timestamp>2002-07-23 17:48:31-04</timestamp>
    <packet>
      <iphdr saddr="192.168.1.100" daddr="192.168.1.2" proto="1" ver="4"
  hlen="5" len="60" id="37123" ttl="100" csum="519">
        <icmphdr type="8" code="0" csum="23612">

  <data>6162636465666768696A6B6C6D6E6F707172737475767761626364656667686 9</data>
        </icmphdr>
      </iphdr>
    </packet>
  </event>

</file>
```

You need an XML parser and a DTD file to interpret data logged into the XML file. You can also load data files in your XML enabled web browser as shown in Figure 4-3.

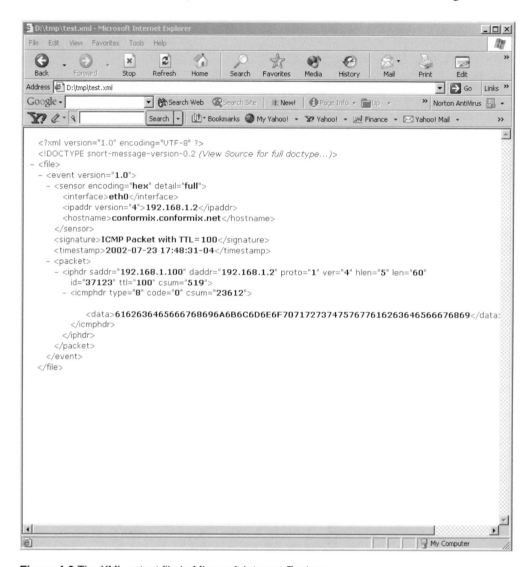

Figure 4-3 The XML output file in Microsoft Internet Explorer.

There are a few things that you can do in Internet Explorer with XML documents. For example, if you want to hide the packet details, you can click on the hyphen character; all details for the packet will be hidden and the hyphen character will be replaced by the plus character. This is shown in Figure 4-4. To display the details again, you can click on the plus character.

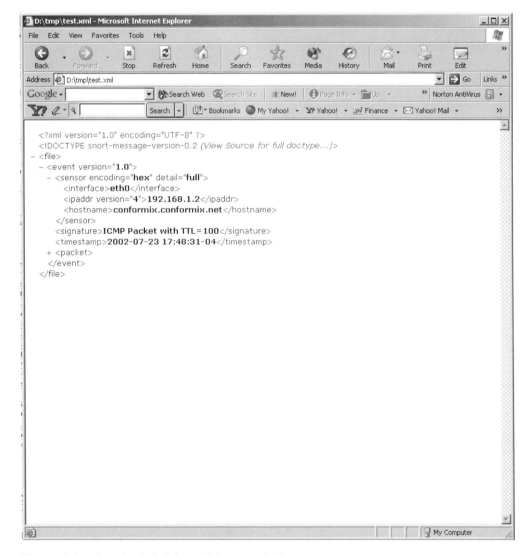

Figure 4-4 Hiding details in Microsoft Internet Explorer.

The plus and the hyphen character can be clicked in all places on the XML document to hide or reveal details about a particular section of the XML document. For more information on XML, you can consult any of the available texts or go to the XML web site at http://www.xml.org.

4.2.7 Logging to Databases

Databases are used with Snort to store log and alert data. Logging data to files in the disk is fine for smaller applications. However, keeping log data in disk files is not appropriate when you have multiple Snort sensors or you want to keep historical data as well. Databases also allow you to analyze data generated by Snort sensors. For example, if you want to find the top 15 alerts that are generated most frequently, you can use SQL statements for the database. Finding the same information from log files is difficult. Similarly, if you want to find the most active attackers in the month of November 2002, it is very easy to find out that information from a database.

You can use multiple types of databases with Snort including Oracle and MySQL. Using the database is discussed in detail in the next chapter. For the sake of completeness of discussion about output modules, consider the following line.

```
output database: log, mysql, user=rr password=rr \
   dbname=snort host=localhost
```

This line configures MySQL to be used as the database running on the same machine where Snort is running. All messages are logged to the database named "snort" which you need to create manually before you can start using it. Snort will access this database using user name "rr" and password "rr". Note that rr is not a UNIX user, it is a database user. You have to create this user name and password yourself as well. Refer to Chapter 5 for details about how to configure MySQL database for use with Snort.

The general format for using the database is as follows:

```
output database: <log | alert>, <database_type>, \
   <parameter_list>
```

The database type is mysql, postgressql, oracle and so on. List of parameters that can be used is shown in Table 4-2. Parameters are separated with a space character in the configuration file (`snort.conf`). Most of these parameters are optional.

Table 4-2 List of Parameters for the Database

Parameter	Description
host	Host where database server is running.
port	Port number used by the database server.
dbname	Name of the database.
user	Name of the database user.
password	Password for the user. If you don't want to use a password, you can omit this parameter (a bad idea!).
sensor_name	Name of the sensor used by Snort. This is useful when many Snort sensors are logging to the database and later on you want to know which alert is related to a particular sensor. This name is also used by tools like ACID to distinguish different sensors.
detail	You can use either *full* or *fast* detail. By default *full* detail is saved to the database.
encoding	You can use ASCII, hex, or base64 encoding for data.

To enable support of databases, you need to compile Snort with database support enabled. The following configure script enables MySQL database support in Snort.

```
./configure --prefix=/opt/snort --with-mysql=/usr/lib/mysql
```

Refer to Chapter 2 for details on how to build Snort.

4.2.8   CSV Output Module

Comma-separated text files are sometimes useful when you want to import data into other software packages like databases and spreadsheets, e.g., Microsoft Excel. Using the CSV output module, you can save output data to a CSV file. The general format of the CSV file is as follows:

```
output csv: <filename> <formatting_options>
```

The file is created in the logging directory which is /var/log/snort by default. Formatting options are used to define what information should be stored in the CSV file and in what order. If you use the keyword "default" in the formatting option, all parameters about the alert are stored in the file.

```
output csv: csv_log default
```

The output file generated after using this line in `snort.conf` file is something like the following:

```
07/23-18:24:03.388106 ,ICMP Packet with
  TTL=100,ICMP,192.168.1.100,,192.168.1.2,,0:2:3F:33:C6:98,0:E0:29:89:
  28:59,0x4A,,,,,,100,0,51367,60,20,8,0,,
07/23-18:25:51.608106 ,GET
  matched,TCP,192.168.1.2,1060,192.168.10.193,,0:E0:29:89:28:59,0:6:25
  :5B:29:ED,0x189,***AP***,0x55BCF404,0x8CBF42DD,,0x16D0,64,0,35580,37
  9,20,,,,
07/23-18:25:52.008106 ,GET
  matched,TCP,192.168.1.2,1061,192.168.10.193,,0:E0:29:89:28:59,0:6:25
  :5B:29:ED,0x1D0,***AP***,0x55628967,0x8D33FB74,,0x16D0,64,0,63049,45
  0,20,,,,
07/23-18:25:52.478106 ,GET
  matched,TCP,192.168.1.2,1061,192.168.10.193,,0:E0:29:89:28:59,0:6:25
  :5B:29:ED,0x1D0,***AP***,0x55628B01,0x8D33FC1B,,0x1920,64,0,63051,45
  0,20,,,,
07/23-18:25:52.708106 ,GET
  matched,TCP,192.168.1.2,1061,192.168.10.193,,0:E0:29:89:28:59,0:6:25
  :5B:29:ED,0x1EF,***AP***,0x55628C9B,0x8D33FCC1,,0x1D50,64,0,63053,48
  1,20,,,,
```

Each line in the output consists of fields as listed in Table 4-3.

Table 4-3 CSV Options

Name	Description
Timestamp	Time stamp including date and time.
Msg	Message which is taken from the msg option of the rule.
Proto	Protocol.
Src	Source IP address.
Srcport	Source port number. No port number is present in ICMP packets.
Dst	Destination IP address.
Dstport	Destination port.
ethsrc	Source Ethernet address.
ethdst	Destination Ethernet address.
ethlen	Length of Ethernet frame.
tcpflags	If the protocol is TCP, this part contains TCP flags.
tcpseq	TCP sequence number in TCP packets.
tcpack	TCP acknowledgement number.

Table 4-3 CSV Options (continued)

Name	Description
tcplen	TCP length.
tcpwindow	TCP window size.
ttl	TTL value in the IP header.
tos	Type of Service field of IP header.
id	Packet ID.
dgmlen	Datagram length.
iplen	Length part in the IP header.
icmptype	Type field in ICMP header.
icmpcode	Code part in ICMP header.
icmpid	ID part of ICMP header.
icmpseq	ICMP sequence.

You can use only a few of these options in the CSV file as required. The following line in `snort.conf` will record only timestamp, msg, source, and destination IP addresses.

```
output csv: csv_log timestamp,msg,src,dst
```

The log entries will look like the following:

```
07/23-19:31:27.128106 ,GET matched,192.168.1.2,192.168.10.193
07/23-19:31:27.278106 ,GET matched,192.168.1.2,192.168.10.193
```

4.2.9 Unified Logging Output Module

Unified output is good for high-speed logging. You can have alerts and logs going into separate files. The general format of these modules is as follows:

```
output alert_unified: filename <alert_file>, \
   limit <max_size>
output log_unified: filename <log_file>, \
   limit <max_size>
```

The size of the file is expressed in Mbytes. You should enable both alert and log files to keep a complete record of data because the alert file does not contain detailed information about the packets. The following is an example of enabling unified output from Snort. These two lines in the `snort.conf` file enable unified output.

```
output alert_unified: filename unified_alert, limit 50
output log_unified: filename unified_log, limit 200
```

If no path is specified, the files are created in /var/log/snort directory. In the above example, the alert file will not grow more than 50 MBytes and the maximum size of the log file will be 200 MBytes. The number of seconds as returned by the time() function are added at the end of file name so that when you restart Snort, new files are created. Some typical names for alert and log files are:

```
unified_alert.1039992424
unified_log.1039992424
```

Unified log files are in binary format and you can use utilities to view these. For simple hexadecimal display, you can use the hexdump utility on Linux. Barnyard is another tool for this purpose. Refer to the Barnyard web site at http://sourceforge.net/projects/barnyard/. This tool is discussed in Chapter 6 also.

4.2.10 SNMP Traps Output Module

The SNMP traps output module is very useful to send alerts as SNMP traps to a centrally managed network operations center. Snort SNMP output module can generate both SNMPv2 and SNMPv3 traps. The general format of SNMPv2 trap is as follows:

```
output trap_snmp: alert, <sensor_ID>, {trap|inform} \
    -v <snmp_version> -p <port_number> <hostname> <community>
```

The following line sends SNMP version 2C traps to host 192.168.1.3 on port 162, which is the standard port for SNMP traps. The community name used is "public".

```
output trap_snmp: alert, 8, trap -v 2c -p 162  \
    192.168.1.3 public
```

You should modify community to a different string. "Public" is the default community name and is known to everyone in the SNMP world. Refer to the example lines provided in snort.conf file for SNMP version 3 traps.

To enable SNMP support in Snort, you have to compile it into Snort at the time you run the configure script. The following configure script command line can be used for this purpose.

```
./configure --prefix=/opt/snort --with-snmp --with-openssl
```

You also need to compile OpenSSL support in Snort. Refer to Chapter 2 for more information about how to build Snort.

4.2.11 Log Null Output Module

This output plug-in causes alert entries not to be logged. For example, you can create a rule type to send SNMP traps without logging these messages. However, I would not recommend using it. You should always have a record of alerts so that if you want to take any action against intruders, you have some evidence of the IDS activities.

4.3 Using BPF Fileters

Berkley Packet Filter (BPF) is a mechanism of filtering data packets at the data link layer level. These filters are extensively used with the tcpdump program to filter data that you want to capture. You can use BPF filters with Snort as well. When using BPF filters, Snort rules are applied only to those packets that pass BPF filters. This way you can save some CPU time by not applying Snort rules to packets that are of no interest. For example, the BPF filters can be used to compare a particular byte from the starting offset of the IP header, TCP header or UDP header.

You can place BPF filters in a file and use that file on the command line when starting Snort. Let us suppose you want to apply Snort only on packets for which the Type of Service (TOS) field in the IP header is not equal to 0. The TOS field is the second byte in the IP header. For this purpose, you can create a file bpf.txt with the following line in it:

```
ip[1] != 0
```

Number 1 is the offset starting from the IP header part of the data packet. The offset starts from 0, so byte number 1 is the TOS field. For the structure of the IP header, refer to Appendix C.

After creating this file, you can use the following command line to start Snort to enable the filter.

```
snort -F bpf.txt -c /opt/snort/etc/snort.conf
```

Only those packets in which the TOS field has some value other than 0 will reach Snort detection engine. A TOS value equal to 0 shows normal data traffic and any other value is used for high priority data packets.

4.4 References

1. Classless Inter-Domain Routing or CIDR. RFC 1519 at http://www.rfc-editor.org/rfc/rfc1519.txt

2. Transmission Control Protocol RFC 793 at http://www.rfc-editor.org/rfc/rfc793.txt

3. The nmap at it web site http://www.nmap.org

4. The Internet Protocol RFC 791 at http://www.rfc-editor.crg/rfc/rfc791.txt

5. The Internet Control Message Protocol at http://www.rfc-editor.org/rfc/rfc792.txt

6. The nmap utility at http://www.nmap.org/

7. Simple Network Markup Language SNML info at http://www.cert.org/kb/snortxml/

8. Barnyard at http://sourceforge.net/projects/barnyard/

9. ACID_XML at http://www.maximumunix.org

10. XML at http://www.xml.org

11. Snot at http://www.sec33.com/sniph/

## CHAPTER 5

Using Snort with MySQL

All systems need some type of efficient logging feature, usually using a database at the backend. Snort can be made to work with MySQL, Oracle or any other Open Database Connectivity (ODBC) compliant database.[1] You already know from the discussion of output modules in the previous chapter that you can save logs and alerts to a database. Logging to a database is very useful for maintaining history data, generating reports and analyzing information. By using other tools like Analysis Control for Intrusion Detection (ACID), discussed in the next chapter, you can get very useful information from the database about attack patterns. For example, you can get a report about the last fifteen unique attacks, information about hosts that are continuously attacking your network, the distribution of attacks by different protocols, and so on.

Since MySQL is a freely available database and works perfectly well on Linux and other operating systems, this is a natural choice for Snort. Some different scenarios for using a database with Snort are:

- You can install and run the MySQL database server on the same machine where Snort is running, as shown in Figure 5-1.

---

1.   ODBC provides a standard way for clients to connect to a database. Refer to ODBS FAQ at http://www.ensyncsolutions.com/odbc_faq.htm or http://www.odbc.org for more information.

- You can also install the MySQL server on a different machine and configure Snort to log to that database, as shown in Figure 5-2.
- You can have multiple Snort sensors to log to a centralized database server running MySQL server, as shown in Figure 5-3.

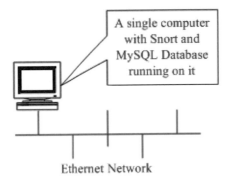

Figure 5-1 A single computer running Snort and MySQL database server.

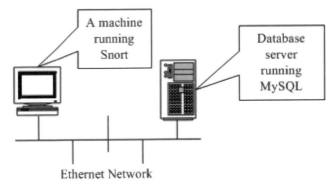

Figure 5-2 A computer running Snort logging to a separate MySQL database server.

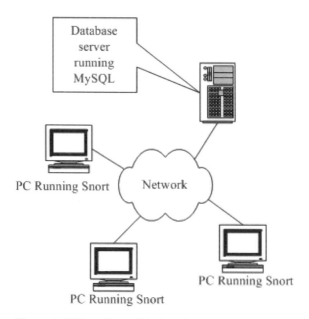

Figure 5-3 Many Snort PCs logging data to a centralized MySQL database server.

The scheme you choose depends on your particular requirements. For example, if you are running only one sensor and don't have any pre-existing database server, it is a natural choice to install the database on the Snort machine itself. However if you have many Snort machines, it makes sense to set up a centralized database server as shown in Figure 5-3.

If you are running a separate database server and are logging to it from remote Snort machines, you can send data without any security or you can use some type of encryption. A possible scheme using the Stunnel package is discussed at the end of this chapter. Using Stunnel, you can encrypt all data between the Snort machine and the database server. This system also helps to pass data through firewalls, because you can use the ports that are already open in the firewall with Stunnel.

Before you start logging to MySQL database, you have to create a database on the database server for Snort. After creating the database, you have to create tables where Snort data is logged. The table schema used with the database is available from http://www.incident.org/snortdb/ for your review. However, you don't need to create tables manually because Snort comes with a script that will do the entire job for you. To work with MySQL, you may have to recompile Snort with MySQL support, as will be explained later in this chapter.

After going through this chapter, you should be able to install Snort and MySQL so that all of the Snort activity is logged to the database. You should also be able to set up a centralized database server and enable multiple Snort machines to log to this server. The last part of this chapter provides information about using the Stunnel packet for secure data exchange between Snort machine and a remote database server.

5.1 Making Snort Work with MySQL

There are a few basic steps to make Snort work with MySQL. A high level step-by-step approach to build a Snort-MySQL system follows. Details of each step will be presented later in the chapter.

1. Compile Snort with MySQL support and install it. Make sure that Snort is working properly by creating some alert messages. You have to use --with-mysql command line argument with the configure script as mentioned in Chapter 2.
2. Install MySQL and use mysql client to make sure the database is available. See Appendix C for basic information about how to get started with MySQL.
3. Create a database on the MySQL server for Snort. I have named this database "snort." You may choose any name for the database. This is explained later in this chapter.
4. Create a user name and password in the database. The user name will be used by Snort to log data.
5. Create tables in this database using scripts that came with Snort distribution in the contrib directory.
6. Modify the snort.conf file to enable the database plug-in as explained later. You will use the database name, user name and password for the database that you just created.
7. Restart Snort. If everything goes well, Snort will start logging to the database.
8. Generate some alerts and use the mysql client program to make sure that alerts are being logged into the database.

The rest of the chapter will provide explanations about how to perform all of these steps. The next chapter discusses the use of ACID, which will make real use of the work that you do in this chapter.

5.1.1   Step 1: Snort Compilations with MySQL Support

Snort must be compiled with `--with-mysql` if you want to use MySQL database with Snort. This is done with the help of the `configure` script as explained in Chapter 2. A typical `configure` script command line follows:

```
./configure --prefix=/opt/snort --with-mysql=/usr/lib/mysql
```

When you run the configure script, I would recommend adding support for other components such as SNMP, which is very useful. MySQL libraries must be present in `/usr/lib/mysql` directory for successful compilation. Refer to Chapter 2 for details.

5.1.2   Step 2: Install MySQL

I would suggest installing the MySQL database packages that come with RedHat or other Linux distributions. MySQL is also available for Microsoft Windows platforms. This is the easiest way to install the database. However you can also download MySQL database server and client software in the source code form from its web site at http://www.mysql.org and compile and install it yourself. However, this is recommended only for very experienced users.

5.1.3   Step 3: Creating Snort Database in MySQL

Once you have compiled Snort with MySQL support, the next step is to create MySQL database where Snort can log data. Before you start using MySQL, make sure that MySQL server is running on the machine that is being used as the database server. You can use `ps -ef | grep mysql` command for this purpose. If this command shows MySQL processes, it means that the server is running. If you are using a single machine, you can have the database server running on the machine where Snort is installed. As mentioned earlier, you can also have a separate database server. For the purpose of this book, I have used a single machine and all components including Snort and MySQL server are installed on it.

You can download and install the latest MySQL server from http://www.mysql.org web site or get the RPM package that is part of your RedHat installation disk. For people running Snort on Microsoft Windows machines, it is better to get the binary installable package. You can use the `root` database user to create the `snort` database and grant needed privileges to the `rr` user.

The `mysql` client program is used to connect to the database server. You can use any name for the Snort database and any name for the user to access this database. For the purpose of this book, we are creating a database named "`snort`" and a user "`rr`" to access this database. Assuming MySQL server is running on localhost, a typical mysql session to create the database and check its status is as follows:

```
[root@laptop]# mysql -h localhost -u root -p
Enter password:
Welcome to the MySQL monitor.  Commands end with ; or \g.
Your MySQL connection id is 40 to server version: 3.23.36

Type 'help;' or '\h' for help. Type '\c' to clear the buffer

mysql> create database snort;
Query OK, 1 row affected (0.00 sec)

mysql> use snort
Database changed
mysql> status
--------------
mysql  Ver 11.13 Distrib 3.23.36, for redhat-linux-gnu (i386)

Connection id:          41
Current database:       snort
Current user:           root@localhost
Current pager:          stdout
Using outfile:          ''
Server version:         3.23.36
Protocol version:       10
Connection:             Localhost via UNIX socket
Client characterset:    latin1
Server characterset:    latin1
UNIX socket:            /var/lib/mysql/mysql.sock
Uptime:                 1 hour 56 min 29 sec

Threads: 1  Questions: 107  Slow queries: 0  Opens: 14   Flush
tables: 1  Open tables: 7 Queries per second avg: 0.015
--------------
mysql>
```

The following commands are used in this session:

• The command "mysql -h localhost -u root -p" is used to connect mysql client to a database server running on localhost. The "-u root" part shows the database user name used to connect to the database. The "-p" part is used to enter user password on the next line. A welcome message is displayed after login and you get the "mysql>" prompt where you can issue other commands.

- The command "create database snort;" creates a new database in the MySQL server with the name "snort". You can use any name of your choice for the database.
- The "use snort" command is used to start using the newly created database.
- The "status" command shows current status of the database server. It shows that the currently opened database is "snort."

To end the mysql client session, you can use the "exit" command at the MySQL prompt.

5.1.4 Step 4: Creating MySQL User and Granting Permissions to User and Setting Password

Using the database user root to access the Snort database is not recommended. For this purpose, you will create a new user "rr". The next command creates a user with name rr. The same command also grants the following permissions to all tables in the snort database we recently created.

- CREATE, used to create new objects
- INSERT, used to insert data into the database
- DELETE, used to delete data from the database
- UPDATE, used to modify records
- SELECT, used to display and select records

We shall use this user to access the Snort database. This user name and password are also used in the snort.conf file when you configure output database module.

```
mysql> grant CREATE,INSERT,DELETE,UPDATE,SELECT on snort.* to
  rr@localhost;
Query OK, 0 rows affected (0.00 sec)

mysql>
```

The permission for this newly created user is granted only for the database Snort. A single command creates the user and grants permission.

Now you need to assign a password to this user. The following command assigns a password "rr78x" to this user.

```
mysql> set password for rr = password('rr78x');
Query OK, 0 rows affected (0.00 sec)

mysql>
```

This password is used in the `snort.conf` file along with the user name with MySQL output module configuration. You have now set values for the following fields of the MySQL output plug-in in `snort.conf` file:

- Database name, which is `snort`
- Database user name which is `rr`
- Database user password which is `rr78x`
- The host where database server is running, which is the same machine where Snort is installed. If both Database server and Snort are running on the same machine, you will use "`localhost`" as the host name.

5.1.5   Step 5: Creating Tables in the Snort Database

After creating a database user and a Snort database, you now have to create the tables required to store data in the database. Fortunately you can use the script `create_mysql` in the `contrib` directory and it will create all of the necessary tables for you. The `contrib` directory is present when you download Snort in the source code form from its web site http://www.snort.org and extract its source files. The `create_mysql` script is present along with other useful stuff in this directory. For example, scripts to create database schema in other types of database servers are also found in this directory.

The following command uses this script to create all database tables in the `snort` database.

```
[root@laptop]# mysql -h localhost -u rr -p snort < contrib/
create_mysql
Enter password:
[root@laptop]#
```

Different command line options are used with this command.

- The "`-h localhost`" part of the command is used to tell the `mysql` client that the database server is running on the same machine as the client.
- The "`-u rr`" part is used to specify database user name to log into the database server. This is the same user that you created previously.
- The "`-p`" part shows that you will enter the password for user `rr` in the next line.
- The "`snort`" part of the command line shows that the database that will be used to create tables is "`snort`."

- The last part "<contrib./create_mysql" specifies a file name and shows that mysql client will read commands from this file.

To display what tables have been created, use the following session:

```
[root@laptop]# mysql -h localhost -u rr -p snort
Enter password:
Reading table information for completion of table and column
names
You can turn off this feature to get a quicker startup with -A

Welcome to the MySQL monitor.  Commands end with ; or \g.
Your MySQL connection id is 46 to server version: 3.23.36

Type 'help;' or '\h' for help. Type '\c' to clear the buffer


mysql> show tables;

+------------------+
| Tables_in_snort  |
+------------------+
| data             |
| detail           |
| encoding         |
| event            |
| icmphdr          |
| iphdr            |
| opt              |
| reference        |
| reference_system |
| schema           |
| sensor           |
| sig_class        |
| sig_reference    |
| signature        |
| tcphdr           |
| udphdr           |
+------------------+
16 rows in set (0.00 sec)

mysql>
```

The "show tables" command lists all the tables in the currently open database. There are sixteen tables created in the table by the create_mysql script as listed above. The first table name in the list is data and the last one in the list is udphdr. Each of these tables keeps part of the information about Snort activity.

- The data table contains the payload for each packet that triggers an alert.
- The detail table contains information about how much detail is logged with a packet. By default it has only two rows. The first row is "fast" and the second one is "full". You can think of this information as the logging mode described in previous chapters.
- The encoding table shows the types of encoding used when logging data packets. By default it contains three types of logging: hex, base64 and ASCII.
- The event table lists all events and stores a timestamp for these events.
- The icmphdr table contains information about the ICMP header of packets that are logged into the database. It contains information including ICMP type, ICMP code, ICMP ID, ICMP sequence number and so on. For more information about ICMP headers, refer to RFC 792 and Appendix C.
- The iphdr table contains all fields of the IP header for logged data packets. The information includes source and destination IP addresses, IP protocol version, IP header length, type of service (TOS) value, time to live (TTL) value and so on. More information about IP headers can be found in RFC 791 and Appendix C.
- The opt table contains options.
- The reference and reference_system tables contain information about reference sites used to get more information about a vulnerability. This is the same information that is used inside Snort rules using the ref keyword as discussed in Chapter 3.
- The schema tables shows the version of database schema.
- The sensor table contains information about different sensors that are logging data to the Snort database. If there is only one Snort sensor, the table contains only one row. Similarly, the table contains one row for each sensor.
- The sig_class contains information about different classes of Snort rules as discussed in Chapter 3. As an example, it contains entries like "attempted-recon", "misc-attack" and so on.
- The sig_reference table links signatures to different online reference sites.
- The signature table contains information about signatures that generated alerts.
- The tcphdr table contains information about the TCP header of a packet, if the logged packet is of TCP type. For more information about TCP header, refer to RFC 793 and Appendix C.
- The udphdr table contains information about UDP header part of the packet if the logged packet is of UDP type. This information contains UDP source and destination ports, length and checksum. For more information about UDP header, refer to RFC 768 and Appendix C.

If you are wondering about the structure of each table, you can display different fields in each table. The following command shows the structure of the iphdr table:

```
mysql> describe iphdr;
+-----------+----------------------+------+-----+---------+-------+
| Field     | Type                 | Null | Key | Default | Extra |
+-----------+----------------------+------+-----+---------+-------+
| sid       | int(10) unsigned     |      | PRI | 0       |       |
| cid       | int(10) unsigned     |      | PRI | 0       |       |
| ip_src    | int(10) unsigned     |      | MUL | 0       |       |
| ip_dst    | int(10) unsigned     |      | MUL | 0       |       |
| ip_ver    | tinyint(3) unsigned  | YES  |     | NULL    |       |
| ip_hlen   | tinyint(3) unsigned  | YES  |     | NULL    |       |
| ip_tos    | tinyint(3) unsigned  | YES  |     | NULL    |       |
| ip_len    | smallint(5) unsigned | YES  |     | NULL    |       |
| ip_id     | smallint(5) unsigned | YES  |     | NULL    |       |
| ip_flags  | tinyint(3) unsigned  | YES  |     | NULL    |       |
| ip_off    | smallint(5) unsigned | YES  |     | NULL    |       |
| ip_ttl    | tinyint(3) unsigned  | YES  |     | NULL    |       |
| ip_proto  | tinyint(3) unsigned  |      |     | 0       |       |
| ip_csum   | smallint(5) unsigned | YES  |     | NULL    |       |
+-----------+----------------------+------+-----+---------+-------+
14 rows in set (0.00 sec)

mysql>
```

For people who want to go into details of how data is stored, database schema provides great information. You can view complete database schema at http://www.incident.org/snortdb/.

5.1.5.1 Creating Extra Tables

When you are using some other programs with database and Snort to map service numbers to service names, additional mapping information is needed. For example, TCP port 23 is used for Telnet. However the tcphdr table contains only the port number, not the textual description. If you want to display source and destination ports as text "Telnet port" instead of "23", you need this information. Snort comes with an additional script that adds more tables and populates them with this information. To create these extra tables, get `snortdb-extra.zip` file in the `contrib` directory and unzip it. Use the following command to create the additional tables and add data to them.

```
[root@laptop]# mysql -h localhost -u rr -p snort < contrib/
snortdb-extra
Enter password:
[root@laptop]#
```

The command creates three tables, protocols, services, and flags. These tables contain descriptive information for different protocols, services and flags. The script also populates the tables with data. A description of these tables is provided in the `snortdb-extra` script. The list of new tables follows:

```
mysql> show tables;

+------------------+
| Tables_in_snort  |
+------------------+
| data             |
| detail           |
| encoding         |
| event            |
| flags            |
| icmphdr          |
| iphdr            |
| opt              |
| protocols        |
| reference        |
| reference_system |
| schema           |
| sensor           |
| services         |
| sig_class        |
| sig_reference    |
| signature        |
| tcphdr           |
| udphdr           |
+------------------+
19 rows in set (0.01 sec)

mysql>
```

There are now nineteen tables instead of sixteen. The services table is quite large and it contains entries for 65535 services, both for TCP and UDP. The total number of rows in this table is 131072 which makes it quite a big table. Creation of this table may take a few seconds on the database server when you run the `snortdb-extra` script.

5.1.5.2   Sample Entries in Snort Database Tables

To give you an idea of what type of entries are present in different tables in the Snort database, let us select some items from the database and display them.

Following are some entries from table sig_class.

```
mysql> select * from sig_class;
+--------------+-------------------------+
| sig_class_id | sig_class_name          |
+--------------+-------------------------+
|            9 | attempted-recon         |
|            8 | misc-attack             |
|            7 | bad-unknown             |
|            6 | web-application-activity |
+--------------+-------------------------+
4 rows in set (0.00 sec)

mysql>
```

The select command pulls out data from a database and displays it on the screen. You can use the select command after connecting to database using the mysql client. For more information on MySQL commands, refer to Appendix B.

The following are some records in reference_system table.

```
mysql> select * from reference_system;
+---------------+-----------------+
| ref_system_id | ref_system_name |
+---------------+-----------------+
|             8 | nessus          |
|             7 | cve             |
|             6 | arachnids       |
|             5 | bugtraq         |
+---------------+-----------------+
4 rows in set (0.02 sec)

mysql>
```

The following output of the select command shows records in encoding table.

```
mysql> select * from encoding;
+---------------+---------------+
| encoding_type | encoding_text |
+---------------+---------------+
|             0 | hex           |
|             1 | base64        |
|             2 | ascii         |
+---------------+---------------+
3 rows in set (0.00 sec)

mysql>
```

The following output of the select command lists all entries in the services table for port numbers between 20 and 30.

```
mysql> select * from services where port<30 and port>20;
+-------+----------+---------+-------------------------+
| port  | protocol | name    | description             |
+-------+----------+---------+-------------------------+
|    21 |        6 | ftp     | File Transfer [Control] |
|    21 |       17 | ftp     | File Transfer [Control] |
|    22 |        6 | -       | Unassigned              |
|    22 |       17 | -       | Unassigned              |
|    23 |        6 | telnet  | Telnet                  |
|    23 |       17 | telnet  | Telnet                  |
|    24 |        6 | -       | Unassigned              |
|    24 |       17 | -       | Unassigned              |
|    25 |        6 | smtp    | Simple Mail Transfer    |
|    25 |       17 | smtp    | Simple Mail Transfer    |
|    26 |        6 | -       | Unassigned              |
|    26 |       17 | -       | Unassigned              |
|    27 |        6 | nsw-fe  | NSW User System FE      |
|    27 |       17 | nsw-fe  | NSW User System FE      |
|    28 |        6 | -       | Unassigned              |
|    28 |       17 | -       | Unassigned              |
|    29 |        6 | msg-icp | MSG ICP                 |
|    29 |       17 | msg-icp | MSG ICP                 |
+-------+----------+---------+-------------------------+
18 rows in set (1.14 sec)

mysql>
```

5.1.6   Step 6: Modify snort.conf Configuration File

After configuring the database and creating tables and user, you need to edit the snort.conf file. These lines in the file will enable logging of log messages to the MySQL database:

```
output database: log, mysql, user=rr password=rr78x \
    dbname=snort host=localhost
```

In the above line, name of the database is snort and the MySQL server is running on localhost. The user for the database is rr and it has a password rr78x. If the user has no password, the line should be like the following:

```
output database: log, mysql, user=rr dbname=snort \
    host=localhost
```

The database is located on MySQL server running on the localhost, the machine where Snort is installed. If you have a separate database server, you can specify the name of the server on this line in the snort.conf file. For example, if the database server is not the same as where Snort is running, you can use the following lines in the `snort.conf` file.

```
output database: log, mysql, user=rr password=rr78x \
    dbname=snort host=192.168.1.23
```

The MySQL database server for the above example is running on host 192.168.1.23. If many Snort sensors are installed and all of them are logging data to the same database server 192.168.1.23, all of the sensors must have the same line in their `snort.conf` files. The database server must be running before starting Snort.

5.1.7   Step 7: Starting Snort with Database Support

When you start Snort after database configuration, the starting message shows what database is being used. The boldface lines show database related information.

```
[root@laptop]# /opt/snort/bin/snort -c /etc/snort/snort.conf
Log directory = /var/log/snort

Initializing Network Interface eth0


        --== Initializing Snort ==--
Decoding Ethernet on interface eth0
Initializing Preprocessors!
Initializing Plug-ins!
Initializing Output Plugins!
Parsing Rules file /etc/snort/snort.conf


+++++++++++++++++++++++++++++++++++++++++++++++++++++++
Initializing rule chains...
No arguments to frag2 directive, setting defaults to:
    Fragment timeout: 60 seconds
    Fragment memory cap: 4194304 bytes
Stream4 config:
    Stateful inspection: ACTIVE
    Session statistics: INACTIVE
    Session timeout: 30 seconds
    Session memory cap: 8388608 bytes
    State alerts: INACTIVE
    Scan alerts: ACTIVE
    Log Flushed Streams: INACTIVE
No arguments to stream4_reassemble, setting defaults:
    Reassemble client: ACTIVE
    Reassemble server: INACTIVE
    Reassemble ports: 21 23 25 53 80 143 110 111 513
    Reassembly alerts: ACTIVE
    Reassembly method: FAVOR_OLD
```

```
Back Orifice detection brute force: DISABLED
Using LOCAL time
database: compiled support for ( mysql )
database: configured to use mysql
database:              user = rr
database: database name = snort
database:               host = localhost
database:    sensor name = 10.100.1.111
database:       sensor id = 1
database: schema version = 105
database: using the "log" facility
886 Snort rules read...
886 Option Chains linked into 99 Chain Headers
0 Dynamic rules
+++++++++++++++++++++++++++++++++++++++++++++++++++++

Rule application order: ->activation->dynamic->alert->pass-
>log

       --== Initialization Complete ==--

-*> Snort! <*-
Version 1.8.6 (Build 105)
By Martin Roesch (roesch@sourcefire.com, www.snort.org)
```

The name of the database, the name of user and the host where the database is installed are all listed in the output. The schema version is saved in the schema table in MySQL database.

5.1.8   Step 8: Logging to Database

After configuring the database properly, you should check if log and alert messages are being saved in the database tables. We use the following two rules for Snort to test the database.

```
alert ip any any -> any any (ipopts: lsrr; msg: \
   "LSRR Options set"; logto: "test";)
alert icmp any any -> 192.168.1.0/24 any (fragbits: D; \
   msg: "Dont Fragment bit set";)
```

To test these rules, we use the following two commands on a Microsoft Windows machine. I have used Windows XP Home Edition for the sake of experiment.

```
ping -n 1 -f 192.168.1.2
ping -n 1 -j 192.168.1.2 192.168.1.2
```

The first command sends an ICMP echo packet with the don't fragment (DF) bit set and thus triggers the second rule. The second command sends an ICMP packet with Loose Source Record Routing (lsrr) option set, which triggers the first rule. Both of these commands create alert messages. The alert messages are recorded in the database as you can see in different tables. For example, the icmphdr table contains ICMP headers corresponding to these alert messages.

```
mysql> select * from icmphdr;
+-----+-----+-----------+-----------+-----------+---------+-----------+
| sid | cid | icmp_type | icmp_code | icmp_csum | icmp_id | icmp_seq |
+-----+-----+-----------+-----------+-----------+---------+-----------+
|   1 |   1 |         8 |         0 |     18780 |    NULL |      NULL |
|   1 |   2 |         0 |         0 |     20828 |    NULL |      NULL |
|   1 |   3 |         8 |         0 |     18524 |    NULL |      NULL |
+-----+-----+-----------+-----------+-----------+---------+-----------+
3 rows in set (0.00 sec)

mysql>
```

In the output of the select command, different fields of the ICMP header are present, including ICMP type and ICMP code. The signature table contains messages and other options from these messages as shown below:

```
mysql> select * from signature;
+--------+----------------------+--------------+--------------+---------+------
---+
| sig_id | sig_name             | sig_class_id | sig_priority | sig_rev |
sig_sid |
+--------+----------------------+--------------+--------------+---------+------
---+
|      1 | Dont Fragment bit set |            0 |         NULL |    NULL |
NULL |
|      2 | LSRR Options set      |            0 |         NULL |    NULL |
NULL |
+--------+----------------------+--------------+--------------+---------+------
---+
2 rows in set (0.00 sec)

mysql>
```

Note that the sig_name field in the signature table contains the same information as you used in the "msg" part of the two Snort rules defined earlier. You can test other tables as well. When you go to the next chapter and start using ACID, you will find out that you don't need to use the command line mysql client anymore. ACID provides a web interface that can be used to view and manage tables on a web browser.

5.2 Secure Logging to Remote Databases Securely Using Stunnel

The MySQL database server is listening to port number 3306. If your database server is not on the same machine where Snort is running, you have to log messages on a remote database server. From a security point of view, you may want to encrypt traffic between Snort and the database server. Stunnel or Secure Tunnel is an open source package available from http://www.stunnel.org that provides you a secure tunnel between two hosts.

Get the latest version from the web site and install it on both the Snort machine and the database server. You have to run it on both the Snort machine (client) and the database server to establish a tunnel. On the database server, use the following command:

```
stunnel -P/tmp/ -p stunnel.pem -d 3307 -r localhost:3306
```

If the `stunnel` directory is not present in the PATH variable, use the full path name with the command. The command will redirect all incoming connections on port 3307 to port 3306 where MySQL server is listening.

On the Snort machine, use the following command:

```
stunnel -P/tmp/ -c -d 3306 -r SERVER_NAME:3307
```

Replace SERVER_NAME with the name or IP address of the server. This command will redirect all connection on local port 3306 (where MySQL database server is supposed to listen to) to port number 3307 on the remote server.

The net effect is that Stunnel is getting all packets on local port 3306 and forwarding them to port 3306 on the remote host by using port number 3307 in a secure way. Make sure that MySQL server is not running on the hosts where Snort is running because MySQL server may already have occupied port 3306 and Stunnel will not be able to bind to it.

After creating this setup, you can configure Snort so that it assumes that MySQL database server is running on the local machine. In fact, Snort will *think* that MySQL server is running locally but Stunnel will transfer all the communication to the remote database server.

This setup is also very useful when you have many sensors logging to a central database server.

N O T E You can log to a remote MySQL database without using Stunnel. Single or multiple sensors can log to a central database server without the requirement of any secure tunnel. Stunnel just provides security of your data while it goes from sensors to the database server.

5.3 Snort Database Maintenance

From time to time, you need to perform some operations on the database to keep it running efficiently. Table optimization enhances the database efficiency. You can optimize individual tables using the optimize command. The following command optimizes the data table.

```
mysql> optimize table data;
+------------+----------+----------+----------+
| Table      | Op       | Msg_type | Msg_text |
+------------+----------+----------+----------+
| snort.data | optimize | status   | OK       |
+------------+----------+----------+----------+
1 row in set (58.10 sec)

mysql>
```

You can create a script to optimize all tables. For this purpose, save the following commands in a file optimize.sql.

```
optimize table data;
optimize table detail;
optimize table event;
optimize table icmphdr;
optimize table iphdr;
optimize table opt;
```

Use the following command to run this script:

```
mysql -h localhost -u rr -prr78x snort < optimize.sql
```

I have not used all table names in the script. You can use all table names by creating additional lines if you like.

You should set this command as a cron job to run everyday so that the database is optimized every 24 hours.

5.3.1 Archiving the Database

If your database grows very large, you may want to archive it. One method is to back up the database, drop it and recreate a new database. Another way is to back up the existing data into archive tables and then clean these tables. Some scripts are available at http://www.dirk.demon.co.uk/utils/ for this purpose. Please download the scripts from this web site and read the text file that comes with them for more information.

5.3.2   Using Sledge Hammer: Drop the Database

If you really want to create a new database and want to destroy all data in the current database, you can drop it using the following command after connecting to the database using mysql client.

```
drop database snort;
```

You can use the same procedure discussed earlier in this chapter to create a new database. But do it only if you really know what you are doing. You have been warned!

5.4 References

1. Snort database schema at http://www.incident.org/snortdb/
2. MySQL at http://www.mysql.org
3. Stunnel is available from http://www.stunnel.org
4. ODBC FAQ at http://www.ensyncsolutions.com/odbc_faq.htm
5. ODBC project at http://www.odbc.org

Using ACID
and SnortSnarf
with Snort

nalysis Console for Intrusion Databases (ACID) is a tool used to analyze and present Snort data using a web interface. It is written in PHP. It works with Snort and databases like MySQL, as you have learned in the last chapter, and makes information available in the database to the user through a web server. In addition to Snort, the tool can be used with other security-related products like firewalls and networking monitoring.

This chapter provides information about ACID and discusses how to install it with MySQL and Snort to view and analyze the intrusion detection data logged by Snort into the database. You will go through a step-by-step procedure to install ACID and use it. The graphical representation of captured data is very useful for analysis purposes.

In addition to ACID, the chapter also provides basic information about SnortSnarf, another tool that can be used with a web server. SnortSnarf is able to parse Snort log files and generate HTML pages that can be viewed using a web browser. I assume that you are able to install and run Apache web server as well as MySQL database server, which are required in order to use the tools discussed in this chapter.

6.1 What is ACID?

ACID consists of many Pretty Home Page (PHP) scripts and configuration files that work together to collect and analyze information from a database and present it through a web interface. A user will use a web browser to interact with ACID. You have to have a web server, database server, PHP and some other tools installed on your system to make it work. For the sake of this book, I am using a RedHat Linux 7.1 machine. I have installed Apache web server, PHP, and MySQL, which are part of the RedHat distribution. The database is configured to work with Snort as explained in Chapter 5. The latest version of ACID is available from http://www.cert.org/kb/acid/.

ACID offers many features:

1. Searching can be done on a large number of criteria like source and destination addresses, time, ports and so on, as shown in Figure 6-7.
2. Packet viewing is used to view different parts of packet. You can view different header parts as well as the payload. Refer to Figure 6-6 for an example of ICMP packet.
3. Alerts can be managed by creating alert classes, exporting and deleting and sending them to an e-mail address.
4. Graphical representation includes charts based upon time, protocol, IP addresses, port numbers and classifications.
5. Snapshots can be taken of the alerts database. As an example, you can view alerts for the last 24 hours, unique alerts, frequent alerts and so on. Refer to Figure 6-7 for detail on snapshots.
6. You can go to different whois databases on the Internet to find out who owns a particular IP address that is attacking your network. You can then contact the responsible person to stop it. The whois database contains information about owners of domain names and IP addresses.

All of these facilities are available through the web browser. You point the web browser to a URL to access ACID screens. For example, I can use http://www.conformix.com/acid/ on my intranet site to view logs. The web pages are written in PHP. Support packages like GD library and PHPLOT are used to print graphs on the web pages. PHP connects to the backend MySQL database to get and update data. For this purpose, you have to provide the database user name and password.

The big picture of the whole system including Snort, MySQL, Web server, PHP and web browser is shown in Figure 1-1 in Chapter 1. The following is a brief, step-by-step description of what happens when an intruder attempts to get into your network.

- An intruder tries to get into your network.
- A Snort sensor installed in your network detects intruder activity based on its rules. It then uses information in the `snort.conf` file to log data into MySQL database. You have to provide the database user name, password, hostname or IP address of the database server and database name in `snort.conf` file.
- A web server is installed where MySQL server is running.
- A user starts the browser, connects to the web server and starts requesting PHP web pages.
- The PHP engine connects to the database using the database user name, password, and database name and gets information from the database server.
- The web server processes this information and sends back a reply to the web browser, where a user can view intrusion data.
- A user can then perform different operations on this data via the web pages.

The rest of this chapter describes how to install and configure all of these tools to build a web-based user interface.

6.2 Installation and Configuration

Since ACID needs additional packages, like PHPLOT, GD library and so on, to work, you need to make sure that everything is installed properly. Fortunately you can install different components independently from each other in no particular order. The following step-by-step process makes it easy to put everything in place.

- Install and test Snort. You have already done it in Chapter 2.
- Install and test MySQL. Please see Chapter 5 for reference. After installing MySQL, you have to create a database and tables so that Snort can log its activity into the database. After that you have to configure Snort using `snort.conf` file so that it logs its data to the database server.
- Install Apache. I would suggest using the RPM package that is part of RedHat installation media. You can also download the latest version of Apache web server from http://www.apache.org.
- Download ACID from http://www.cert.org/kb/acid/ and uncompress it in `/var/www/html` directory. This process creates a directory named `acid` under `/var/www/html` directory. The Apache package that is part of the RedHat distribution has its HTML files under `/var/www/html` directory. Depending on your distribution, the directory may be different on your

machine. If you download Apache in source code form and compiled it yourself, you can choose a particular directory for this purpose during the compilation process. Just keep in mind that you have to install ACID under the directory where Apache is looking for HTML files.

- Get and Install PHP. You can download it from http://www.php.net or you can use the RPM package that is part of the RedHat distribution. Set `display_errors` variable in `/etc/php.ini` to Off. If you are using a precompiled or RPM version of Apache, PHP may already have been built into it as a module.

- Get and install GD library from http://www.boutell.com/gd/. This is also available on RedHat installation CDs in the RPM form and I would recommend using the RPM file. It is installed as `/usr/lib/libgd.so` file.

- Download PHPLOT from http://www.phplot.com and uncompress it in `/var/www/html` directory. This is used to create graphics in the web pages.

- Download ADODB from http://php.weblogs.com/adodb and install it in `/var/www/html` directory. ADODB is an object oriented library written in PHP and is used to connect to the database. ADODB Frequently Asked Questions (FAQ) are available at http://php.weblogs.com/adodb_faq.

Let us carry out the process of installing these components. At this point I assume that you have:

- Installed MySQL database server as discussed in the last chapter.
- Installed and configured Snort so that it logs data into the Snort database.
- Installed Apache, GD library, and PHP as part of RedHat Linux installation.

Now download and install the software as mentioned below:

- Download ACID file `acid-0.9.6b21.tar.gz` from http://www.cert.org/kb/acid/ and put it in `/opt` directory.
- Download ADODB file `adodb221.tgz` from http://php.weblogs.com/adodb and put it in `/opt` directory.
- Download PHPLOT file `phplot-4.4.6.tar.gz` from http://www.phplot.com and put it in `/opt` directory.
- Move to `/var/www/html` directory.
- Use the command "`tar zxvf /opt/acid-0.9.6b21.tar.gz.`" This will create a directory /var/www/html/acid and put all ACID files under it.

- Use the `cd` command to go to `/var/www/html/acid` directory.
- Use the command "`tar zxvf /opt/adodb221.tgz`" to extract ADODB files. The command will create a directory `/var/www/html/acid/adodb` and put all ADODB files under this directory.
- Use the command "`tar zxvf /opt/phplot-4.4.6.tar.gz`" to extract PHPLOT files. This will create a directory `/var/www/html/acid/phplot-4.4.6` and put all PHPLOT files under this directory.
- Create another database `snort_archive` using "`create database snort_archive;`" command after starting mysql client using the procedure described in Chapter 5. You have already created a database with the name "`snort`" and a user with the name "`rr`" as discussed in Chapter 5. The new `snort_archive` database is used by ACID to archive old data. The new database is not required by Snort to log data. If you don't want to archive old data using ACID, you can skip this step and the next step as well.
- Grant permissions to user `rr` to manage `snort_archive` database using the command "`grant CREATE,INSERT,DELETE,UPDATE,SELECT on snort_archive.* to rr@localhost;`".
- Create tables in this database using the command "`mysql -u rr -p snort_archive <contrib/create_mysql`" as described in Chapter 5.
- Set `display_errors` variable in `/etc/php.ini` to Off.

Now you have to configure ACID so that it can interact with the MySQL database. The configuration process also enables Snort to use the PHPLOT package. The configuration process is simple and includes setting up different parameters in the `acid_conf.php` configuration file which is located in the same directory where you uncompressed the ACID files. For the examples in this book, the file is located in the `/var/www/html/acid` directory. You have to put information about the following items in this file:

- Location of ADODB files. In our case this path is `./adodb`. This is because all ADODB files are located in adodb directory under the directory where `ACID` files are located.
- Type of database server. For the example in this book the type of server is "`mysql`".
- MySQL database name for Snort log data.
- MySQL database server name or IP address.
- MySQL database user name and password.

- Name of the archive database if you are using one.
- Database server name where archive database is located. In our case both snort and snort_archive databases are located on localhost.
- Database user name and password to access snort_archive database.
- Location of PHPLOT files. In our case this is ./phplot-4.4.6. This is because all PHPLOT files are located in phplot-4.4.6 directory under the directory where ACID files are located.

This information is present in the start of the acid_conf.php file. The typical opening lines of this file in my installation are as follows:

```
<?php

$ACID_VERSION = "0.9.6b21";

/* Path to the DB abstraction library
 *   (Note: DO NOT include a trailing backslash after the
 *   directory)
 *   e.g. $foo = "/tmp"        [OK]
 *        $foo = "/tmp/"       [OK]
 *        $foo = "c:\tmp"      [OK]
 *        $foo = "c:\tmp\"     [WRONG]
 */
$DBlib_path = "./adodb";

/* The type of underlying alert database
 *
 *   MySQL          : "mysql"
 *   PostgresSQL : "postgres"
 *   MS SQL Server : "mssql"
 */
$DBtype = "mysql";

/* Alert DB connection parameters
 *   - $alert_dbname   : MySQL database name of Snort
 *                       : alert DB
 *   - $alert_host     : host on which the DB is stored
 *   - $alert_port     : port on which to access the DB
 *   - $alert_user     : login to the database with
 *                       : this user
 *   - $alert_password : password of the DB user
 *
 *   This information can be gleaned from the Snort database
 *   output plugin configuration.
 */
```

```
$alert_dbname   = "snort";
$alert_host     = "localhost";
$alert_port     = "";
$alert_user     = "rr";
$alert_password = "rr78x";

/* Archive DB connection parameters */
$archive_dbname   = "snort_archive";
$archive_host     = "localhost";
$archive_port     = "";
$archive_user     = "rr";
$archive_password = "rr78x";

/* Type of DB connection to use
 *   1  : use a persistant connection (pconnect)
 *   2  : use a normal connection (connect)
 */
$db_connect_method = 1;

/* Path to the graphing library
 *   (Note: DO NOT include a trailing backslash after the
directory)
 */
$ChartLib_path = "./phplot-4.4.6";
```

Note that you have used the same user name, password, and database name as we used in snort.conf file. The following is a description of data located in the acid_conf.php file.

The following line in acid_conf.php file sets up the location of ADODB files:

```
$DBlib_path = "./adodb";
```

The following line in acid_conf.php file sets up the type of database:

```
$DBtype = "mysql";
```

The following lines in acid_conf.php file set up the main Snort database information where Snort logs its data:

```
$alert_dbname   = "snort";
$alert_host     = "localhost";
$alert_port     = "";
$alert_user     = "rr";
$alert_password = "rr78x";
```

The following lines in `acid_conf.php` file set up archive database information where ACID archives data. This part is not necessary for Snort or ACID operation. It is required only if you want to archive data using ACID.

```
$alert_dbname   = "snort_archive";
$alert_host     = "localhost";
$alert_port     = "";
$alert_user     = "rr";
$alert_password = "rr78x";
```

The following line in `acid_conf.php` file sets up the location of PHPLOT files.

```
$ChartLib_path = "./phplot-4.4.6";
```

After going through this practice, make sure that Snort, MySQL server, and Apache server are running. Now you are ready to start using the web interface of ACID.

6.3 Using ACID

If you have installed everything as mentioned above, you should be able to access ACID by going to URL http:/<your_web_server>/acid/. My web server is running on IP address 192.168.1.2, so I can go the URL http://192.168.1.2/acid/.

The first time you go to this URL, ACID needs to do some setup tasks and you will see a web window like the one shown in Figure 6-1.

At this screen, click the Setup page link and you will move to the DB Setup page shown in Figure 6-2.

In Figure 6-2, click the "Create ACID AG" link so that ACID can create its own table to support Snort. ACID creates its own tables in the main Snort database and uses these tables for its own housekeeping data. More discussion about ACID tables is presented later in this chapter. Figure 6-3 shows the result of creating these new tables.

As shown in Figure 6-3, you can click the "Main Page" link towards the bottom of the page to go to the main ACID page. Web pages shown in Figures 6-1, 6-2 and 6-3 will not be displayed the next time you start using ACID.

Figure 6-1 Invoking ACID for the first time.

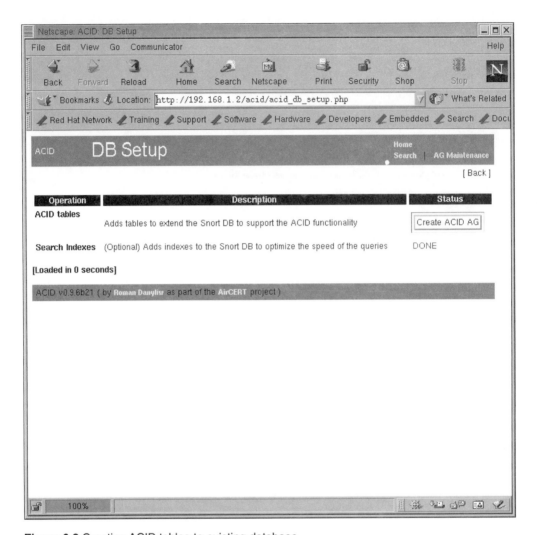

Figure 6-2 Creating ACID tables to existing database.

Figure 6-3 The result of creating additional tables in the Snort database to support ACID.

6.3.1   ACID Main Page

The ACID main page provides an overview of currently available data. It has different sections to display information in groups. You can view traffic profiles by different protocols, get a snapshot of sensors, search data and so on, as shown in Figure 6-4. You are encouraged to explore the different links found on this page.

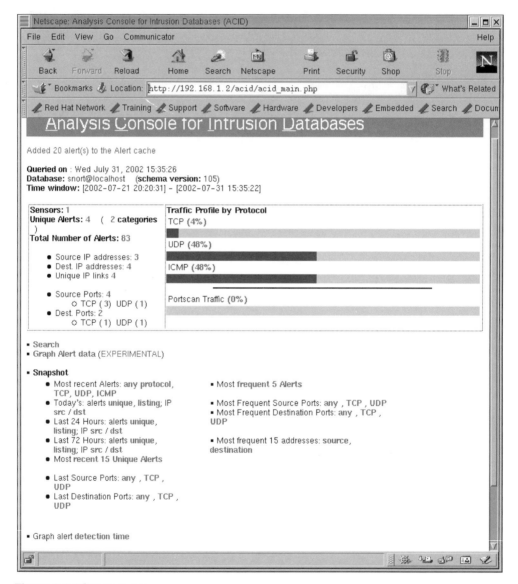

Figure 6-4 ACID main page.

By clicking different links on the web page shown in Figure 6-4, you can view a great deal of information.

- List of sensors that are logging data to the database.
- Number of unique alerts and their detail.
- Total number of alerts and their detail.
- Source IP addresses for the captured data. This shows who is trying to hack into your network. By following the subsequent links, you can also find the owner of the source IP address by looking up whois databases.
- Destination IP addresses for captured data.
- Source and destination ports.
- Alerts related to a particular protocol, like TCP alerts, UDP alerts and ICMP alerts.
- Search alert and log data for particular entries.
- Most frequent alerts.
- Plot alert data, which is still experimental.

In the following screen shots, you will learn a few important things. But this is just an overview of what ACID can do for you. The more time you spend using ACID, the more you will learn about different methods of analyzing Snort data. As you learn new things, you will appreciate how arranging Snort data in different ways makes a lot more sense compared to just looking at log files.

6.3.2 Listing Protocol Data

From the main page, you can click on a protocol to get information about packets logged for that particular protocol. Figure 6-5 shows a screen shot for ICMP protocol. The bottom part of the screen shows the last fifteen individual packets that have been logged into the database. You can click on any one of these lines at the bottom to find out more details about a particular packet.

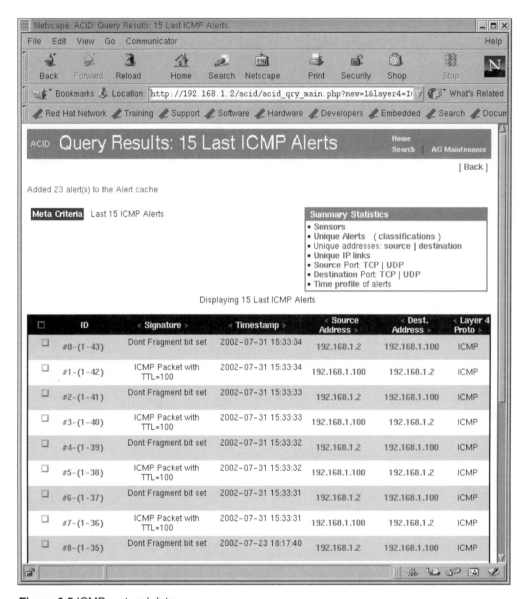

Figure 6-5 ICMP protocol data.

6.3.3   Alert Details

Figure 6-6 shows details about a particular ICMP packet that you would see when you click on an alert as shown in Figure 6-5. As you can see, there are different sections on the page. Each section displays a particular layer of the data packet. The topmost section provides general information about the alert. The IP section displays all parts of the IP header. The ICMP header displays ICMP data, followed by the payload. Payload is displayed both in hexadecimal and ASCII text. Refer to Appendix C for information about different protocol headers.

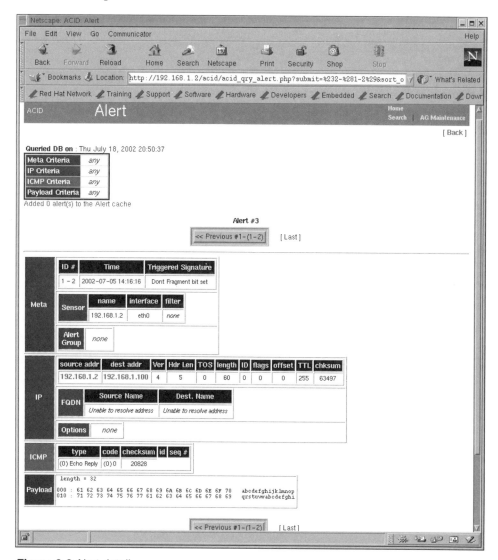

Figure 6-6 Alert detail.

Navigation buttons are provided in this window that can be used to move to next and previous alerts. Different colors are used to indicate different headers of the packet, which makes it very easy to understand visually.

6.3.4 Searching

One important feature of ACID is that it can be used to search the captured log and alert data based on parameters such as:

- A particular sensor when you are using a central database to log data from many Snort sensors.
- Time of alert using start and ending time. This is very useful if you want to look at alerts that occurred within a specific period of time.
- Source and destination addresses.
- Different fields in the IP packet header.
- Transport layer protocols.
- String of data in the payload area of the IP packet.

If you look at the screen shot shown in Figure 6-7, you can see that searching for data in the database is very easy. All the criteria that you specify in this screen are translated to a SQL statement that is passed to the MySQL database server. Results of your query are displayed when you click the "Query DB" button.

For example, if you want to search all alerts for which the signature field contains the string "ATTACK RESPONSE", you can fill out information as shown in Figure 6-8.

The result of this search is shown in Figure 6-9, where all alerts containing this string are displayed. You can click a particular alert line to find out more information about that alert.

I would strongly recommend spending some time with the search methods of ACID to get acquainted to it.

Snort can also be used to find fully qualified names for source and destination addresses found in captured data. Figure 6-10 shows unique destination IP addresses and hostnames. For the sake of this screen shot and to create some data in the database, I had to use a rule that creates an alert for all outgoing HTTP requests. Of course it is not intrusion activity, but it does provide some data in the Snort database.

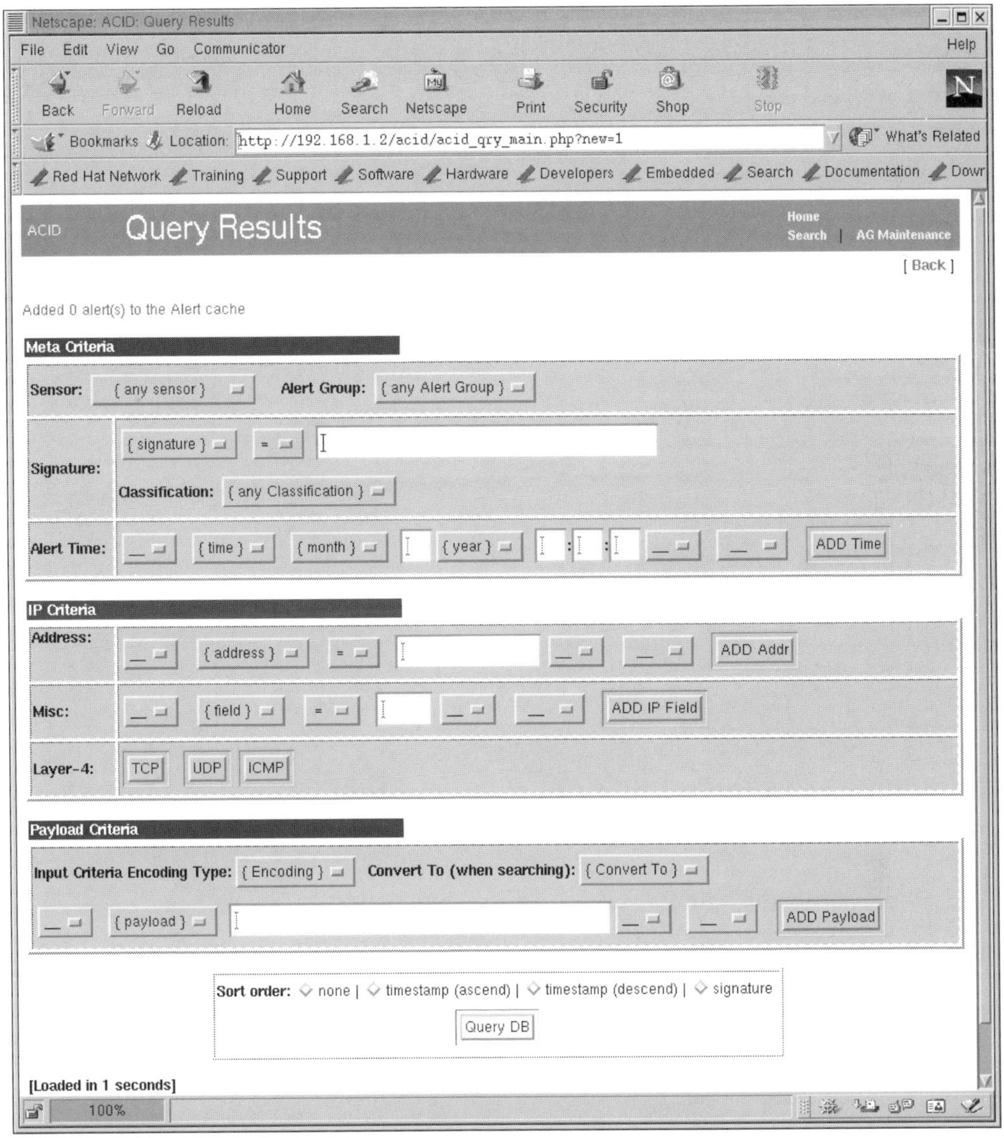

Figure 6-7 Searching database using ACID.

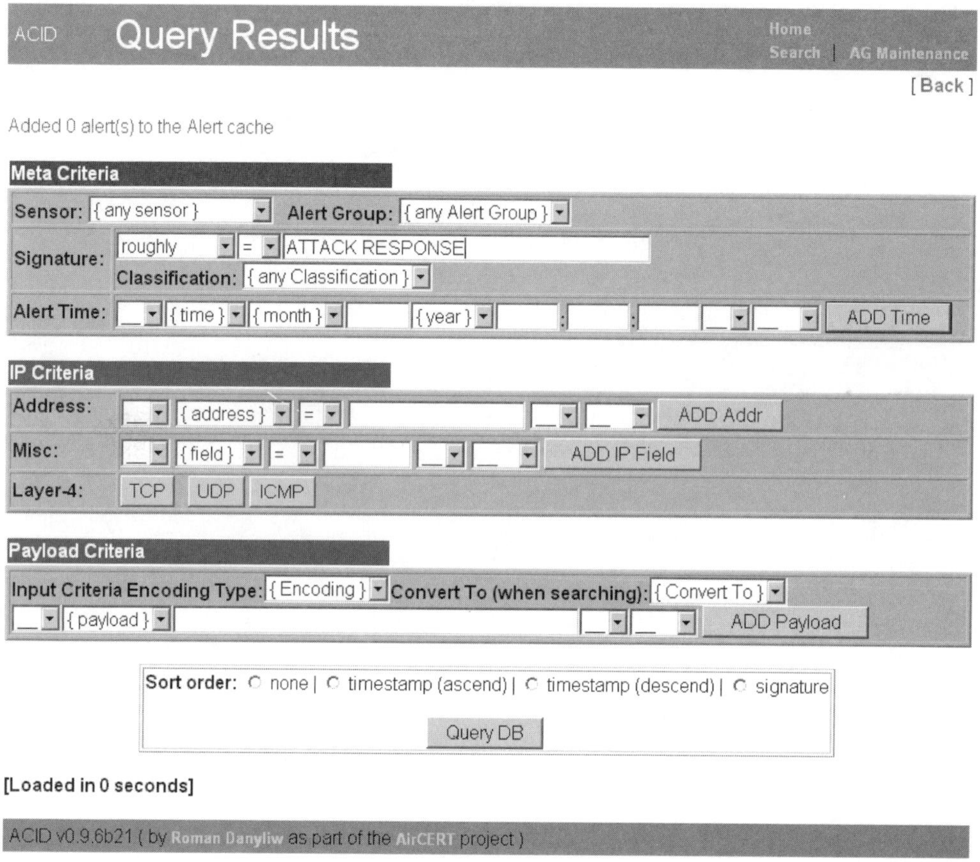

Figure 6-8 Searching for all alerts that contain "ATTACK RESPONSE" string in the signature.

Displaying alerts 1-6 of 6 total

☐	ID	< Signature >	< Timestamp >	< Source Address >	< Dest. Address >	< Layer 4 Proto >
☐	#0-(1-607)	ATTACK RESPONSES id check returned root	2002-12-24 20:10:02	192.168.1.2	255.255.255.255	ICMP
☐	#1-(1-608)	ATTACK RESPONSES id check returned root	2002-12-24 20:10:02	255.255.255.255	192.168.1.2	ICMP
☐	#2-(1-609)	ATTACK RESPONSES id check returned root	2002-12-24 20:10:03	192.168.1.2	255.255.255.255	ICMP
☐	#3-(1-610)	ATTACK RESPONSES id check returned root	2002-12-24 20:10:03	255.255.255.255	192.168.1.2	ICMP
☐	#4-(1-611)	ATTACK RESPONSES id check returned root	2002-12-24 20:10:03	192.168.1.2	255.255.255.255	ICMP
☐	#5-(1-612)	ATTACK RESPONSES id check returned root	2002-12-24 20:10:03	255.255.255.255	192.168.1.2	ICMP

Action			
{action} ▼	Selected	ALL on Screen	Entire Query

[Loaded in 0 seconds]

ACID v0.9.6b21 (by Roman Danyliw as part of the AirCERT project)

Figure 6-9 Result of query used in Figure 6-8.

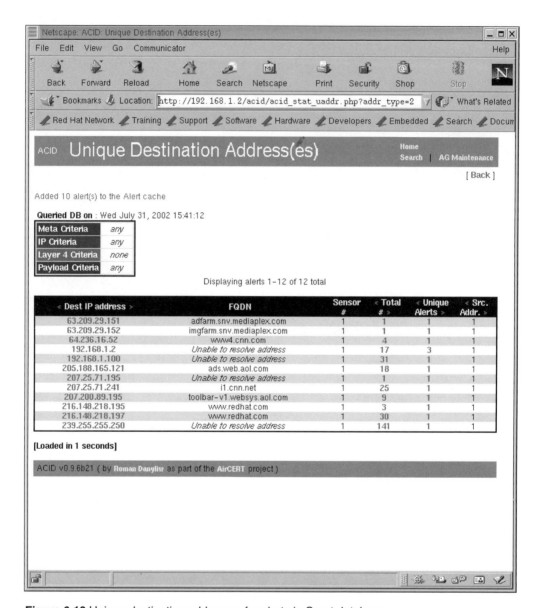

Figure 6-10 Unique destination addresses for alerts in Snort database.

6.3.5   Searching whois Databases

To get whois information about a particular address, you can click on any address and select a particular whois database, like American Registry for Internet Numbers (ARIN) at http://www.arin.net. The response to such a query for IP address 66.236.16.52 is shown in Figure 6-11.

This information is very important for incident response. This is usually the first step to finding out the owner of the attacking IP address and his/her contact number. After finding this information, you can contact the owner to stop bad guys from probing your network.

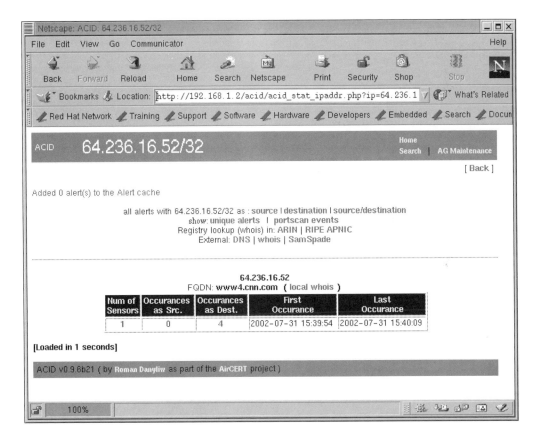

Figure 6-11 Response to whois query.

6.3.6   Generating Graphs

Generating graphs is still experimental in ACID at the time of writing this book. I have included it for the sake of introducing this interesting feature. You can go to the ACID main page where a link is provided to generate graphs. When generating graphs, you can select data and type of graph. For example, you can generate a line or bar graph for alerts in the last five days. Figure 6-12 shows a sample bar graph for the alert data.

ACID uses the PHPLOT package on the backend side to generate these graphs. You can also use another package, JPGRAPH in place of PHPLOT. JPGRAPH has a different licensing scheme and there may be some restrictions for using it in commercial environment.

N O T E   The functionality described in this section is just an overview of ACID capabilities. In addition to the tasks presented here, you can also use ACID to archive data, delete data from the database and so on.

6.3.7   Archiving Snort Data

You have created a new database called `snort_archive` in the previous sections to archive the data from the main Snort database. Using ACID, you can either move alerts from the main database to the archive database or just copy them. For example, if you want to move all alerts from the main database to the archive database, click the number next to "Total Number of Alerts" on the main ACID page. The next page displays all of the alerts in the database. If the number of alerts is more than 50, then only the first 50 alerts are displayed. Now you can use the bottom part of the screen to archive the alerts as shown in Figure 6-13. Note that only the bottom part of the browser window is shown in this figure.

If you click the "Entire Query" button in Figure 6-13, all alerts will be moved to the archive database. The result of this action is shown in Figure 6-14.

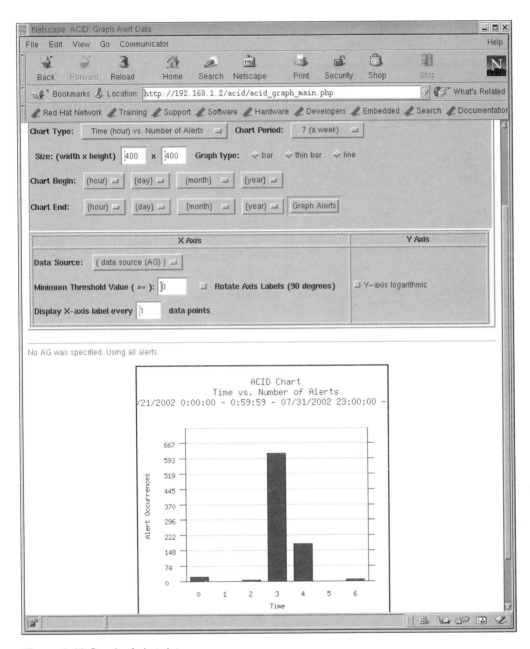

Figure 6-12 Graph of alert data.

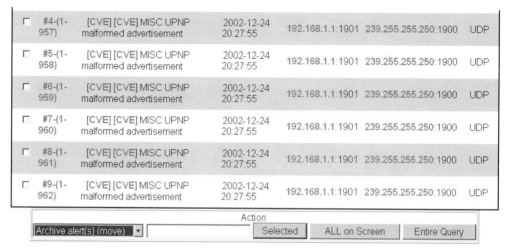

[Loaded in 31 seconds]

ACID v0.9.6b21 (by Roman Danyliw as part of the AirCERT project)

Figure 6-13 Moving alerts to the archive database.

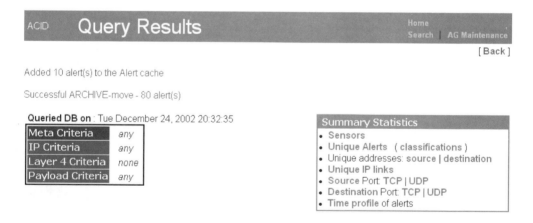

Figure 6-14 Result of moving alert data to archive database.

6.3.8 ACID Tables

When you start using ACID for the first time, it creates its own tables in the Snort database. These tables are used for housekeeping functions of ACID. For example, you can create new alert groups called (AG) in ACID and ACID keeps a record in its own tables. This section shows a list of MySQL database tables before and after configuring ACID. The following is a list of tables as they appear before using ACID for the first time.

```
mysql> show tables;
+------------------+
| Tables_in_snort  |
+------------------+
| data             |
| detail           |
| encoding         |
| event            |
| flags            |
| icmphdr          |
| iphdr            |
| opt              |
| protocols        |
| reference        |
| reference_system |
| schema           |
| sensor           |
| services         |
| sig_class        |
| sig_reference    |
| signature        |
| tcphdr           |
| udphdr           |
+------------------+
19 rows in set (0.01 sec)

mysql>
```

The following is a list of tables after the creation of ACID tables in the database. The user name that was used for ACID must have permission to create new tables. Refer to Chapter 5 for information about granting permissions.

```
mysql> show tables;
+-------------------+
| Tables_in_snort   |
+-------------------+
| acid_ag           |
| acid_ag_alert     |
| acid_event        |
| acid_ip_cache     |
| data              |
| detail            |
| encoding          |
| event             |
| flags             |
| icmphdr           |
| iphdr             |
| opt               |
| protocols         |
| reference         |
| reference_system  |
| schema            |
| sensor            |
| services          |
| sig_class         |
| sig_reference     |
| signature         |
| tcphdr            |
| udphdr            |
+-------------------+
23 rows in set (0.00 sec)

mysql>
```

The first four tables in the list show the newly created ACID tables.

6.4 SnortSnarf

SnortSnarf is another tool to display Snort data using a web interface. It is available from its web site at http://www.silicondefense.com/software/snortsnarf/index.htm. Basically it is a Perl script and you can run it after downloading without going through any compilation process. It can parse Snort log files as well as extract data from MySQL database. The following command parses /var/log/snort/alert file and places the newly generated HTML files in the /var/www/html/snortsnarf directory where they can be viewed later using a web browser.

```
snortsnarf.pl /var/log/snort/alert -d /var/www/html/snortsnarf
```

The following command extracts data from MySQL database running on the `localhost`. It uses a user name `rr` and password `rr78x` to login to the database.

```
snortsnarf.pl rr:rr78x@snort@localhost -d /var/www/html/snortsnarf
```

To get data from a database, you have to define the following parameters on the command line:

- Database user name
- Password
- Database name
- Host where database server is running
- Port number for the database server. By default the port number is 3306 and this parameter is optional.

The general format of defining these parameters is:

```
user:passwd@dbname@host:port
```

You can run SnortSnarf from a cron script on a periodic basis. Figure 6-15 shows the main page created by SnortSnarf. It provides basic information about alert data.

Figure 6-16 shows the information about a particular alert that is displayed when you click a link as shown in Figure 6-15.

Figure 6-17 shows a screen shot for searching whois databases or DNS lookup when you need to get more information about an IP address.

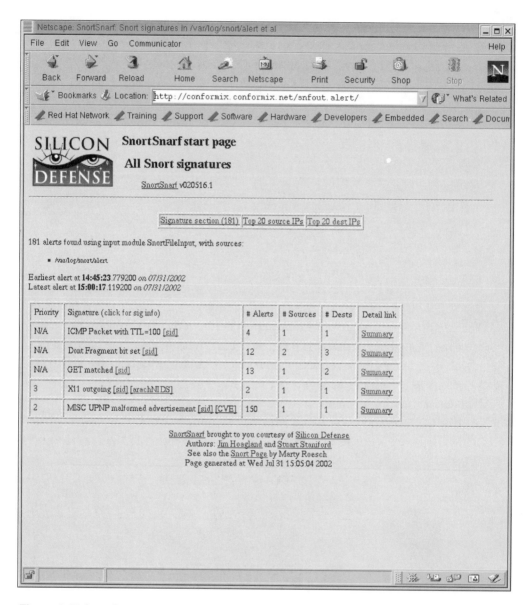

Figure 6-15 SnortSnarf main page.

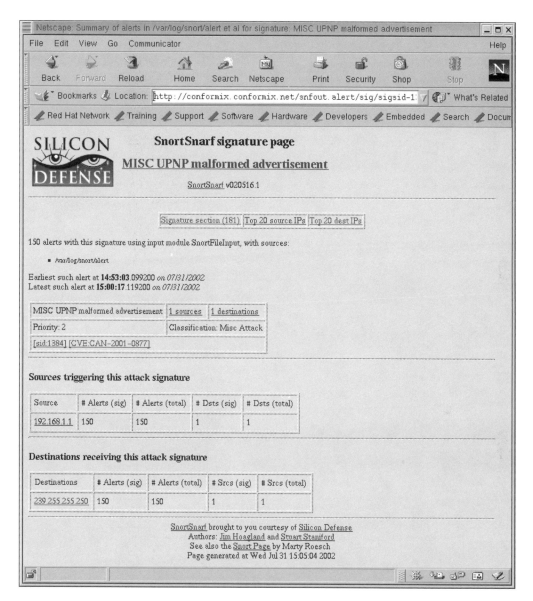

Figure 6-16 Detail of a particular alert in SnortSnarf.

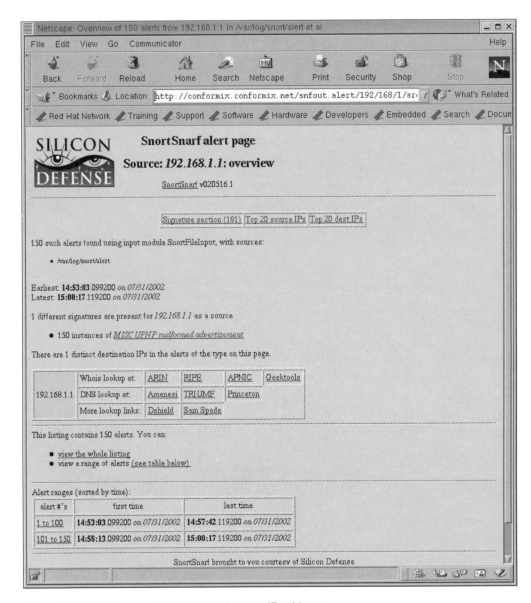

Figure 6-17 Getting more information about an IP address.

6.5 Barnyard

Barnyard is a new tool which is intended to parse binary log files generated by Snort when you use the unified logging module. Barnyard is still in experimental form at the time of writing this book. You can download the latest version from the Snort web site and read the included file about installation and use of the tool. Basically you have to carry out the following three steps to compile and install it.

1. Run the configure script with a prefix command line parameter to define the directory where you intend to install it. A typical command line may be "`con-figure --prefix=/opt/barnyard`".
2. Run the `make` command.
3. Run the `make install` command to install it.

You also need to edit the `barnyard.conf` file before using the tool. I am omitting a detailed discussion because the process may change significantly by the time you read this book.

W A R N I N G At the time of writing this book, Barnyard is still in the development process and the installation may differ significantly in the final release of the package.

6.6 References

1. ACID is available from http://www.cert.org/kb/acid/
2. Apache web site at http://www.apache.org
3. PHP web site at http://www.php.net
4. GD library at http://www.boutell.com/gd/
5. PHPLOT package at http://www.phplot.com
6. ADODB package at http://php.weblogs.com/adodb
7. SnortSnarf at http://www.silicondefense.com/software/snortsnarf/index.htm
8. ADODB FAQ at http://php.weblogs.com/adodb_faq

## CHAPTER 7

Miscellaneous Tools

At this point you have built your completely working Snort system with database backend and web-based user interface. This chapter introduces a few useful tools that you can use with this system to make management simple and to enhance the capabilities of your system. You will also learn how to make your system secure. These components are briefly introduced below.

IDS Manager is a Microsoft Windows-based GUI tool to manage Snort rules and the Snort configuration file `snort.conf`. Using this tool, you can carry out different tasks like:

- Downloading the current configuration file `snort.conf` and rules from an operational Snort sensor.
- Modifying the configuration file and rules.
- Uploading the modified configuration to the sensor.

Using IDS Manager, you can manage multiple Snort sensors. The only catch is that it uses SSH server, which must be running on the Snort sensor.

SnortSam is another tool that can integrate Snort with firewalls. Using this package with Snort, you can modify firewall configuration. The usefulness of this technique is still debatable as it may open up the firewall for denial of service (DoS) attacks.

Another topic discussed in this chapter is the security of the web server where ACID is installed. Up to now you have not done anything to secure the web server. Anybody can access the ACID console and delete the data collected by Snort. Here you will learn a few methods of securing the web server itself.

7.1 SnortSam

SnortSam is a tool used to make Snort work with most commonly used firewalls. It is used to create a Firewall/IDS combined solution. You can configure your firewall automatically to block offending data and addresses from entering your system when intruder activity is detected. It is available from http://www.snortsam.net/ where you can find the latest information. The tool consists of two parts:

1. A Snort output plug-in that is installed on the Snort sensor.
2. An agent that is installed on a machine close to Firewall or Firewall itself. Snort communicates to the agent using the output plug-in in a secure way.

At the time of writing this book, the tools support the following firewalls:

• IP filter-based firewalls
• Checkpoint Firewall-1
• Cisco PIX
• Netscreen

The output plug-in, which is compiled with Snort, provides new keywords that can be used to control firewall behavior. For compiling Snort, refer to Chapter 2.

In a typical scheme where you are using Checkpoint Firewall, you can run the SnortSam agent on the firewall itself. Figure 7-1 shows a typical scheme where a Snort sensor is controlling two Checkpoint firewalls. These firewalls may be running on Linux, Windows or other UNIX platforms supported by Checkpoint.

In a typical situation where you don't have a Checkpoint firewall, you will run the agent on another system, located close to the firewall. Depending on the type of your firewall, you will add plug-ins to the SnortSam agent to control a particular type of firewall. For example, to control a Cisco router access list, you will use the relevant plug-in available from the SnortSam web site. The scheme is shown in Figure 7-2 where the sensor sends messages to the agent system where the SnortSam agent is running. The

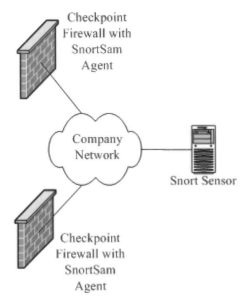

Figure 7-1 Running SnortSam on Checkpoint Firewall.

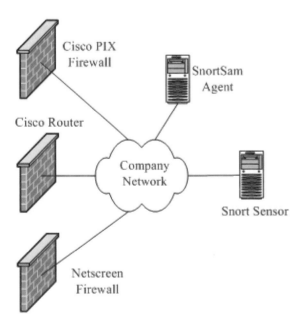

Figure 7-2 Running SnortSam with a separate agent to control multiple firewalls.

agent system will then update configuration of the firewall or routers depending on the policy.

Documentation, examples, and information about how to install SnortSam are available on its web site. You can find information about the changes you need to make for a particular type of firewall in the `snort.conf` file. You should think twice about modifying firewall policy; it may lead to Denial of Service (DoS) attacks. For example, if someone sends you a message resulting in the blocking of root name server addresses, your DNS server will fail.

7.2 IDS Policy Manager

IDS policy manager is a Microsoft Windows based GUI. It is used to manage the Snort configuration file and Snort rules on a sensor. It is available from its web site http://activeworx.com/idspm/. At the time of writing this book, beta version 1.3 is available from this web site and it supports Snort versions up to 1.9.0. You can download the software and install it using normal Windows installation procedures. When you start the software, a window like the one shown in Figure 7-3 is displayed.

As you can see, this window is initially empty. It has three tabs at the bottom, as explained below:

- The "Sensor Manager" tab shows the sensors that you are managing with this tool. Initially there is no sensor listed in the window because you have to add sensors after installing IDS Manager. This is the default tab when you start the Policy Manager.
- The "Policy Manager" tab shows configured policies. A policy includes `snort.conf` file parameters (variables, input and output plug-ins, include files) as well as a list of rules that belong to that policy.
- The "Logging" tab shows log messages.

You can click on any of these tabs to switch to a particular window. To add a new sensor, you can click on the "Sensor" menu and chose the "Add Sensor" option. A pop-up window like the one shown in Figure 7-4 appears where you fill out information about the sensor.

Figure 7-3 IDS Policy Manager Window.

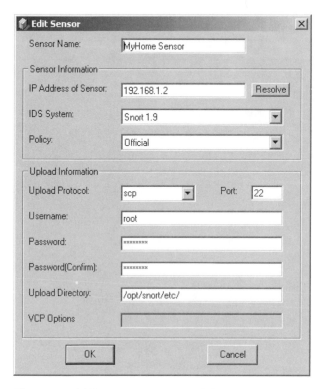

Figure 7-4 Adding a new sensor to IDS Policy Manager.

The screen shot shown in Figure 7-4 is taken after filling out information in blank fields. You have to enter the following information about a sensor:

- Sensor name, which is "MyHome Sensor" in this example.
- IP address of sensor which is 192.168.1.2. You have to fill out the IP address of your sensor in this box.
- The "IDS System" box is used to specify which version of Snort is being used on the sensor. Different Snort versions have slightly different parameters for input and output plug-ins as well as keywords used in rules. It's important to use correct information in this option.
- The policy name is "Official". You can use a different name for the policy. The sensor policy is downloaded and stored on the machine where IDS Policy Manager is being installed.
- The "Upload Information" section includes parameters that are needed to transfer files from and to the sensor.

- The SCP method uses SSH server running on the sensor. User name and password are used to log in to the Snort sensor to upload and download files. The "Upload Directory" shows the location of the `snort.conf` file on the Snort sensor. Since the location of other rule files is mentioned in the `snort.conf` file, you don't need to specify names and locations of other rule files.

After entering this information, you can click "OK" to add the sensor. After adding the sensor, the first task is to download policy from the sensor you added in the previous step. For this purpose, you can use the "Download Policy from Sensor" option in the "Sensor" menu. After downloading the policy, you can click on the "Policy Manager" tab at the bottom of the screen to edit the policy. When you click here, you will see the screen with a list of currently available policies. Since you used "Official" as the name of the policy while adding the sensor, this policy must be present in the list.

To edit the policy, double click the policy name and a Policy Editor window will appear, as shown in Figure 7-5.

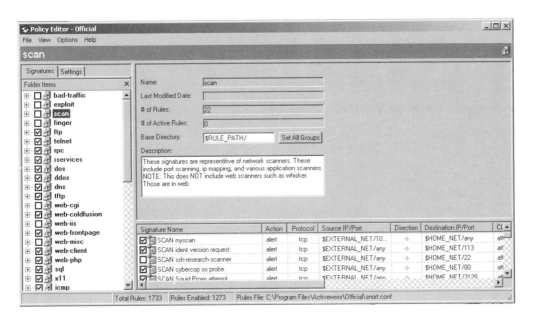

Figure 7-5 The Policy Editor window with list of rules.

On the left hand side of the window shown in Figure 7-5 is a list of different classes of rules used on the sensor. The right hand side of the window shows a description of the class and individual rules included in that class. To modify a rule, you can double click that rule and a window like the one shown in Figure 7-6 will appear where you can modify different parts of a rule.

The pull-down menus in the right side of the window shown in Figure 7-6 make it very easy to modify rules. For example, to modify protocol used in the rule, you can click the pull-down menu button and a list of supported protocols will appear.

To modify other parts of the `snort.conf` file, you can click the "Settings" tab on the top left side of the window. A window like the one shown in Figure 7-7 appears where you can modify input and output plug-ins and values of different variables.

As you can see in the screen shot in Figure 7-7, the database user name and passwords are displayed. These are the same ones we used in Chapter 5 while configuring the MySQL database.

After making changes to the policy, you can close this window. Now you can upload it to the sensor using options in the "Sensor" menu of the main menu.

IDS Policy Manager makes it very easy to modify sensor policies. It does almost all of the tasks that are discussed in Chapter 3 and Chapter 4.

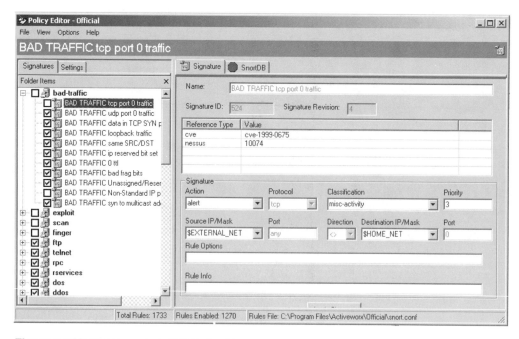

Figure 7-6 Modifying a rule in IDS Policy Manager.

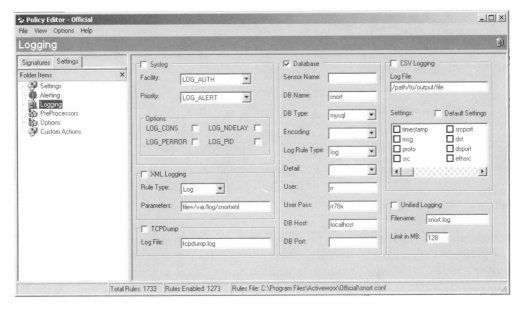

Figure 7-7 The Policy Editor window with `snort.conf` settings.

7.3 Securing the ACID Web Console

As you have seen in Chapter 6, ACID is a very useful tool for viewing and managing data generated by the Snort sensors. However, there is one issue that is not yet resolved—security of ACID. If the web server running ACID is not secure, anybody can go to the ACID web pages and modify, archive, and delete data in the database using ACID. As you have seen, the user name and password are hard coded in the ACID configuration file `acid_conf.php` and the person viewing ACID web pages does not need to know the database user name and password to delete information from the database. There are multiple methods that you can adopt to achieve security.

7.3.1 Using a Private Network

There are different ways to make ACID secure. One way is to use a private network for all Snort sensors and the centralized database server where ACID and Apache are installed so that their IP addresses are not visible from the Internet. This scheme is still vulnerable to the internal users who have access to this private network.

7.3.2 Blocking Access to the Web Server on the Firewall

Another method is to block access to your web server from the firewall so that nobody from the Internet can access the web server. Again this scheme is still vulnerable to internal users.

7.3.3 Using iptables

Another way is to use `iptables` to allow only your own computer to access port 80 on the web server. This is the most secure method because it protects your web server and ACID from both internal and external users. You can use a simple command to block all incoming connections except your own workstation, which has an IP address 192.168.1.100.

```
iptables -A INPUT -s ! 192.168.1.100 -j DROP
```

The command is case sensitive. This command blocks all connections except ones from host 192.168.1.100, which is your own workstation where you use the web browser. This is not a comprehensive tutorial on how to use the `iptables` command. You can either use the "`man iptables`" command to get more information about iptables-based firewalls or read Rusty's guide for iptables at http://www.netfilter.org/unreliable-guides/packet-filtering-HOWTO/index.html.

Once you use the above command, nobody from any other host will be able to access ANY service on the machine where you used this command. All existing connections will be dropped. You are warned!

7.4 Easy IDS

Easy IDS is an integrated system available from http://www.argusnetsec.com for the Linux operating system. It has all of the necessary components to build a complete IDS quickly. These components are precompiled and configured for easy installation. The package includes:

- Snort
- Apache Web server
- MySQL server
- ACID
- PHPLOT
- ADODB

The installation script installs all of these components and creates startup and shutdown script links. This is a good choice for people who want to get something running quickly. At the time of writing this book, you have to ask for an evaluation CD from the company to test it. It may be available for free download from the company web site in the future.

7.5 References

1. SnortSam at http://www.snortsam.net/
2. Activeworx web site at http://activeworx.com/idspm/
3. Rusty's Unreliable Guides at http://www.netfilter.org/unreliable-guides/
4. Easy IDS at http://www.argusnetsec.com

Introduction to tcpdump

Tcpdump is a packet capture tool. It can grab packets flowing on the network, match them to some criteria and then dump them on the screen or into a file. It is available on most of the UNIX platforms. On Linux machines, you need to be the root user to run tcpdump. If you save the captured data in a file, you can view the file later using tcpdump. Since Snort can also store data in the tcpdump format in files, it becomes an interesting tool for many people to view Snort files that have been created in the tcpdump format.

The typical output of the command when used on the command prompt without any argument is as follows:

```
[root@conformix]# tcpdump
Kernel filter, protocol ALL, TURBO mode (575 frames), datagram packet
  socket
tcpdump: listening on all devices
13:05:52.216049 eth0 < rr-laptop.6001 > dti414.1245: P
  1578894642:1578894674(32) ack 3347166818 win 63520
  <nop,nop,timestamp 453029 53292014> (DF)
13:05:52.216049 eth0 > dti414.1245 > rr-laptop.6001: . 1:1449(1448) ack
  32 win 63712 <nop,nop,timestamp 53292021 453029> (DF)
13:05:52.216049 eth0 > dti414.1245 > rr-laptop.6001: P 1449:2045(596)
  ack 32 win 63712 <nop,nop,timestamp 53292021 453029> (DF)
13:05:52.216049 eth0 < rr-laptop.6001 > dti414.1245: . 32:32(0) ack
  2045 win 64240 <nop,nop,timestamp 453029 53292021> (DF)
```

```
13:05:52.226049 eth0 > dti414.1245 > rr-laptop.6001: . 2045:3493(1448)
   ack 32 win 63712 <nop,nop,timestamp 53292022 453029> (DF)
13:05:52.226049 eth0 > dti414.1245 > rr-laptop.6001: P 3493:4089(596)
   ack 32 win 63712 <nop,nop,timestamp 53292022 453029> (DF)
13:05:52.226049 eth0 < rr-laptop.6001 > dti414.1245: . 32:32(0) ack
   4089 win 64240 <nop,nop,timestamp 453029 53292022> (DF)
```

You can use a number of command line switches with the command. A list of switches is available on the manual pages. The important switch to use with Snort is -r <filename>, where filename is the file containing Snort data. Simple Snort log files can't be used with this option. Only the files that are created in the tcpdump format can be read by the command.

Getting Started with MySQL

MySQL is probably the most popular open source database. It is available for Linux and you can download and install it on your Linux machine. The package is available in source code format as well as binary files. The easiest way to install it is to download the RPM file and install it on your Linux machine. I have used RedHat Linux 7.1 on my machine and installed the MySQL package that came with it.

MySQL has two basic parts, the server and the utilities used to administer the server and connect to it. If you install the RPM package, the startup script will be copied into the `/etc/init.d` directory which you use to start the database at boot time. Client utilities are available to manage the database.

MySQL is an easy database to use. This appendix contains some very basic commands that you can use to get started with the database. This is not a MySQL manual or tutorial by any means. Comprehensive information about MySQL can be obtained from http://www.mysql.com/doc/ web site.

For New Users of MySQL

The MySQL server daemon, `mysqld`, can be started using the startup script. It listens to incoming connection requests from clients. The package comes with `mysql` client program that you can use to connect to the database and carry out some system administration tasks as well as add/update/delete records in the database. You can have multiple databases and at the time of connection you can define to which database you want to connect.

Starting and Stopping MySQL Server

You can start and stop MySQL Server using startup script `/etc/init.d/` `mysqld` on Linux machines. This script is shown below:

```
#!/bin/bash
#
# mysqld This shell script takes care of starting
# and stopping
#        the MySQL subsystem (mysqld).
#
# chkconfig: - 78 12
# description:MySQL database server.
# processname: mysqld
# config: /etc/my.cnf
# pidfile: /var/run/mysqld/mysqld.pid

# Source function library.
. /etc/rc.d/init.d/functions

# Source networking configuration.
. /etc/sysconfig/network

# Source subsystem configuration.
[ -f /etc/sysconfig/subsys/mysqld ] && . /etc/sysconfig/subsys/mysqld


prog="MySQL"

start(){
    touch /var/log/mysqld.log
    chown mysql.mysql /var/log/mysqld.log
    chmod 0640 /var/log/mysqld.log
    if [ ! -d /var/lib/mysql/mysql ] ; then
        action $"Initializing MySQL database: " /usr/bin/
  mysql_install_db
        ret=$?
```

```
            chown -R mysql.mysql /var/lib/mysql
            if [ $ret -ne 0 ] ; then
             return $ret
            fi
       fi
       chown mysql.mysql /var/lib/mysql
       chmod 0755 /var/lib/mysql
       /usr/bin/safe_mysqld  --defaults-file=/etc/my.cnf >/dev/null 2>&1
   &
       ret=$?
       if [ $ret -eq 0 ]; then
           action $"Starting $prog: " /bin/true
       else
               action $"Starting $prog: " /bin/false
       fi
       [ $ret -eq 0 ] && touch /var/lock/subsys/mysqld
       return $ret
}

stop(){
         /bin/kill `cat /var/run/mysqld/mysqld.pid  2> /dev/null ` > /
   dev/null 2>&1
       ret=$?
       if [ $ret -eq 0 ]; then
           action $"Stopping $prog: " /bin/true
       else
               action $"Stopping $prog: " /bin/false
       fi
       [ $ret -eq 0 ] && rm -f /var/lock/subsys/mysqld
       [ $ret -eq 0 ] && rm -f /var/lib/mysql/mysql.sock
       return $ret
}
restart(){
    stop
    start
}

condrestart(){
    [ -e /var/lock/subsys/mysqld ] && restart || :
}

reload(){
    [ -e /var/lock/subsys/mysqld ] && mysqladmin reload
}

# See how we were called.
case "$1" in
```

```
  start)
    start
    ;;
  stop)
    stop
    ;;
  status)
    status mysqld
    ;;
  reload)
    reload
    ;;
  restart)
    restart
    ;;
  condrestart)
    condrestart
    ;;
  *)
    echo $"Usage: $0 {start|stop|status|reload|condrestart|restart}"
    exit 1
esac

exit $?
```

To start the server, use the following commands:

```
/etc/init.d/mysqld start
```

When you start MySQL for the first time, you will see the following messages on your screen:

```
[root@conformix /root]# /etc/init.d/mysqld start
Initializing MySQL database:                        [  OK  ]
Starting MySQL:                                      [  OK  ]
[root@conformix /root]#
```

The next time you start MySQL, it will not show the first line of output because it only needs to initialize its own database the first time you start it.

To stop the database, use the following command:

```
[root@conformix /root]# /etc/init.d/mysqld stop
Stopping MySQL:                                      [  OK  ]
[root@conformix /root]#
```

If the script is not available on your platform, you can create a similar script yourself for your particular UNIX platform.

MySQL Server Configuration File

At startup time, the server uses its configuration file /etc/my.cnf as mentioned in this startup script. The default configuration file that came with my distribution of Linux 7.1 is shown below:

```
[mysqld]
datadir=/var/lib/mysql
socket=/var/lib/mysql/mysql.sock

[mysql.server]
user=mysql
basedir=/var/lib

[safe_mysqld]
err-log=/var/log/mysqld.log
pid-file=/var/run/mysqld/mysqld.pid
```

Database Storage Files

Each database is stored in a directory under /var/lib/mysql top level directory (configurable through my.cnf file). For example, if you use "snort" as the database name, all files in this database will be located in the directory /var/lib/mysql/snort. You have used a script to create tables in this database in Chapter 5. The typical contents of this directory after creating all tables is as follows:

```
[root@laptop]# ls -l /var/lib/mysql/snort
total 4080
-rw-rw----    1 mysql     mysql          8614 Apr 30 14:30
data.frm
-rw-rw----    1 mysql     mysql             0 Apr 30 14:30
data.MYD
-rw-rw----    1 mysql     mysql          1024 Apr 30 14:30
data.MYI
-rw-rw----    1 mysql     mysql          8606 Apr 30 14:30
detail.frm
-rw-rw----    1 mysql     mysql            40 Apr 30 14:30
detail.MYD
-rw-rw----    1 mysql     mysql          2048 Apr 30 14:30
detail.MYI
-rw-rw----    1 mysql     mysql          8614 Apr 30 14:30
encoding.frm
-rw-rw----    1 mysql     mysql            60 Apr 30 14:30
encoding.MYD
-rw-rw----    1 mysql     mysql          2048 Apr 30 14:30
encoding.MYI
```

```
-rw-rw----    1 mysql    mysql         8642 Apr 30 14:30
event.frm
-rw-rw----    1 mysql    mysql            0 Apr 30 14:30
event.MYD
-rw-rw----    1 mysql    mysql         1024 Apr 30 14:30
event.MYI
-rw-rw----    1 mysql    mysql         8802 Apr 30 14:39
flags.frm
-rw-rw----    1 mysql    mysql        17476 Apr 30 14:39
flags.MYD
-rw-rw----    1 mysql    mysql         1024 Apr 30 14:39
flags.MYI
-rw-rw----    1 mysql    mysql         8738 Apr 30 14:30
icmphdr.frm
-rw-rw----    1 mysql    mysql            0 Apr 30 14:30
icmphdr.MYD
-rw-rw----    1 mysql    mysql         1024 Apr 30 14:30
icmphdr.MYI
-rw-rw----    1 mysql    mysql         8920 Apr 30 14:30
iphdr.frm
-rw-rw----    1 mysql    mysql            0 Apr 30 14:30
iphdr.MYD
-rw-rw----    1 mysql    mysql         1024 Apr 30 14:30
iphdr.MYI
-rw-rw----    1 mysql    mysql         8728 Apr 30 14:30
opt.frm
-rw-rw----    1 mysql    mysql            0 Apr 30 14:30
opt.MYD
-rw-rw----    1 mysql    mysql         1024 Apr 30 14:30
opt.MYI
-rw-rw----    1 mysql    mysql         8624 Apr 30 14:39
protocols.frm
-rw-rw----    1 mysql    mysql         6248 Apr 30 14:39
protocols.MYD
-rw-rw----    1 mysql    mysql         1024 Apr 30 14:39
protocols.MYI
-rw-rw----    1 mysql    mysql         8630 Apr 30 14:30
reference.frm
-rw-rw----    1 mysql    mysql            0 Apr 30 14:30
reference.MYD
-rw-rw----    1 mysql    mysql         1024 Apr 30 14:30
reference.MYI
-rw-rw----    1 mysql    mysql         8618 Apr 30 14:30
reference_system.frm
-rw-rw----    1 mysql    mysql            0 Apr 30 14:30
reference_system.MYD
```

```
-rw-rw----    1 mysql    mysql        1024 Apr 30 14:30
reference_system.MYI
-rw-rw----    1 mysql    mysql        8580 Apr 30 14:30
schema.frm
-rw-rw----    1 mysql    mysql          13 Apr 30 14:30
schema.MYD
-rw-rw----    1 mysql    mysql        2048 Apr 30 14:30
schema.MYI
-rw-rw----    1 mysql    mysql        8706 Apr 30 14:30
sensor.frm
-rw-rw----    1 mysql    mysql           0 Apr 30 14:30
sensor.MYD
-rw-rw----    1 mysql    mysql        1024 Apr 30 14:30
sensor.MYI
-rw-rw----    1 mysql    mysql        8648 Apr 30 14:39
services.frm
-rw-rw----    1 mysql    mysql     3686536 Apr 30 14:39
services.MYD
-rw-rw----    1 mysql    mysql        1024 Apr 30 14:39
services.MYI
-rw-rw----    1 mysql    mysql        8614 Apr 30 14:30
sig_class.frm
-rw-rw----    1 mysql    mysql           0 Apr 30 14:30
sig_class.MYD
-rw-rw----    1 mysql    mysql        1024 Apr 30 14:30
sig_class.MYI
-rw-rw----    1 mysql    mysql        8730 Apr 30 14:30
signature.frm
-rw-rw----    1 mysql    mysql           0 Apr 30 14:30
signature.MYD
-rw-rw----    1 mysql    mysql        1024 Apr 30 14:30
signature.MYI
-rw-rw----    1 mysql    mysql        8616 Apr 30 14:30
sig_reference.frm
-rw-rw----    1 mysql    mysql           0 Apr 30 14:30
sig_reference.MYD
-rw-rw----    1 mysql    mysql        1024 Apr 30 14:30
sig_reference.MYI
-rw-rw----    1 mysql    mysql        8888 Apr 30 14:30
tcphdr.frm
-rw-rw----    1 mysql    mysql           0 Apr 30 14:30
tcphdr.MYD
-rw-rw----    1 mysql    mysql        1024 Apr 30 14:30
tcphdr.MYI
-rw-rw----    1 mysql    mysql        8704 Apr 30 14:30
udphdr.frm
```

```
-rw-rw----     1 mysql     mysql                 0 Apr 30 14:30
udphdr.MYD
-rw-rw----     1 mysql     mysql              1024 Apr 30 14:30
udphdr.MYI
[root@laptop]#
```

As you may have figured out, there are three files related to each table in the database. To find out how many databases are present on your system, just list the directories under /usr/lib/mysql.

Basic MySQL Commands

This section presents some very basic MySQL commands. These commands are required to do basic operations with the database.

Creating a Database

First of all you have to login to create a database. You can login as user "root" to MySQL server as shown below. This root user is not the Linux root user. It is related to MySQL database only.

```
[root@conformix /root]# mysql -u root
Welcome to the MySQL monitor.  Commands end with ; or \g.
Your MySQL connection id is 1 to server version: 3.23.36

Type 'help;' or '\h' for help. Type '\c' to clear the buffer

mysql>
```

At the mysql> prompt, you can use MySQL commands. The following command creates testdb.

```
mysql> create database testdb;
Query OK, 1 row affected (0.01 sec)

mysql>
```

When you create a database, a directory is created under /var/lib/mysql to store database files. In this case the name of the directory is /var/lib/mysql/ testdb.

Displaying a List of Databases

At the command prompt, you can use the show databases command to list available databases.

```
mysql> show databases;
+----------+
| Database |
+----------+
| mysql    |
| test     |
| testdb   |
+----------+
3 rows in set (0.00 sec)

mysql>
```

This command shows that three databases exist. The names of these databases are
mysql, test and testdb.

Connecting to a Database

To connect to a database, you can use the use command by providing the name of
the database as the argument to this command. The following command starts using
testdb as the database.

```
mysql> use testdb;
Database changed
mysql>
```

In some cases you can also use the following command:

```
mysql> connect testdb
Reading table information for completion of table and column
names
You can turn off this feature to get a quicker startup with -A

Connection id:    3
Current database: testdb

mysql>
```

Creating Tables

The following command creates a table with the name customer. The table contains four columns.

```
mysql> create table customers (name varchar(20), address
varchar(40), phone varchar(10), dob date);
Query OK, 0 rows affected (0.00 sec)

mysql>
```

Column names and their data types are defined in the command. When you create
a table, three files are created in the directory that corresponds to the database. In this

case, files are created in /var/lib/mysql/testdb directory as shown in the following command.

```
[root@conformix]# ls /var/lib/mysql/testdb
customers.frm  customers.MYD  customers.MYI
[root@conformix]#
```

The names of these files start with the name used for the table.

Listing Tables

The show tables command lists currently defined tables in the database.

```
mysql> show tables;
+------------------+
| Tables_in_testdb |
+------------------+
| customers        |
+------------------+
1 row in set (0.01 sec)

mysql>
```

Displaying Table Information

You can display information about each table column by using the describe command. The following command displays information about recently created table customers.

```
mysql> describe customers;
+---------+-------------+------+-----+---------+-------+
| Field   | Type        | Null | Key | Default | Extra |
+---------+-------------+------+-----+---------+-------+
| name    | varchar(20) | YES  |     | NULL    |       |
| address | varchar(40) | YES  |     | NULL    |       |
| phone   | varchar(10) | YES  |     | NULL    |       |
| dob     | date        | YES  |     | NULL    |       |
+---------+-------------+------+-----+---------+-------+
4 rows in set (0.01 sec)

mysql>
```

Adding Data to Tables

Data can be added to a table using the insert command. The following command adds one row to the customers table.

```
mysql> insert into customers values ('Boota', '135 SB,
Sargodha', '001-946-15', '1970-01-01');
Query OK, 1 row affected (0.06 sec)

mysql>
```

Displaying Data in Tables

The `select` command retrieves data from one or more tables. In its simplest form, the following command displays all records in the customers table.

```
mysql> select * from customers;
+-------+------------------+------------+------------+
| name  | address          | phone      | dob        |
+-------+------------------+------------+------------+
| Boota | 135 SB, Sargodha | 001-946-15 | 1970-01-01 |
+-------+------------------+------------+------------+
1 row in set (0.00 sec)

mysql>
```

For more information on the `select` command, use any SQL language reference.

Deleting Data from Tables

The `delete` command removes data from the table. The following command deletes records from the `customer` table where the name of the customer is Boota.

```
mysql> delete from customers where customers.name='Boota';
Query OK, 1 row affected (0.00 sec)

mysql>
```

Switching from One Database to Another

You can use the `use` commands to switch to another database. The following command starts using `mysql-test` database.

```
mysql> use mysql-test
Reading table information for completion of table and column
names
You can turn off this feature to get a quicker startup with -A

Database changed
mysql>
```

Creating a User

The simplest way to create a user is to grant the user some access rights to a database. If the user does not already exist, it will be created. The following command creates a user `rrehman` and grants all access rights on the `testdb` database.

```
mysql> grant all on testdb.* to rrehman;
Query OK, 0 rows affected (0.00 sec)

mysql>
```

This command creates a row in the user table in `mysql` database for user `rreh-man` and grants permission for everything to user `rrehman` on database `testdb`.

Setting Password for a User

You can assign a password to the user upon creation. The following command creates a user `rrehman` and assigns a password `boota`.

```
grant all on testdb.* to rrehman identified by 'boota';
```

To assign a password later on, use the following command:

```
mysql> set password for rrehman = password('kaka');
Query OK, 0 rows affected (0.00 sec)

mysql>
```

Granting Permissions

The `grant` command is used to grant different levels of permissions to users. Refer to the following command where different permissions are assigned to a user `rr` on `localhost`.

```
mysql> grant CREATE,INSERT,DELETE,UPDATE,SELECT on snort.* to
rr@localhost;
Query OK, 0 rows affected (0.00 sec)

mysql>
```

Using mysqladmin Utility

The `mysqladmin` utility is used for database administration. A complete discussion is beyond the scope of this book. The following output of the command shows some of the tasks that it is capable of doing.

```
[root@conformix /root]# mysqladmin
mysqladmin  Ver 8.18 Distrib 3.23.36, for redhat-linux-gnu on i386
Copyright (C) 2000 MySQL AB & MySQL Finland AB & TCX DataKonsult AB
This software comes with ABSOLUTELY NO WARRANTY. This is free software,
and you are welcome to modify and redistribute it under the GPL license

Administration program for the mysqld daemon.
Usage: mysqladmin [OPTIONS] command command....

  -#, --debug=...          Output debug log. Often this is
  'd:t:o,filename`
  -f, --force              Don't ask for confirmation on drop database;
  with
```

```
                        multiple commands, continue even if an error
occurs
-?, --help             Display this help and exit
--character-sets-dir=...
                       Set the character set directory
-C, --compress         Use compression in server/client protocol
-h, --host=#           Connect to host
-p, --password[=...] Password to use when connecting to server
                       If password is not given it's asked from the tty
-P --port=...  Port number to use for connection
-i, --sleep=sec Execute commands again and again with a sleep between
-r, --relative         Show difference between current and previous
values
                       when used with -i. Currently works only with
                       extended-status
-E, --vertical         Print output vertically. Is similar to --
relative,
                       but prints output vertically.
-s, --silent           Silently exit if one can't connect to server
-S, --socket=...Socket file to use for connection
-t, --timeout=...Timeout for connection to the mysqld server
-u, --user=#           User for login if not current user
-v, --verbose          Write more information
-V, --version          Output version information and exit
-w, --wait[=retries]  Wait and retry if connection is down

Default options are read from the following files in the given order:
/etc/my.cnf /var/lib/mysql/my.cnf ~/.my.cnf
The following groups are read: mysqladmin client
The following options may be given as the first argument:
--print-defaults  Print the program argument list and exit
--no-defaults           Don't read default options from any options file
--defaults-file=# Only read default options from the given file #
--defaults-extra-file=# Read this file after the global files are read

Possible variables for option --set-variable (-O) are:
connect_timeout         current value: 0
shutdown_timeout        current value: 3600

Where command is a one or more of: (Commands may be shortened)
  create databasenameCreate a new database
  drop databasenameDelete a database and all its tables
  extended-status         Gives an extended status message from the
  server
  flush-hosts             Flush all cached hosts
  flush-logs              Flush all logs
  flush-status            Clear status variables
```

```
flush-tables          Flush all tables
flush-threads         Flush the thread cache
flush-privileges      Reload grant tables (same as reload)
kill id,id,... Kill mysql threads
password new-password Change old password to new-password
ping                  Check if mysqld is alive
processlist           Show list of active threads in server
reload                Reload grant tables
refresh               Flush all tables and close and open logfiles
shutdown              Take server down
status                Gives a short status message from the server
start-slave           Start slave
stop-slave            Stop slave
variables              Prints variables available
version               Get version info from server
[root@conformix]#
```

You can use different options on the command line. For example "mysqladmin version" will show the version number for the utility.

Packet Header Formats

S nort rules use the protocol type field to distinguish among different protocols. Different header parts in packets are used to determine the type of protocol used in a packet. In addition, rule options can test many of the header fields. This appendix explains headers of different protocols. These packet headers are explained in detail in RFCs. Understanding different parts of these packet headers is very important for writing effective Snort rules.

IP Packet Header

The basic IPv4 header consists of 20 bytes. An options part may be present after these 20 bytes. This optional part may be up to forty bytes long. Structure of IP header is present in Figure C-1.

V	IHL	TOS		Total Length	
ID			F	Frag Offset	
TTL		Protocol		Header Checksum	
Source Address					
Destination Address					

Figure C-1 IP header

Detailed information about the IP packet header can be found in RFC 791 which is available from ftp://ftp.isi.edu/in-notes/rfc791.txt and many other places including the RFC editor web site. A brief explanation of different fields in the IP packet header is found in Table C-1.

Table C-1 IP Packet Header Fields

Field	Explanation
V	Version number. The value is 4 for IPv4. Four bits are used for this part.
IHL	This field shows length of IP packet header. This is used to find out if the options part is present after the basic header. Four bits are used for IHL and it shows length in 32-bit word length. The value of this field for a basic 20-bytes header is 5.
TOS	This field shows type of service used for this packet. It is 8 bits in length.
Total Length	This field shows the length of the IP packet, including the data part. It is 16 bits long.
ID	This field packet identification number. This part is 16 bits long.
F	This part is three bits long and it shows different flags used in the IP header.
Frag Offset	This part is thirteen bits long and it shows fragment offset in case an IP packet is fragmented.
TTL	This is time to live value. It is eight bits long.
Protocol	This part shows transport layer protocol number. It is eight bits long.
Header Checksum	This part shows header checksum, which is used to detect any error in the IP header. This part is sixteen bits long.
Source Address	This is the 32 bit long source IP address.
Destination Address	This is the 32 bit long destination IP address.

ICMP Packet Header

ICMP header is completely explained in RFC 792, which is available from ftp://ftp.isi.edu/in-notes/rfc792.txt for download. Figure C-2 shows basic structure of ICMP header. Note that depending upon type of ICMP packet, this basic header is followed by different parts.

Type	Code	Checksum
ICMP Information		

Figure C-2 Basic ICMP header

An explanation of the fields in a basic ICMP header is provided in Table C-2.

Table C-2 ICMP Packet Header Fields

Field	Explanation
Type	This part is 8 bits long and shows the type of ICMP packet.
Code	This part is also 8 bits long and shows the sub-type or code number used for the packet.
Checksum	This part is 16 bits long and is used to detect any errors in the ICMP packet.

The ICMP information part is variable depending upon the value of the type field. For example, the ping command uses ICMP ECHO REQUEST type packet. This packet header is shown in Figure C-3.

Type	Code	Checksum
Identifier		Sequence Number

Figure C-3 ICMP packet used in ping command.

For a complete list of ICMP packet types, refer to RFC 792.

TCP Packet Header

TCP packet header is discussed in detail in RFC 793 which is available at ftp://
ftp.isi.edu/in-notes/rfc793.txt for download. Figure C-4 shows structure of TCP header.

Source Port				Destination Port
Sequence Number				
Acknowledgement Number				
Offset	Reserved	Flags		Window
Checksum				Urgent Pointer
Options and Padding				

Figure C-4 TCP header

Different parts of TCP header are explained in Table C-3. Again for a detailed
explanation of TCP, refer to the RFC 793.

Table C-3 TCP Packet Header Fields

Field	Explanation
Source Port	This part is 16 bits long and shows source port number.
Destination Port	This is a 16-bit long field and shows the destination port number.
Sequence Number	This is the sequence number for the TCP packet. It is 32 bits long. It shows the sequence number of the first data octet in the packet. However if SYN bit is set, this number shows the initial sequence number.
Acknowledgement Number	This number is used for acknowledging packets. It is 32 bits long. This number shows the sequence number of the octet that the sender is expecting.
Offset	This is a 4- bit field and shows the length of the TCP header. Length is measured in 32-bit numbers.
Reserved	Six bits are reserved.
Flags or Control bits	The flags are six bits in length and are used for control purposes. These bits are URG, ACK, PSH, RST, SYN and FIN. A value of 1 in any bit place indicates the flag is set.
Window	This is 16 bits long and is used to tell the other side about the length of TCP window size.

Table C-3 TCP Packet Header Fields (continued)

Field	Explanation
Checksum	This is a checksum for TCP header and data. It is 16 bits long.
Urgent Pointer	This field is used only when the URG flag is set. It is 16 bits long.
Options	This part is of variable length.

UDP Packet Header

The UDP packet header is simple and is described in RFC 768. It has four fields as shown in Figure C-5. Each field is 16 bits long. Names of all fields are self-explanatory.

Source Port	Destination Port
Length	Checksum

Figure C-5 UDP packet header

ARP Packet Header

ARP packets are used to discover the hardware or MAC addresses when the IP address is known. In any LAN, you will see a lot of ARP packets being transmitted. This is because each host has to find out the MAC address of the destination host before sending data. The ARP is a broadcast protocol and its packet header is shown in Figure C-6.

HW Address Type		Protocol Address Type	
HW Addr Len	Proto Addr Len	Operation	
Source Hardware Address			
Source Hardware Address (Continued)		Source Protocol Address	
Source Protocol Address (Continued)		Target Hardware Address	
Target Hardware Address (Continued)			
Target Protocol Address			

Figure C-6 ARP header

Different fields in the ARP packet header are described in Table C-4.

Table C-4 ARP Packet Header Fields

Field	Explanation
HW Address Type	The HW Address type is a 16 bit long field and it shows the type of hardware. Since most of LANs are Ethernet-based, its value is 1. For IEEE 802 networks, its value is 6. For IPSec tunnel, the value is 31.
Protocol Address Type	The protocol address type shows the protocol used in the network layer. The value of this field is 0x800 for IP.
HW Addr Len	This field shows the length of the hardware address in number of bytes. This field is 8 bits long.
Proto Addr Length	This field shows the length of the protocol address. This field is also 8 bits long.
Operation or Opcode	This field is 16 bits long and is used for the type of ARP packet. A value of 1 indicates a request packet and a value of 2 indicates a reply packet.
Source hardware address	This is a 48 bit long field in the case of Ethernet. However its length is variable.
Source protocol address	This is a 32 bit field in the case of IPv4 packets. However its length is variable.
Target hardware address	This is 48 bits long in Ethernet and its length is variable.
Target protocol address	This is 32 bits in the case of IPv4 and its length is variable.

Glossary

T his appendix defines some of the most commonly used terms in this book.

Alert A message generated when any intruder activity is detected. Alerts may be sent in many different forms, e.g., pop-up window, logging to screen, e-mail and so on.

DMZ Demilitarized zone.

HIDS Host Intrusion Detection System. A system that detects intruder activity for a host.

IDS Intrusion Detection System. A system that detects any intruder activity. Snort is an example of an IDS.

IDS Signature A pattern that we want to look for in a data packet. Based upon a particular signature we can define appropriate action to take.

NIDS Network Intrusion Detection System. This is an intrusion detection system that works for a network. Usually a device (computer or a dedicated device) is placed at an appropriate location in the network to detect any intruder activity.

Rule Header The first part of each Snort rule. It contains information about action, protocol, source and destination addresses, port numbers and direction.

Snort Configuration File The `snort.conf file`, which is the main configuration file for Snort. It is read at the time when Snort starts.

Snort Rule   A way of conveying intruder signatures to Snort.

TOS   Type of Service field used in IPv4 packet header.

Trust Levels   Different levels of trust may be imposed in different trust zones (see Trust Zone). For example, a financial database may be at a different trust level than a company public web server.

Trust Zone   An area of your network where you apply the same security policy. For example, all publicly accessible hosts (WWW and e-mail servers) may be placed in a demilitarized zone (DMZ).

TTL   Time to Live field used in IP packet header.

SNML DTD

This is the DTD file used for Snort XML based messages.

```
<?xml version="1.0" encoding="UTF-8"?>

<!-- * Simple Network Markup Language (SNML)
     *  Version 0.2
     *
     * snml.dtd
     * Copyright (C) 2001, 2002 Carnegie Mellon University
     *
     * This program is free software; you can redistribute it and/or
     * modify it under the terms of the GNU General Public License as
     * published by the Free Software Foundation; either version 2 of
     * the License, or (at your option) any later version.
     *
     * This program is distributed in the hope that it will be useful,
     * but WITHOUT ANY WARRANTY; without even the implied warranty of
     * MERCHANTABILITY or FITNESS FOR A PARTICULAR PURPOSE.  See the
     * GNU General Public License for more details.
     *
     * You should have received a copy of the GNU General Public
     * License along with this program; if not, write to the Free
     * Software Foundation, Inc., 59 Temple Place - Suite 330, Boston,
     * MA 02111-1307, USA.
  -->

<!-- This DTD defines a simple XML exchange format for Network
     Intrusion Detection Systems.
```

The snml can stand for "Snort Markup Language" when used with
the snort IDS or as the "Simple Network Markup Language" when
used in multi-vendor IDS environments.

Comments or questions can be directed to:

            Roman Danyliw <rdd@cert.org>
 -->

<!DOCTYPE snml-message-version-0.2 [<!ELEMENT report (event*)>

<!ELEMENT event (sensor, signature, reference?, timestamp, packet)>

<!--
 | The sensor element contains information that can be used to
 | uniquely identify the source which detected the event.
 | It always contains a hostname. Optionally, a
 | sensor filter, a data source filename, or an ip address
 | and network interface may be given.
 -->
<!ELEMENT sensor ((file|(ipaddr, interface?)), hostname, filter?)>

<!--
 | sensor attributes
 | format = encoding format of the packet payload (data)
 | detail = defines which protocol fields will be present
 | fast - limited information
 | full - the full packet will be present
 -->
<!ATTLIST sensor
          format (base64|ascii|hex) #REQUIRED
          detail (fast|full)   #REQUIRED
>

<!-- This field contains an ordinary hostname -->
<!ELEMENT hostname (#PCDATA)>

<!-- This contains a file name with a full path -->
<!ELEMENT file (#PCDATA)>

<!--
 | Contains a string representing a network interface
 | e.g., eth0, ppp0, hme0, etc.
 -->
<!ELEMENT interface (#PCDATA)>

```
<!--
 | A string representing a tcpdump filter that is normally passed
 | in on the command line. e.g. "not net 10.1.1.0/24"
 -->
<!ELEMENT filter (#PCDATA)>

<!--
 | The signature is free-form text describing the event. In snort,
 | it is the string contained in the "msg" rule option
 -->
<!ELEMENT signature (#PCDATA)>

<!--
 | signature attributes
 |  id       = unique identifier of this signature (0..2^32-1)
 |  revision = revision number of this signature
 |  class    = classification identifier of this signature (numeric)
 | priority = numeric priority of this event - (0..255)
 -->
<!ATTLIST signature
          id          CDATA    #IMPLIED
          revision    CDATA    #IMPLIED
          class       CDATA    #IMPLIED
          priority    CDATA    #IMPLIED
>

<!--
 | A reference provides a mechanism to refer to an external
 | database for information related to this signature or event.
 -->
<!ELEMENT reference (#PCDATA)>

<!--
 | reference attribute
 |    system   = the external database referenced
 |                 - cve       : Common Vulnerabilities and Exposures
 |                                 (http://cve.mitre.org)
 |                 - bugtraq   : Bugtraq
 |                                 (http://www.securityfocus.com/bid)
 |                 - arachnids : arachNIDS
 |                                 (http://www.whitehats.com/ids)
 |                 - mcafee    : McAfee
 |                                 (http://vil.nai.com)
 |                 - url       : custom URL
 -->
<!ATTLIST reference
          system    CDATA    #REQUIRED
```

```
>

<!--
 | The timestamp must conform to ISO-8601 standard.
 |    e.g., ISO-8601: 1999-08-04 00:01:23-05
 -->
<!ELEMENT timestamp (#PCDATA)>

<!--
 | A packet can be logged without being decoded using "raw"
 | mode. This encoding should only be used when a packet is
 | received containing protocols which cannot be decoded.
 -->
<!ELEMENT packet (raw|iphdr)>

<!--
 | IP address (in dot-quad notation).
 |    e.g., 10.1.2.3
 |  Note: Domain names are not valid.
 |
 |  The version attribute is the version of IP address
 |  (should be 4 or 6).
 -->
<!ELEMENT ipaddr (#PCDATA)>
<!ATTLIST ipaddr
          version   CDATA   #REQUIRED
>

<!-- raw contains a base64 representation of a packet -->
<!ELEMENT raw (#PCDATA)>

<!--
 | IPv4 header
 |    saddr   = source IP address      - IP address  IP  (192.168.1.2)
 |    daddr   = destination IP address - IP address  IP  (192.168.1.2)
 |    ver     = version of ip          - 1 byte INT (0 - 15)
 |    hlen    = header length in 32 bit words
 |                                      - 1 byte INT (0 - 15)
 |    tos     = type of service        - 1 byte INT (0 - 255)
 |    len     = total length of the packet
 |                                      - 2 byte INT (0 - 65535)
 |    id      = identification         - 2 byte INT (0 - 65535)
 |    flags   = fragment flags         - 1 byte INT (0 - 7)
 |    off     = fragment offset        - 2 byte INT (0 - 65535)
 |    ttl     = time to live           - 1 byte INT (0 - 255)
 |    proto   = protocol               - 1 byte INT (0 - 255)
 |    csum    = checksum               - 2 byte INT (0 - 65535)
```

```
  -->
<!ELEMENT iphdr ((tcphdr|udphdr|icmphdr), option*)>
<!ATTLIST iphdr
          saddr    CDATA   #REQUIRED
          daddr    CDATA   #REQUIRED
          ver      CDATA   #REQUIRED
          hlen     CDATA   #IMPLIED
          tos      CDATA   #IMPLIED
          len      CDATA   #IMPLIED
          id       CDATA   #IMPLIED
          flags    CDATA   #IMPLIED
          ttl      CDATA   #IMPLIED
          off      CDATA   #IMPLIED
          ttl      CDATA   #IMPLIED
          proto    CDATA   #REQUIRED
          csum     CDATA   #IMPLIED
>

<!--
  | IP or TCP option
  |   option = option code            - 1 byte INT (0 - 255)
  |   len     = length of option data - 1 byte INT (0 - 255)
  -->
<!ELEMENT option (#PCDATA)>
<!ATTLIST option
          code     CDATA   #REQUIRED
          len      CDATA   #IMPLIED
>

<!--
  | TCP header information
  |   sport    = source port          - 2 byte INT (0 - 65535)
  |   dport    = destination port     - 2 byte INT (0 - 65535)
  |   seq      = sequence number      - 4 byte INT (0 - 4294967295)
  |   ack      = acknowledgment number - 4 byte INT (0 - 4294967295)
  |   off      = data offset          - 1 byte INT (0 - 15)
  |   res      = reserved field       - 1 byte INT (0 - 63)
  |   flags    = represents TCP flags - 1 byte INT (0 - 255)
  |   win      = window               - 2 byte INT (0 - 65535)
  |   csum     = checksum             - 2 byte INT (0 - 65535)
  |   urp      = urgent pointer       - 2 byte INT (0 - 65535)
  -->
<!ELEMENT tcphdr (data, option*)>
<!ATTLIST tcphdr
          sport    CDATA   #REQUIRED
          dport    CDATA   #REQUIRED
          seq      CDATA   #IMPLIED
```

```
                  ack        CDATA  #IMPLIED
                  off        CDATA  #IMPLIED
                  res        CDATA  #IMPLIED
                  flags      CDATA  #REQUIRED
                  win        CDATA  #IMPLIED
                  csum       CDATA  #IMPLIED
                  urp        CDATA  #IMPLIED
>


<!--                                                    `
  | UDP header information
  |    sport    = source port              - 2 byte INT (0 - 65535)
  |    dport    = destination port         - 2 byte INT (0 - 65535)
  |    len      = length field of UDP header
  |                                        - 2 byte INT (0 - 65535)
  |    csum     = checksum                 - 2 byte INT (0 - 65535)
  -->
<!ELEMENT udphdr (data)>
<!ATTLIST udphdr
          sport      CDATA  #REQUIRED
          dport      CDATA  #REQUIRED
          len        CDATA  #IMPLIED
          csum       CDATA  #IMPLIED
>


<!--
  | ICMP header
  |    type     = icmp type                - 1 byte INT (0 - 255)
  |    code     = icmp code                - 1 byte INT (0 - 255)
  |    csum     = checksum                 - 2 byte INT (0 - 65535)
  |    id       = identifier               - 2 byte INT (0 - 65535)
  |    seq      = sequence number          - 2 byte INT (0 - 65535)
  -->
<!ELEMENT icmphdr (data)>
<!ATTLIST icmphdr
          type    CDATA #REQUIRED
          code    CDATA #REQUIRED
          csum    CDATA #IMPLIED
          id      CDATA #IMPLIED
          seq     CDATA #IMPLIED
>

<!-- Packet payload -->
<!ELEMENT data (#PCDATA)>

]>
```

INDEX

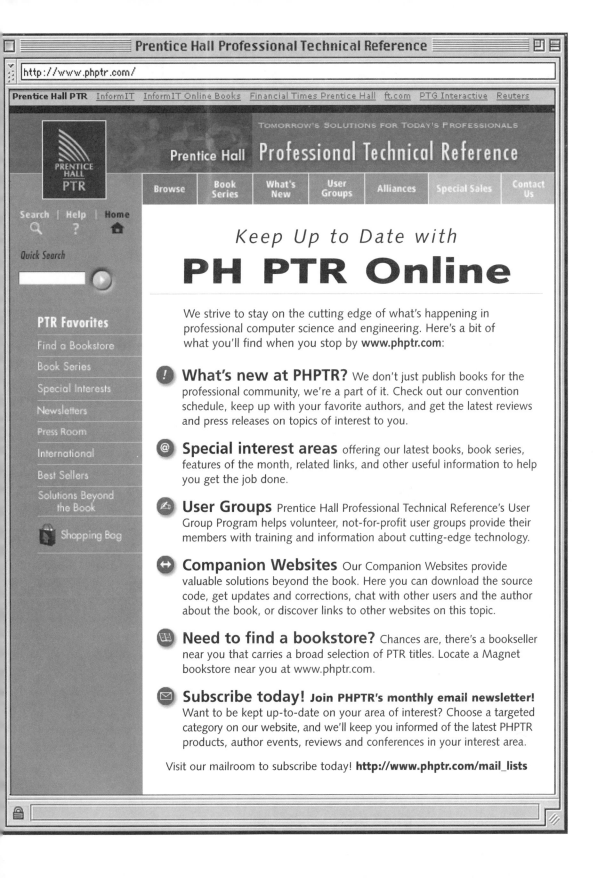

Keep Up to Date with
PH PTR Online

We strive to stay on the cutting edge of what's happening in professional computer science and engineering. Here's a bit of what you'll find when you stop by **www.phptr.com**:

(!) **What's new at PHPTR?** We don't just publish books for the professional community, we're a part of it. Check out our convention schedule, keep up with your favorite authors, and get the latest reviews and press releases on topics of interest to you.

(@) **Special interest areas** offering our latest books, book series, features of the month, related links, and other useful information to help you get the job done.

(✍) **User Groups** Prentice Hall Professional Technical Reference's User Group Program helps volunteer, not-for-profit user groups provide their members with training and information about cutting-edge technology.

(↔) **Companion Websites** Our Companion Websites provide valuable solutions beyond the book. Here you can download the source code, get updates and corrections, chat with other users and the author about the book, or discover links to other websites on this topic.

(📖) **Need to find a bookstore?** Chances are, there's a bookseller near you that carries a broad selection of PTR titles. Locate a Magnet bookstore near you at www.phptr.com.

(✉) **Subscribe today!** **Join PHPTR's monthly email newsletter!** Want to be kept up-to-date on your area of interest? Choose a targeted category on our website, and we'll keep you informed of the latest PHPTR products, author events, reviews and conferences in your interest area.

Visit our mailroom to subscribe today! **http://www.phptr.com/mail_lists**